International Custom and the Continental Shelf

A Study in the Dynamics of Customary Rules of International Law

by

ZDENEK J. SLOUKA

With a foreword by

OLIVER J. LISSITZYN

MARTINUS NIJHOFF / THE HAGUE

MARTINUS NIJHOFF — PUBLISHER — THE HAGUE

This book comes at a time when the entire deep ocean floor is being rapidly and effectively politicized, and when the United Nations is laboring to secure international order and peace on thebottom of the sea. The author analyzes the initial and crucial stages of this process with two primary aims: first, to reexamine from a new perspective the origins of the modern regimes of the continental shelf; second, to contribute to modern theory of the formation of customary rules of international behavior.

Two sets of questions are raised.

The first set is empirically oriented: In the beginning, who acted how and when on the continental shelves of theworld? What was the technological, political and social environment of this state activity? How did states communicate to one another their policies, and to what extent did they rely on the mutually raised expectations? How well did we understand this process of the formation of international legal order while it was in progress, and how widely did expert observers agree on the meaning of what they saw taking place under the oceans? The study demonstrates the need to go beyond formal pronouncements and acts of governments when one studies interaction of states, and to inquire into the technological, economic, social and political substrata of international behavior.

The second set of questions moves the study onto the level of international legal and political theory. Under givenconditions, how do customary rules of international law emerge and grow, and how are they perceived and identified? Is there any "twilight zone" between international politics and law, does some mystery shroud the origins of customary rules of international conduct – or do we fail to comprehend some of the processes involved simply because we often look at the wrong things from the wrong angle? The book questions the feasibility of studying legal conse-quences of state interaction in a global, general perspective stimulated by a desire for universal rules. Responding to this problem, the author introduces a "bilateral approach" to the study of international systems of order as a part of a new theory contributing to the solution of the "mys-teries" of international customary law.

About the Author: Professor Zdenek J. Slouka is on the faculty of Columbia University in the Department of Political Science. He received his Ph.D. from Columbia University (international law and relations); previously he did graduate work in international law and politics at New York University, and in political sociology at Masaryk University, Czechoslovakia. Specializing in studies of the relation of science, technology and international law and politics, he is also Research Associate of the Institute for the Study of Science in Human Affairs at Columbia University.

1968. XII and 186 pages. Guilders 25.20

Voor Nederland *f* 26.25

INTERNATIONAL CUSTOM AND THE CONTINENTAL SHELF

INTERNATIONAL CUSTOM AND THE CONTINENTAL SHELF

A STUDY IN THE DYNAMICS OF CUSTOMARY RULES OF INTERNATIONAL LAW

by

ZDENEK J. SLOUKA

MARTINUS NIJHOFF / THE HAGUE / 1968

ISBN 978-94-011-8488-5 ISBN 978-94-011-9210-1 (eBook)
DOI 10.1007/978-94-011-9210-1

Softcover reprint of the hardcover 1st edition 1968

To Olga and Mark

ACKNOWLEDGMENTS

As any study of scholarly nature, this book has its roots in the work of many others and, undoubtedly, contains many weaknesses of its own. And the author, while sharing ultimate responsibility for this work with no one, has many more intellectual debts to repay than can be mentioned. Yet, some are truly outstanding: To the late Clyde Eagleton, for an early and inspiring introduction to the general field of this volume. To Philip C. Jessup, for opening new and unexplored dimensions of a significant area of inquiry into the behavior of states, and for his comments, friendly and incisive, on an initial paper leading to this study. Finally and primarily, to Oliver J. Lissitzyn: for sharing so generously not only in the entire process through which a study is conceived and planned; but also for his patience, encouragement, understanding and criticism, through all the stages of this work. Nor should a significant debt to an institution be left out: while, today, some seek to restructure Columbia University by means painfully real, and for purposes painfully unreal, I wish to thank that institution for providing this author, together with so many others, with an environment effectively stimulating inquiry, with a climate of a free, searching quest of knowledge and understanding, unlimited and uninhibited. Two more debts can never really be repaid but must be acknowledged: To my wife Olga for the untiring and multiple aid she provided as a professional information specialist and, non-professionally yet just as or more effectively, as a reader, indexer, critic, and a soothsayer. And, of course, to Mark: for being quiet to allow some flights of abstract speculation, and for sounding off to bring one down to earth.

Ardsley, 1968 Zdenek J. Slouka

FOREWORD

One of the reasons for the speed with which international law has been changing in recent years has been the acceleration in the development of technology. New technological capabilities create opportunities for new kinds of economic activities which in turn require new legal norms to regulate them. Many such norms are formulated by express agreement and embodied in multilateral treaties. Much of contemporary air and space law is being developed by this method. For various reasons, however, the treaty-making process is not always adequate for the development of new law, at least in its initial stages. Express agreement of a substantial majority of states on norms formulated with some precision requires much time and effort. Eighteen years have passed, for example, since the United Nations International Law Commission began its work on the law of the sea which led to the formulation of four conventions at the Geneva Conference of 1958 on this subject. Ten years after this Conference, none of the four conventions has been ratified or acceded to by a majority of the states of the world. It is not surprising, therefore, that in some fields new law first emerges as a set of customary norms of varying degrees of clarity and general acceptance. But the nature of the process of development and change of customary norms has remained inadequately understood and explained in the theory of international law. Some eminent jurists have called it "a mystery."

One of the fields of international law in which the impact of new technology has been particularly evident is the law of the sea. Among the new legal phenomena in this field are the norms comprising "the doctrine of the continental shelf." First proclaimed by the President of the United States in 1945, this doctrine, which seeks to regulate the extraction of natural resources from the subsoil and the seabed adjacent to the coast of a state but beyond the limits of its territorial sea, has gained extensive if not universal acceptance in its essential features even by states which have not yet ratified the Geneva Convention of 1958 on the Continental Shelf. It has been widely applied in the practice of states. The process by which this set of norms has been emerging may help us understand the "mystery" of change in customary international law.

In his monograph, Professor Slouka subjects to a minute examination the claims and activities of states through which the contemporary regime of the continental shelf began to take shape. He stresses the bilateral character of the legal relationships which initially emerged in the course of the process and invokes the concept of estoppel to explain how some (though not necessarily all) customary norms of international law come into being. The value of the monograph is thus twofold. It describes in great factual detail the emergence of the doctrine of the continental shelf; and by its new and challenging theory it makes a notable contribution to the solution of the legal "mystery" of international custom. It can be recommended both to practitioners concerned with the evolution and present state of the law of the sea and to scholars seeking to understand the dynamics of international law.

O. J. Lissitzyn

CONTENTS

CHAPTER I

INTERNATIONAL CUSTOM: ITS STATICS AND DYNAMICS

The purpose of this case study in the dynamics of international customary law is twofold: first, to inquire into some of the processes through which states, by acting or failing to act in respect of a specific international issue, narrow their choice of policies in that particular sphere up to the point of being bound by legal rules of established international custom; secondly, and necessarily, such an inquiry is also an examination of the methods through which the existence and scope of a customary rule could be ascertained with a clarity sufficient to endow the rule with normative significance.

It has been said that the problem of custom is so intimately connected with all the fundamental problems of law that it is impossible to treat these latter questions without an exhaustive study of the former.[1] And it has also been noted that, as a result, many writers study the phenomenon of custom not as such, but with a view to finding in it the confirmation of their general theory of law.[2] As already implied by the opening statement of the purpose of this study, we do not seek to solve "the mystery of custom oscillating inconclusively between being a law-creating source of legal rules and mere evidence of pre-existing law." [3] Our aim is simpler: to determine, by reference to a specific case evolving under specific circumstances, the variety and effectiveness of factors influencing the growth of international custom.

Robert Ago defines customary law, or *ius non scriptum,* as primarily "the type of norm which, not having been manifested by an appropriate creative act, can only be recognized as existing by the outward manifestations of its functioning in the conscience of members of the social body" [4] – but

[1] W. Henrich, "Zur Problematik des Gewohnheitsrechts," *Receuil d'Etudes sur les Sources du Droit en l'Honneur de François Gény*, vol. 2 (Paris: Recueil Sirey, 1934), p. 276.

[2] L. Kopelmanas, "Custom as a Means of the Creation of International Law," 18 *British Year Book of International Law* 128 (1937).

[3] H. Lauterpacht, *The Development of International Law by the International Court of Justice* (New York: Praeger, 1958), p. 379.

[4] R. Ago, "Positive Law and International Law," 51 *American Journal of International Law* 723 (1957).

what, then, are those outward manifestiations? According to Briggs, "the proper way to express the process by which customary international law is created is to say that a particular pattern of state conduct hitherto legally discretionary, has acquired obligatory force through its general acceptance by states as a legal obligation" [5] – but what does actually constitute acceptance and how general must it be? Sorensen observed that, in a certain sense, the creation of a customary rule is an inverted process of the application of an existing rule; to apply a rule is to determine one's action in conformity with an abstract norm – "la concrétion de son contenu" – while a customary rule rises by having its elements abstracted from the actual conduct of the subjects of law.[6] But what elements may be abstracted from which conduct, and how? Standard textbooks on international law do, of course, state the traditional requirements for the coming into existence of a new customary rule, namely, according to Hudson, the following:

(a) concordant practice by a number of States with reference to a type of situation falling within the domain of international relations; (b) continuation or repetition of the practice over a considerable period of time; (c) conception that the practice is required by, or consistent with, prevailing international law; and (d) general acquiescence in the practice by other States.[7]

On the whole, writers in the field of international law agree that this statement of requirements is generally correct, even though in individual instances they may stress or deemphasize one requirement or another.

Yet there is an area marked by a much more conspicuous agreement of writers, jurists and political practitioners: it is hardly ever disputed that the rise of customary rules is shrouded in mystery, and their existence difficult to ascertain. Jenks speaks of the "uncertain status of established custom," [8] a contradiction in itself. Lauterpacht comments on "the complexities – indeed the mysteries – of the rise of binding customary law from amidst the amorphous . . . manifestations of conduct" [9] and admits that the ascertainment of the existence of a customary rule "may, in the last resort, be one of impression" rather than of exact definition and precise determination.[10] On a different level – that of practical application of rules – the uncertainty clearly manifests itself. Asked to express his views as to the position, under inter-

[5] H. W. Briggs, "The Columbian-Peruvian Asylum Case and Proof of Customary International Law," 45 *American Journal of International Law* 730 (1951).

[6] M. Sørensen, *Les Sources du Droit International: Étude sur la Jurisprudence de la Cour Permanente de Justice Internationale* (Copenhagen: Munksgaard, 1946), p. 85.

[7] H. W. Briggs, *The Law of Nations*, 2nd edition (New York: Appleton-Century-Crofts, 1952), p. 25.

[8] C. W. Jenks, *The Common Law of Mankind* (New York: Praeger, 1958) p. 30.

[9] Lauterpacht, *op. cit.* (note 3), p. 390.

[10] *Ibid.*, p. 377.

national law, of balloons and circling satellites, the then United States Secretary of State Dulles referred to the whole subject as "a mystery wrapped in an enigma"; he further stated that "the legal position is quite obscure" and, significantly, that he would not be able to answer what the legal position is "because I do not believe that the legal position has even been codified." [11]

The desire for a code as an orderly, systematic compilation of law, instead of unwritten rules "variously understood and applied by different judges and administrative officials" [12] is natural but not helpful; it underlines, rather than solves, the problem of determining and applying customary international law, particularly since the past experience is not favorable to anything like an attempt at a large-scale codification by convention.[13] A code, to be of any practical value, must be systematic and logical; yet the practice of states from which the code must be abstracted is often without any system and contains contradictions and ambiguities.[14] A code must also be relatively final and definite and, indeed, codification attempts have met with a measure of success in areas of international law that had behind them a long history of reasonably stable development; yet it is precisely in the still developing, dynamic and often turbulent spheres of international law and politics where the absence of a written code is most conspicuous and most difficult to overcome.

Apart from codification, international tribunals are sometimes looked upon as safe shelters providing some protection from the uncertainties and ambiguities of international custom. To Cheng, decisions of international courts constitute the most important means for the determination of rules

[11] Press release 68 of 7 February 1956, 34 *Department of State Bulletin* 280–281.

[12] P. M. Brown, "The Codification of International Law," 29 *American Journal of International Law* 26 (1935).

[13] A. D. McNair, *The Development of International Justice* (New York: New York University Press, 1954), p. 20.

[14] Julius Stone, discussing problems of international law and communication, speaks of "the fact that conscious efforts by States to restate and codify even the less controversial aspects of international law have, on the whole, tended to decrease rather than increase the area of assumed agreement. For it is often the very ambiguities and uncertainties for future application conveyed by existing formulations of customary law which permit State representatives to accept the rule as binding between them. Restatement and codification inevitably seek to clarify and fix these ambiguities and uncertainties, thus stimulating resistances, conscious or unconscious, arising from comtemplation of hypothetical future situations which otherwise might not have impeded consensus." J. Stone, "Problems Confronting Sociological Enquiries concerning International Law," 89 *Recueil des Cours* 99–100 (1956-I). According to McNair, commenting on the 1930 Geneva Conference and its attempts to codify the law of territorial waters and responsibility of states, "this well-prepared, well-meant, but premature attempt at codification did positive harm, because so far from promoting uniformity of views among Governments, it promoted disunity. Certain rules of law that were in the course of acquiring general consent were thrown back into the melting pot as the result of the disagreements which emerged." McNair, *op. cit.* (note 13), p. 23.

and principles of international law,[15] while Kopelmanas reasons that "the judge may be considered as the author *par excellence* of custom." [16] Yet, in the absence of an international court system capable of delivering declaratory judgments whenever called upon to do so,[17] opinions of international tribunals and codification attempts offer, on the whole, but a little relief to a governmental decision-maker determining whether and how the scope of his political discretion has been limited by the operation of *ius non scriptum*.

This last problem of determining nationally the existence and scope of customary rules of international law provides the point of orientation for this study. Starting with the proposition that law, to be effective, must be known, we proceed to examine whether the origins of customary rules are really shrouded in mystery, or whether the alleged mystery consists, at least in some cases, of non-elastic preconceptions and tools mechanically applied to a variety of complex tasks for which such preconceptions and tools are not appropriate.

The examination rests on simple and recognized facts characterizing international customary rules: On the fact that they originate in national policies manifested in the conduct of states; and on the fact, secondly, that their growth is evolutionary. Combined, these two facts imply that the growth of customary rules is a process through which political discretion of states gradually narrows down into progressively restrictive, unavoidable, and finally, obligatory patterns.

There is no reason to search in this process for any specific point in time when a general rule of law, in deference to some artificial criteria and in defiance of its own character, suddenly bursts into its legal existence. It has been said that "Until points determined in the operation of policy are negotiated into treaties, they are elements of political action, subjects to all the vicissitudes of unresolved international questions." [18] But such a statement, taken literally, would not only represent a denial of the obligatory character of international custom; it also seeks to draw an artificially sharp line between politics and law as if they were two separate – one might almost say sovereign – realms, one not to intrude onto the other. Yet the very origin of customary rules in the conduct of states rather suggests that, in this

[15] Bin Cheng, *General Principles of Law as Applied by International Courts and Tribunals* (London: Stevens, 1953), p. 191.

[16] Kopelmanas, *op. cit.* (note 2), 141.

[17] E. M. Borchard advocated the establishment of some such system with respect to the effect on treaties of changing circumstances in order to substitute "certainty for uncertainty and clarity for doubt and jeopardy" and to "enlarge the scope of legal control and proportionately narrow the area of political action." E. M. Borchard, "Declaratory Judgments in International Law," 29 *American Journal of International Law* 492 (1935).

[18] D. F. Myers, "The Names and Scope of Treaties," 51 *American Journal of International Law* 597 (1957).

sphere at least, law and politics are indivisible; that they do not oppose each other but in fact cooperate as the stabilizing and the dynamic elements in international life.[19]

However, by adopting this general view one immediately runs into conflicts with the accepted criteria for the coming into existence of customary rules of international law – conflicts in fact so fundamental that they warrant a closer review on whose basis this study may then proceed.

SOME TRADITIONAL CRITERIA OF THE GROWTH OF INTERNATIONAL CUSTOM

Particular and General Rules

The recognition of the gradual process through which national policies grow and become transformed into customary rules of international law profoundly affects one's ability to differentiatie meaningfully between particular and general rules of customary law. As usually understood and employed, the term "general rule" means "a rule universally binding," while one of the prerequisites of that status is "general practice," meaning practice not universal, but preponderant.[20] Avoiding this looseness of language, the traditional view of one of the requirements for the coming into existence of a general customary rule may be simply expressed thus: So many states behave in this specific way that every state should. But, by circumventing the imprecision of words, one does not overcome the pitfalls inherent in that view; the pitfall of injecting a static element into a dynamic process; another of artificially simplifying the natural complexity of international life; and, last but not least, of setting up a psychological bar to the acceptance of full legal effectiveness of customary rules not valid *erga omnes*.

One of the rigidly static elements hides behind the requirement of general practice. To say that a certain practice is sufficiently preponderant among states implies, in fact, a quantitative measurement: it suggests that at a certain point, when the number of states consistently pursuing one specific policy is X, the practice has not achieved the quality of being preponderant, while at the next moment, when the number rises to X plus one, it has achieved the desirable level and every remaining state has been instantly drawn into the closed circle.

[19] Q. Wright, *Problems of Stability and Progress in International Relations* (Berkeley: University of California Press, 1954), p. 272.

[20] *E.g.*, Josef L. Kunz, "The Nature of Customary International Law," 57 *American Journal of International Law* 666 (1953).

This static rigidity is in no way softened by the prevailing vagueness and disagreement as to the number of states whose concordant policies would represent a preponderant practice. Nor does one restore the dynamism of the process by the not unrealistic view that the number of states capable to achieve a sufficiently preponderant practice may be smaller if there are among them great powers, or states with special interest in the area concerned, or traditionally law-abiding states. For all these qualifications still have their mechanically quantitative characteristic in suggesting that while some states count each as one, others may count for more. The impression persists that until a certain figure is attained, nothing of real legal relevance has happened, or only very little, and that a new legal rule springs up only when the mysterious culmination point has been reached.

The artificial simplification behind the requirement of preponderant practice leading to general rules, still further accentuating the deformed static view of a dynamic process, lies in the counting as units of states as if they were inorganic entities each with a set of fully consolidated policies directed equally at all the others. This method obscures the more realistic view which considers as the basic element of international politics and law not the state as a static entity, but the dynamic state-to-state relationship.[21] In cases where it might be necessary to indulge in mathematical exercises in order to discover how preponderant and general a certain practice has become, the relevant question would not be how many states maintain that practice, but in how many instances of state-to-state relationships it exists. In other words, the correct calculation would be not how many states out of the approximately 130 existing ones maintain a certain practice but in how many instances of state-to-state relationships does that practice predominate.

But no matter how one arrives at the quantitative conclusion that there is a sufficient volume – in the words of article 38 of the Statute of the International Court of Justice – of "international custom, as evidence of a general practice accepted as law," what are the intrinsic characteristics, other than the scope of operation, that distinguish the general rule from particular ones? Whether a rule is more general or less, it can always be modified, abandoned or reversed by the action or agreement of any two or more states for the purposes of their own mutual relationship. Consequently, State A

21 At this point it is appropriate to refer to the stimulating studies by Myres S. McDougal viewing international law as a comprehensive process of authoritative decision, or a process of unceasing social interaction – of mutual tolerances, restraints and conflicts of interests. For a recent exposition of McDougal's views see Chapter I in Myres S. McDougal and William T. Burke, *The Public Order of the Oceans: A Contemporary International Law of the Sea* (New Haven: Yale University Press, 1962).

may be bound to observe one rule in relation to State B and another, governing the same matter, in relation to State C. The resolution of a dispute is ultimately governed by finding what is the specific legal relationship of the two states involved. In the 1960 case concerning *Right of Passage over Indian Territory,* Portugal also invoked general international custom in support of its claim of a right of passage over Indian territory as formulated by Portugal. The Court, after emphasizing that it was dealing with a concrete case, refused to examine the existence of the alleged general international custom where there was "a practice clearly established between two States which was accepted by the Parties as governing the relations between them," and added that "such a particular practice must prevail over any general rules." [22]

In the *Norwegian Fisheries* case the Court did enter the question of the existence of general rules of international law; and it declined to consider as universally applicable the rules determining the base-line of territorial waters by the low-water mark following the sinuosities of the coast and, in case of bays, by the ten-mile width. The Court pointed out that

> although the ten-mile rule has been adopted by certain States both in their national law and in their treaties and conventions, and although certain arbitral decisions have applied it as between these States, other States have adopted a different limit. Consequently, the ten-mile rule has not acquired the authority of a general rule of international law.[23]

The Court did not indicate whether it would require as a basis of a general rule of law a universally uniform practice, or whether it would be satisfied with less than that.[24] But of still greater significance to our purposes is the stress the Court laid on the case being one between Norway and the

[22] International Court of Justice, *Reports* 1960, pp. 43–44. As to Portugal's claims based on local custom, it was objected on behalf of India that no local custom could be established between only two states. To this the Court replied: "It is difficult to see why the number of States between which a local custom may be established on the basis of long practice must necessarily be larger than two. The Court sees no reason why long continued practice between two States accepted by them as regulating their relations should not form the basis of mutual rights and obligations between the two States. *Ibid.*, p. 39.

[23] International Court of Justice, *Reports* 1951, p. 131. But nowhere throughout the judgment is there any indication that the Court intended to question the existence of a particular – yet widespread – ten-mile rule, or to detract from its obligatory force. For a view that the attitude of the Court, indicating the acceptance of the standard of universality as the only valid test of the existence of a rule of international law, may be open to the objection that it puts into question the existence of most rules and principles of international law, see Lauterpacht, *op. cit.* (note 3), pp. 191–192. See also note immediately below.

[24] Commenting on the case, Lauterpacht stated: "If universality is to be made the condition of the application of customary rules, it may become doubtful whether many rules would qualify for that purpose" – thus indicating that, in his opinion, the Court did demand universal or almost universal practice as a basis of a general rule of law. *Ibid.*, p. 370.

United Kingdom. Thus the Court stated, rejecting the argument of the British Government that the Norwegian system of delimitation had not been known to it and thus lacked the notoriety essential to provide the basis of an historic title enforceable against it:

The Court is unable to accept this view. As a coastal State on the North Sea, greatly interested in the fisheries in this area, as a maritime Power traditionally concerned with the law of the sea and concerned particularly to defend the freedom of the seas, the United Kingdom could not have been ignorant of the Decree of 1869 which had at once provoked a request for explanations by the French Government. Nor, knowing of it, could it have been under any misapprehension as to the significance of its terms, which clearly described it as constituting the application of a system.

And, concluding, again:

The notoriety of the facts, the general toleration of the international community, Great Britain's position in the North Sea, her own interest in the question, and her prolonged abstention would in any case warrant Norway's enforcement of her system against the United Kingdom.[25]

It is, of course, futile to contemplate how would the Court have ruled had some country other than the United Kingdom been a party to the case – possibly a country far removed from the North Sea; with a coastline and general economic conditions similar to those of Norway; one which determined the shoreward limits of its own territorial waters by the low water mark following the sinuosities of the coast; and, perhaps, with evidence that in at least some instances Norwegian fishermen had taken advantage off its coasts of base-lines so determined and of the consequent extent of the territorial sea. The futility of attempting to suggest which way would then the Court's ruling go lies, obviously, in the artificiality and the resulting simplification of our example; however, seeing that the Court did consider not only general conditions of the case but also, and with emphasis, the bilateral relation of the two parties, one is permitted to say that, possibly, its ruling might have been different if a country other than the United Kingdom stood with Norway before the Court.

This essentially bilateral viewpoint, if consistently maintained, may appear to lead to a certain disintegration or at least to the weakening of customary law. Yet, we submit, an exactly opposite result is more likely. It is most often in the bilateral relations of states that disputes arise, and it is with reference to such relations that they can be most easily settled. Further-

[25] International Court of Justice, *Reports* 1951, pp. 140–141.

more, the unrealistic ideal of universally uniform rules of law, and the corresponding requirement of a general practice leading to such rules, represent a psychological as well as practical hindrance on the way to more orderly relations of states; for when a supposedly general rule of customary law is found not to be so very general, or when bilateral or regional changes in state practice reduce its generality, the impression is created that a law has been weakened and ceased to be binding.

An illustrative example was provided by the reaction to the *Norwegian Fisheries* case of some United States legislators. The Committee on Interior and Insular Affairs of the United States House of Representatives, succumbing to the temptation to use the Court's ruling as a point of departure for a more liberal determination of the base-lines of the territorial sea, stated in one of its reports:

> The decision of the International Court provides an opportunity for the United States, as well as other nations, to reexamine its inland-water policy in light of the principles of the decision. Where Federal agencies had taken a limited position or no position at all, it would seem proper for the Congress to adopt a new position at this time.

The report also said that

> A persuasive argument can be made that any position taken by the United States prior to that decision was based on a mistaken impression as to international law, or at least on inadequate knowledge as to the state of such law . . .[26]

Thus the statement of the Court that there was not a rule of law so general in its application as to bind Norway, with its historical practice and special conditions, was somehow understood as a signal to undertake revisions of policies perhaps even without regard to the existing bilateral and multilateral obligations unaffected by the decision.[27]

[26] United States Congress. House of Representatives. Committee on Interior and Insular Affairs. *Investigation and Study of the Seaward Boundaries of the United States*. Report, 1953 (82nd Cong., 2nd Sess., H. Rept. 2515), p. 13.

[27] Brunson MacChesney, commenting briefly on the *Norwegian Fisheries* case, stated that the decision "will particularly affect the practice of States with respect to the methods for measuring base lines as well as having a significant impact on the extent of internal and territorial waters . . . Even though the decision is not technically a precedent binding in future cases, it has already influenced and will continue to influence in practice the claims of States and the reactions of other States to such claims." U.S. Naval War College, *International Law Situation and Documents* 1956, Brunson MacChesney, ed. (Washington, D.C.: Government Printing Office, 1957), p. 60. The general impact of the decision of the International Court of Justice in the *Norwegian Fisheries* case was clearly in evidence during the 1958 U.N. Conference on the Law of the Sea at Geneva. The draft Convention on the Territorial Sea and the Contiguous Zone, eventually adopted by the Conference, permitted the employment of straight baselines under those conditions that the Court had emphasized. Several delegates at the Conference directly referred to the decision of the Court as an authoritative guide to a generally permissible practice. U.N. Conference on the Law of the Sea, 2 *Official Records* 62–63 and 132–133, Doc. A/CONF.13/38.

Seen from the bilateral viewpoint, on the other hand, every customary rule binding on more than two states appears to consist of a number of specific legal relationships even if it is, in rare cases, a truly universal rule. And that viewpoint then also discloses both the stability and the dynamism of international custom. A decision of an international tribunal denying the validity of an assumed "general" rule in a specific case need not mean that the whole system of law in the area concerned has been shattered. The political decision underlying every change in state practice, when seen from the bilateral perspective, is not an enemy of law and order but a component part in their operation. It may lead to a refinement and individualization of customary rules rather than to their disintegration; even a sizeable change in state practice, seen from the bilateral viewpoint, may mean but the emergence of new or modified rules existing alongside the traditional ones, rather than the creation of a gap, conducive to disorder, in the entire legal system governing the matter in question.

All these considerations underlie one of the leading concepts on which this study is based: that in the case of certain customary rules of international law their classification as general or even universal rules, or as "not-yet-general," is irrelevant or misleading. To state that, as a result of an increasing number of states adopting parallel policies, there is a general customary rule *in fieri, in statu nascendi,* is to present an unverifiable impression of little significance; it is still necessary to determine whether or not the parallel practices of the states in question have not already grown, among some or all of them, into particular legal relations. A statement such as Wilson's, that "there must . . . be adequate evidence that the custom has really become so generally followed that there is no longer reasonable doubt about its jural force" [28] invites the obvious question whether the jural force of a customary rule is really dependent on its "generality," and why.

Duration of Practice as a Static Element

The lapse of time traditionally and often mechanically required for the emergence of international customary rules represents another static factor deforming a theoretical reconstruction of the dynamic process through which customary rules grow. Kopelmanas states that a customary rule "may arise simply from the fact that states in their mutual relations observe a

[21] R. R. Wilson, *The International Law Standard in Treaties of the United States* (Cambridge, Mass.: Harvard University Press, 1953), p. 6.

certain definite attitude for a long period of time." [29] De Visscher stresses "the slow consolidation by the action of time" [30] as an important element in the growth of custom. Discussing the effect of treaties on third parties, McNair considers it undeniable that "after a period of time, to which no fixed duration can be attributed, the mere lapse of time and the acquiescence of other States in the arrangement thus made have the effect of extending the scope of operation of the treaty . . ." [31]

Taken literally, the usual emphasis on the time element again creates the impression that in individual instances a certain duration of practice does lead to a customary rule, while a somewhat shorter period of time would be insufficient; by implication this would mean that up to a certain point in time since the inception of an international practice the development is legally inert, while the mere lapse of some more time injects into it its legal content.

One of the possible reasons for the sometimes unquestioning verbal deference to the proposition that a considerable length of time must elapse for a customary rule to become valid lies in the assumption that a protracted change is more conducive to order while too rapid a development would bring about chaos. Yet in at least some cases a prolonged duration of a certain practice may be completely unproductive. One may consider the following statement:

> Well over one hundred treaties which *have governed or today govern* water uses in international drainage basins have been entered into all over the world. These treaties . . . indicate that there are principles limiting the power of states to use such waters without regard to injurious effects on co-riparians . . . The number of states parties to these treaties, *their spread over time* and geography, and the fact that in these treaties similar problems are resolved in similar ways, make of these treaties and negotiations persuasive evidence of law-creating international practice.[32]

It is not obvious, though, why the "spread over time" of the treaties should strengthen the evidence of law-creating practice. If all the treaties referred to were negotiated, signed and put into effect within a single year or a time still shorter, would not the concentration of parallel acts in that brief period attest much more persuasively to the existence of a law-creating practice?

The crucial point is, of course, in the widespread admission that it is

[29] Kopelmanas, *op. cit.* (note 2) 132.

[30] Charles De Visscher, "Reflections on the Present Prospects of International Adjudication," 50 *American Journal of International Law* 472 (1956).

[31] A. D. McNair, "Treaties Producing Effects Erga Omnes," 2 *Scritti di Diritto Internazionale in Onore di Tomaso Perassi* (Milan: Giuffré, 1957) 2

[32] William L. Griffin, "The Use of Waters of International Drainage Basins under Customary International Law," 53 *American Journal of International Law* 50 (1959). Emphases added.

impossible to fix any specific length of time needed for the emergence of international customary rules, or for the emergence of any one rule. It is true that in the case concerning *Right of Passage over Indian Territory* the International Court of Justice stressed that the practice established between Portugal and India "continued over a period extending beyond a century and a quarter";[33] that in the *Norwegian Fisheries* case the same Court, examining the historic or prescriptive element of the Norwegian system of base-line determination, emphasized the length of time elapsed since the inception of that system in the 19th century.[34] But even in the field of prescriptive rights, where the element of time is thought to play a particularly significant role, its length is indeterminate. According to Lauterpacht's Oppenheim, "no general rule can be laid down" [35] as to the length of time, while Scelle, still more forcefully, stated: ". . . le Droit International ne comporte pas de délais déterminés des prescriptions, et il est un peu naif de la part de certains auteurs d'avoir essayé de les chiffrer (quarante ou cinquante ans) . . ." [36]

The reasons why the duration of practice as one of the elements effecting the emergence of international custom is characterized by so much vagueness, and its impact is so uncertain, become clearer when we examine the preconceptions emphasizing the time element, and the problems it creates.

Systematization and Generalization

The setting-up of the time-length criterion is but a part of the tendency to set relatively firm and generally applicable criteria for the emergence of international customary rules. It is a tendency to discern some order in, or force some order into, an amorphous mass of state acts so as to make them legally legible; the compelling need to determine the existence of a customary rule provides the impulse to systematization and generalization.

Yet it is impossible to overlook that customary law covers an extremely wide range of subjects; that the state acts which initiate customary rules greatly vary in form; and that an even greater variety prevails among states in their geographical and political positions, economic strength, technological standards, and in their ability to keep in touch with developments abroad. In De Visscher's words:

[33] International Court of Justice, *Reports* 1960, p. 40. On other occasions in the same judgment, the Court referred to custom "established on the basis of long practice" and to "a long continued practice."

[34] International Court of Justice, *Reports* 1951, pp. 133ff.

[35] L. Oppenheim, *International Law: A Treatise*, 6th ed., ed. by H. Lauterpacht, vol .1 (London: Longmans, Green & Co., 1947), p. 527.

[36] Georges Scelle, *Manuel de Droit International Public* (Paris: Domat-Montchrestien, 1948), p. 160.

The selection of the factual elements which, viewed as a whole, lead to the admission of the existence of a customary rule is subject to extremely variable considerations; it hardly permits efforts toward systematization.[37]

To state that a long continued practice is necessary for the emergence of customary rules, but to admit that its actual duration is variable, is hardly an acceptable criterion; much rather it is an unnecessary generalization of the undisputed fact that every human act or inactivity can only occur within time, shorter or longer, its length depending on surrounding circumstances.

The Contents of Time

It is more important what transpires within a certain time rather than its mere lapse. Obviously the effects of an authoritative statement of a national policy affecting other states would not linger on indefinitely and even become stronger if the policy were not implemented although it could have been, and if the non-consummated statement of policy met with indifference abroad. Conversely, the adoption by a state of an internationally significant practice which could rapidly involve important public interests and is of a particularly noticeable nature may lead to the emergence of a legal relationship within a very short time; its length could in fact be limited to a period needed, first, for the new practice to become known to other states; second, for the requisite study of the implications of the new practice; and third, for communicating the eventual decision as to the appropriate reaction or the implementation of such a decision.

Some illustration of this problem can again be obtained from the *Norwegian Fisheries* case. The International Court of Justice, rejecting in its judgment the contention of the United Kingdom that the Norwegian system of delimitation had not been known to it, referred to the Norwegian Decree of 1869 "which had at once provoked a request for explanations by the French Government" and expressed the opinion that "the United Kingdom could not have been ignorant" of it.[38] The French request for explanations was dispatched only two months after the promulgation of the Decree, was answered by Norway within six weeks, and the eventual French acceptance of the Norwegian system as resting upon the configuration of the coast and the conditions of the inhabitants was communicated to Norway within another five months.

The mechanically and generally applied requirement of a long duration of a specific state practice thus often only obscures the need to examine the

[37] De Visscher, *op. cit.* (note 30) 473.
[38] International Court of Justice, *Reports* 1951, p. 140.

manifestations of that practice in detail, to judge its circumstances, and to evaluate its consequences.

Duration of Practice and Bilateral Origins of Custom

The stress on the duration of practice as an effective factor in the emergence of customary rules is often due to the traditional tendency to distinguish rigidly between particular and general rules. However, the relativity of time in the growth of customary rules becomes obvious once we admit that even rules which eventually attain general validity may be initiated by the action of only one state acting unilaterally, or by a parallel action of two states, in a sphere not fully regulated by international law or even in a manner inconsistent with the existing law. Resorting again to the law of the sea, it is not difficult to imagine that a state with such intense interests in fishing as Japan would probably estop itself much sooner – through acquiescence – from contesting a newly established practice of a third state affecting international fisheries in the North Pacific than, for instance, a country such as the Union of South Africa, less engaged in fishing and far removed in space. An international tribunal would probably allow much longer time for a South African protest than it would for a Japanese claim in the same situation.

However, the question of international communication and national alertness to changes and new developments in state practice is but one aspect of the problem the bilateral viewpoint tends to clarify. Another emerges from observing the fact that international customary rules binding on several states may be the sum of varied bilateral legal relationships. A specific conduct between two states may be regulated by a tacit agreement, while the same conduct between different sets of two or more states may be ordered by a form of estoppel, local custom or prescription, each becoming effective under different situations.

Provisionally closing the present section on the duration of international practice, it is possible to agree with the following statement by Tunkin:

> Although in fact time plays a big part in the process of formation of a customary norm of international law, juridically the element of time cannot in itself have a decisive significance. Depending on circumstances, a customary norm may take a long time to develop but may also be formed in a short period of time.[39]

[39] G. I. Tunkin, "Remarks on the Juridical Nature of Customary Norms of International Law," 49 *California Law Review* 420 (1961).

The Relative Value of "Opinio Juris sive Necessitatis"

The requirement of *opinio juris* as an indispensable factor in the growth of international customary law has always represented an elusive and controversial issue. It does appear, though, that the considerable difficulties attending the so-called psychological conception of international custom – *i.e.* the consciousness that a specific international practice is pursued with a sense of legal obligation – do not arise from any intrinsic complexity of the factor itself. Those difficulties are again a product of an almost irresistible tendency of some writers and jurists to generalize – so as to infuse some order and symmetry into the asymmetric movement of international law and politics – by devising ever-valid definitions which, being too general, are neither ever-valid nor sufficiently precise to define anything.

The briefest definition of *opinio juris* is to be found in article 38 of the Statute of the International Court of Justice where international custom is described as evidence of a general practice *accepted as law*. The term "accepted" may have an activist meaning; it might imply governmental *acts of acceptance*. But it may also have a number of other meanings; it may signify a willingness of states to accept certain conduct as obligatory and to exclude any other mode of behavior, or the readiness of states to view that conduct, when chosen by others out of two or more alternate courses of behavior, as legally unassailable. The problem arises as soon as one chooses among the various meanings, and attempts to press them into a new and generally valid definition of *opinio juris*.

The activist meaning of the principle of *opinio juris sive necessitatis* appears, for instance, in Basdevant's statement that customary norms "which are born spontaneously, out of the requirements of international law, acquire a positive character *by being recognized* by those with the power to have them applied in international life." [40] Tunkin, representing the prevailing Soviet view[41] of customary law, finds the evidence of *opinio juris* in an expression of the will of the state to abide by a specific rule, in the state's "agreement to regard this or that customary rule as a norm of international law"; what he calls a "dialectical approach" leads him to a somewhat puzzling statement:

[40] J. Basdevant, "Règles Générales du Droit de la Paix," 58 *Recueil des Cours de l'Academie de Droit International* 516 (1936).

[41] For a recent review of Soviet theories and attitudes – and their modifications – toward international customary law, see J. F. Triska and R. M. Slusser, "Treaties and Other Sources of Order in International Relations: The Soviet View," 52 *American Journal of International Law* 699–726 (1958).

Opinio juris signifies that the states treat this or that customary norm as juridically binding. When other states, too, *express a will* in this direction, a tacit agreement is formed to recognize the customary rule as a norm of law.[42]

Finally, the opinion of the Permanent Court of International Justice in the notorious *Lotus* case also points, indirectly, to an activist concept of *opinio juris*. There the Court demanded a positive proof that the abstention of states from a specific conduct was demonstrably due to their consciousness of a legal duty to abstain; in the absence of such a poof the Court found it impossible to confirm the existence of an alleged customary rule ordering the abstentions.[43] However, to demand such a proof is to demand specific and articulate acts of states clearly expressing their consciousness of an obligation not to undertake certain acts.

A different meaning of the requirement of *opinio juris*, less stringent but also less clear, is implied by the definition of *opinio juris* as a "conception that the practice is required by, or consistent with, prevailing international law." [44] Not only is there a fundamental difference between the terms "required by" and "consistent with" – *ie.*, between "obligatory" and "permissible"; it is also highly problematical how the conception may be formed, whether subjectively as an impression or a feeling, or by determining with legal objectivity what international law actually requires. In the latter case, however, why search for any additional *opinio juris* if the conception would represent but the cognizance of a previously and objectively existent legal fact?

Still another meaning of *opinio juris* is implied in the view that the existence of the conviction of legal obligation is sufficiently proven by continuously uniform conduct of states within legally relevant spheres of action. Adopt-

[42] Tunkin, *op. cit.* (note 39) 424. Emphasis added. Concluding his brief examination of the custom-creating factors, the author states: "Agreement between states on the basis of equality is the essence of the norm-formation process in customary international law. It is particularly characteristic of the period of co-existence of states belonging to opposed social systems, since the existence of two opposed systems further accentuates the impossibility of creating norms of law binding upon the states of both systems except by agreement between them based on equality." *Ibid.* 430.

[43] The Court states, while examining an argument advanced by the French Government that an international rule applying to case of ship collisions had grown up according to which criminal proceedings regarding such case come exclusively within the jurisdiction of the flag state: "Even if the rarity of the judicial decisions to be found among the reported cases were sufficient to prove in point of fact the circumstances alleged by the Agent for the Frech Government, it would merely show that States had often, in practice, abstained from instituting criminal proceedings, and not that they recognized themselves as being obliged to do so; for only if such abstention were based on their being conscious of having a duty to abstain would it be possible to speak of an international custom. The alleged fact does not allow one to infer that States have been conscious of having such a duty . . ." Permanent Court of International Justice, *Reports* 1927, Series A, No. 10.

[44] From Hudson's definition of elements required for the emergence of customary international legal rules. See p. 2.

ed by Lauterpacht,[45] this view includes the admission that the frequency or constancy of a specific conduct may be conceived by states as due either to a sense of obligation or to the will to undertake a legal obligation,[46] but in neither case anything more is required as evidence beyond the frequency and uniformity of practice.

All these and many other interpretations of the requirement of *opinio juris* as a custom-creating factor have one common denominator: they are intended to apply to all and any rules of international custom and, in addition, to apply to them from the perspective of general or even universal norms. This high degree of abstraction is mainly responsible for the inconclusiveness of discussions surrounding the requirement of *opinio juris* and for the difficulties in applying it.

We are not thus suggesting that an essentially bilateral view of customary rules, with a particular stress on the dynamics of their growth and operation, does erase all the problems. But in those instances where it can be usefully applied as a method of analysis it does help to reveal the relativity of the requirement of *opinio juris* as well as of other criteria presumed to determine the existence of international customary rules. To illustrate that relativity one may first use the example of customary rules of multilateral effectiveness whose origins may be traced to repetitious clauses in bilateral treaties. Where does the criterion of *opinio juris* come in? Here one may partly agree with Kopelmanas that "when agents of a state sign a treaty, they do not intend to obey existing law. They are making new law . . ." – and with his conclusion that "no *opinio juris* governs the birth of this class of customary rules";[47] but one can agree with these statements only if, first, one defines *opinio juris* as a conception that certain conduct is required by international law and not merely consistent with it, and, second, if one excludes *a priori* treaties whose provisions are declaratory in the sense that they merely confirm an existing legal relationship, perhaps customary in origin, between the parties. And again, in case of third states adopting the practices regulated by a set of bilateral treaties but without any express subjection to them – where does one look for *opinio juris?* How can one determine whether the states adopted the practices for reasons of political or economic expediency or out of a feeling of legal necessity? What political and legal alternatives had been open to them before they adopted the one particular mode of conduct? Having adopted it, what expectations did they create among other states and to what extent have they obligated themselves to fulfil them?

[45] *Op. cit.* (note 3), pp. 380, 385–6.
[46] *Ibid.*, p. 379.
[47] Kopelmanas, *op. cit.* (note 2) 137.

None of these questions can be meaningfully answered *in abstracto*. Answers can be usefully sought only with reference to specific rules operating under specific conditions.

This brief exposition of some of the theoretical problems enveloping the growth and operation of international customary rules not only sets the guidelines for but, in a very real sense, determines the scope of this study. The only approach left open to us for a study in the dynamics of international customary law and for an examination of the methods through which the existence of a customary rule could be ascertained is a case-study approach – the case here selected being that of the rules comprising the contemporary legal regime of the continental shelf. The second important limitation to which this inquiry is necessarily subject is that no generalization applicable to other customary rules is to be derived from such conclusions and findings as we submit in the course of the case-study except perhaps one: that any attempts to generalize in the highly dynamic field of international custom, and the efforts to systematize its creative elements, prove unsound when confronted with practical problems.

THE LAW OF THE CONTINENTAL SHELF IN THEORY

The contemporary legal regime of the continental shelf has been selected as a case for the purposes of this study for a number of reasons: first, that regime is still developing, its various rules have reached different levels of maturity; second, its emergence is fairly recent and, consequently, evidence of its origins is not buried too deep in the history of international relations; last but not unimportant, it was a close study of the continental shelf regime that aroused the author's concern with some problems of the growth of international customary law, and affected the formation of some of the views and concepts expressed or implied in the preceding sections.

Stated as simply as possible, the rules comprising the legal regime of the continental shelf give to the coastal state an exclusive right to put to certain uses, such as the exploitation of the natural resources, the seabed and subsoil under the high seas adjacent to the state's territorial waters; and they impose the obligation on the users that should such uses of the continental shelf be practiced, other lawful users of the continental shelf and of the high seas above it must be protected from consequent damage.

In a sense, the system of rules governing the uses of the continental shelf has an exceptional history and singular characteristics. It has no complex system of historical roots. Its basic principles emerged almost overnight in the form of a doctrine of a great persuasive potential; applied with considerable intensity, the elements of the doctrine rapidly grew into a system of customary rules which, although internally diversified and full of uncertainties and incompatibilities, was still effective as a system of public order. The forces shaping the continental shelf regime – economic, technological and political – are not only identifiable with relative ease; they have also worked in an unusual harmony with one another and in unison with the national and international interests involved. Born and growing during a tense period of multiple international crises heaped upon economic diversity and social revolutions, the legal system of the continental shelf has been little affected by the vicissitudes of international conflicts.

On the more narrowly legal front, the regime of the continental shelf seems to have emerged and grown in an equally favorable climate. Its entry into the system of international law caused no revolutionary changes in that law; no established rules had to be rapidly and completely erased to make room for the new addition. Of course, the legal regime of the continental shelf had to be accommodated in the international law system by subtracting from some established rules into whose family it fitted – the freedom of high sea navigation and fishing in particular. But these changes have been slight, and slow in coming. On the whole, they emphasize rather than undermine the compatibility of the continental shelf regime with other systems of international norms.

The relative simplicity of the history of the rules comprising the legal regime of the continental shelf and, relatively again, their clear-cut legal complexion are exactly those features that make them an instrument eminently suited to some of the stated purposes of this inquiry. One would rightly expect that an examination of the emergence and growth of such a system of rules should show in sharp relief the respective effectiveness of such criteria – allegedly determining the legal status of an international usage – as the generality and duration of the practice of states and its acceptance as a legal necessity or *desideratum* expressed by the term *opinio juris sive necessitatis*; further, one should be able to recognize and evaluate the impact on these criteria of circumstances under which they function, and of the forces that may strengthen, modify, or weaken their operation and legal relevance.

Of course, when using for this inquiry the legal regime of the continental shelf, we are not entering an unexplored corner of international law. In the past eighteen years, writers and jurists paid considerable attention to the continental shelf doctrine. Before embarking upon our own independent inquiry into the problem and before attempting to reconstruct the dynamic process through which the legal regime of the continental shelf emerged and grew, we may briefly yet profitably survey what other students of the continental shelf policies and law have discovered or failed to find with reference to the criteria of the growth of international customary rules.

As we shall see in some detail later, the continental shelf doctrine, reflecting the utility of an international acceptance of some exclusive coastal rights on the adjacent continental shelf, was first formulated by the United States Government in the so-called Truman Proclamation of 28 September 1945. By this unilateral statement of policy, the United States claimed certain exclusive rights on the continental shelf under the high seas adjacent to its territorial waters. In the following months and years, there was a rapidly moving procession of comparable actions undertaken by other states – unilateral declarations, legislative acts, joint proclamations and hemispheric resolutions – and on their trail commenced a theoretical search for legal foundations of the emerging customary regime of the continental shelf. Writers, jurists, expert groups and juridical bodies joined in the effort. Their broad ultimate aim was to determine whether a new regime governing the continental shelf had come into existence, and on what legal bases it could comfortably rest.

The Legal Status of the Doctrine

There was considerable agreement among writers – some exceptions are mentioned below in this section – with a general statement made by C. C. Hyde in 1945 that the "subsoil appurtenant to the coast of a State and extending therefrom into an area beneath the high sea is . . . susceptible to acquisition by that State." [48] However, beyond these terms little agreement appeared possible concerning the conditions and processes through which a state could consummate that susceptibility. One writer even considered that there were ". . . almost as many rationalizations of the concept of the continental shelf as there have been commentators"; [49] but whether this statement slightly exaggerated or not, from 1945 on writers' and students' answers as to the legal validity of the continental shelf doctrine oscillated between emphatic acceptance by some and almost equally emphatic denial by others. At a meeting of the United Nations International Law Commission in 1950, J. M. Yepes of Bogota even asserted that the Truman Pro-

[48] C. C. Hyde, *International Law Chiefly as Interpreted and Applied by the United States*, vol. 1 (Boston: Little, Brown & Co., 1945), p. 481.

[49] D. P. O'Connell, "Sedentary Fisheries and the Australian Continental Shelf," 49 *American Journal of International Law* 194 (1955).

clamation of 1945 itself "... constituted a veritable customary law to which the Commission should give recognition ..." [50] But one need not dwell on exceptional views to see the diversity of conclusions reached.[51]

Until 1950, writers[52] generally display considerable restraint; they do study the many varied aspects of the continental shelf doctrine but do not express definite conclusions as to its legal validity.

In 1950, the United Nations Secretariat transmitted to the International Law Commission a valuable memorandum on the law of the high seas which finds that "the continental shelf doctrine as it emerges from ... [the texts of the various unilateral proclamations] has no support from rules of general international law" [53] but that the proclamations themselves "may constitute the origin of a new law." [54] In that same year, however, a writer as distinguished as Hersch Lauterpacht, in an inquiry both penetrating and inspired, asserted that "the question of the nature of the right over the adjacent submarine areas is to a large extent an academic question ..." [55] since the practice of the continental shelf "has now, in any case, become part of international law." [56] Writing at about the same time, C. H. M. Waldock considered the continental shelf doctrine legally ineffective and incomplete in all respects where it differed from the established rules of the law of effective

[50] U.N. International Law Commission, *Yearbook* 1950, vol. 1 (Summary Records of the Second Session, 67th Meeting, 13 July 1950), p. 218. Professor Yepes later attempted to defend the extensive maritime claims of Chile, Ecuador and Peru in "El Problema del Mar Territorial o Jurisdiccional y de la Plataforma Submarina ante al Nuevo Derecho Internacional," 8 *Revista Universitas* (Bogotá) 45–69 (1955). For comment, see Josef L. Kunz, "Continental Shelf and International Law: Confusion and Abuse," 50 *American Journal of International Law* 839 ff. (1956).

[51] In 1957, a Japanese writer asserted that "almost all the publicists, who separate the regime of the submarine areas from that of the high seas, suffer from incorrect view of space in world community." Shigeru Oda, "The Continental Shelf." 1 *Japanese Annual of International Law* 36 (1957).

[52] *E.g.*, F. A. Vallat, "The Continental Shelf," 23 *British Year Book of International Law* 333–338 (1946); Richard Young, "The Legal Status of Submarine Areas beneath the High Seas," 45 *American Journal of International Law* 225–249 (1951); Cecil J. B. Hurst, "The Continental Shelf," 34 *Transactions of the Grotius Society* 153–169 (1949).

[53] U.N. Secretariat. *Memorandum on the Regime of the High Seas.* Doc. A/CN.4/32 (14 July 1950), p. 95.

[54] *Ibid.*, p. 100.

[55] H. Lauterpacht, "Sovereignty over Submarine Areas," 27 *British Year Book of International Law* 392 (1950).

[56] *Ibid.* 376–377, 414–415, 431. However, the next year the U.N. International Law Commission completed its first draft of the continental shelf articles of which article 2 read: "The Continental Shelf is subject to the exercise by the coastal State of control and jurisdiction for the purpose of exploring it and exploiting its natural resources." And in paragraph 6 of its commentary on the article quoted the ILC stated: "The Commission has not attempted to base on customary law the right of a coastal State to exercise control and jurisdiction for the limited purposes stated in article 2. Though numerous proclamations have been issued over the past decade, it can hardly be said that such unilateral action has already established a new customary law." U.N. International Law Commission, *Yearbook* 1951, vol. 2 (Documents of ILC, Third Session), pp. 141–142.

occupation.[57] Still in 1950, the Committee on "Rights to the Sea Bed and its Subsoil" of the International Law Association recognized that the practice of coastal states to make unilateral proclamations asserting their jurisdiction and control over the adjacent continental shelf "evidently satisfies a need for the development of international law on this subject,"[58] but in general likewise treated the continental shelf doctrine as legally immature.

In the following years and until at least the 1958 United Nations Conference on the Law of the Sea at Geneva, no greater uniformity of views existed on the legal status of the doctrine. As umpire in the dispute between Petroleum Development (Trucial Coast) Ltd. and Sheikh Shakhbut of Abu Dhabi, Lord Asquith of Bishopstone examined the question whether the continental shelf doctrine formed "part and parcel of international law" and, finding that "neither the practice of nations nor the pronouncements of learned jurists give any certain or consistent answer" to many fundamental problems, concluded that

> there are in this field so many ragged ends and unfilled blanks, so much that is merely tentative and exploratory, that in no form can the doctrine claim as yet to have assumed hitherto the hard lineaments or the definitive status of an established rule of International Law.[59]

Several months later,[60] M. W. Mouton expressed his conviction, after a detailed study of the subject, that "there is no rule of International Law concerning the use of the continental shelf and hence no State has 'ipso jure' rights on the shelf." [61] Viewing the problem from Australia, D. P. O'Connell stated in 1955 that "the concept of the continental shelf and the character of the rights asserted in respect of it have crystallized, and . . . a definite pattern has now been set for future development of the law," [62] and that it was legitimate to say that "the continental shelf is a concept of law." [63] Shortly thereafter, Josef Kunz considered the doctrine "a new norm of general customary international law *in fieri, in statu nascendi*"; [64] but "a new norm of interna-

[57] C. H. M. Waldock. "The Legal Basis of Claims to the Continental Shelf," 36 *Transactions of the Grotius Society* 143 (1950).

[58] International Law Association, *Report of the Forty-Fourth Conference*, Copenhagen 1950 (London: I.L.A., 1952), p. 127.

[59] Text of the award, reprinted from 1 *International and Comparative Law Quarterly* 247 (1952), appears in U.S. Naval War College, *op. cit.* (note 27), pp. 137 ff. Quote at p. 149.

[60] The purpose of the present discussion is merely to review the general divergence of conclusions as to the validity of the continental shelf doctrine. For a broad, selective list of articles, reports and special studies dealing with the subject see the appended bibliography.

[61] M. W. Mouton, *The Continental Shelf* (The Hague: Nijhoff, 1952), p. 315.

[62] O'Connell, *op. cit.* (note 49) 185.

[63] *Ibid.* 195.

[64] Kunz, *op. cit.* (note 50) 832.

tional law has not yet come into existence, although we are witnessing the formation of such new norm." [65]

Nor is it possible to turn to the work of the International Law Commission for a persuasive indication as to the legal status of the continental shelf doctrine at any given time. During its extensive work on the law of the sea, the Commission at first attempted to specify which of the provisional articles it drafted fell into the category of rules sufficiently developed in practice, and in which it exercised its authority to progressively develop the law in fields as yet legally unregulated. Later, however, the Commission abandoned the attempt primarily in view of the wide differences of opinion as to whether a subject is already sufficiently developed in practice.[66] But even after the Convention on the Continental Shelf had been signed at Geneva on 29 April 1958, theoretical doubts about the legal existence of a customary rule governing the uses of the continental shelf did not disappear; commenting on the Geneva Conference, Max Sørensen would go no further than to state that "it is arguable that a customary rule of international law has developed" [67] on the basis of national claims to the adjacent shelves and their general acceptance.

The Formative Factors in the Growth of the Law

The divergence of views regarding the legal status of the continental shelf doctrine grew out of a variety of factors, principles and conditions to which individual writers ascribed legally relevant roles – positive or negative – in the growth of the rule. One may, perhaps, agree with O'Connell that "basically the controversy is the old one between those who reason *a priori* and the positivists." [68] But it is unnessary to enter that controversy directly while considering the bases of the different conclusions reached.

[65] *Ibid.* 829–830. At 829, Kunz mentions Lauterpacht and Verdross as two writers who accept, and Mouton, Scelle and Guggenheim as those who deny, the existence of a new rule of general customary law governing the continental shelf.

[66] U.N. International Law Commission, *Yearbook* 1956, vol. 2 (Documents of ILC, Eighth Session), p. 256.

[67] Max Sørensen, "Law of the Sea," 520 *International Conciliation* 227 (November 1958). Emphasis added. It is also interesting to consider the studied vagueness in the statement made by the United States delegation's representative in Committee IV (Continental Shelf) of the U.N. Conference on the Law of the Sea: "Prior to very recent years, the legal status of the continental shelf, outside the recognized territorial sea was, in considerable measure, undefined. But the progress of events now requires an expansion of international law in this area. Much of the work of Committee IV lies in the realm of the 'progressive development of international law' . . ." UN Doc. A/CONF.13/C.4/SR.10, pp. 4–5. Also, Marjorie M. Whiteman, "Conference on the Law of the Sea: Convention on the Continental Shelf," 52 *American Journal of International Law* 632 (1952).

[68] O'Connell, *op. cit.* (note 49) 194.

It is interesting to note that considerable disagreement clouded the assumed effects of even such traditional requirements for the legal validity of a customary rule as the nature, scope and intensity, clarity, duration and legal meaning of state practice regarding the continental shelf. A general survey of the views expressed suffices to illustrate the depth of that disagreement.

The Nature of State Practice

One is mildly surprised that throughout the 1945-1958 period, the state practice mainly discussed, analyzed and evaluated by the writers was the practice of issuing proclamations and various enactments relating to the continental shelf.

The theoretical preoccupation with that particular type of state practice was by itself enough to lead to considerable difficulties and further disagreements. The old question of the declaratory or constitutive character of the unilateral acts of governments was raised, and the usual set of answers largely depending on the theoretical orientation of each individual writer followed. Mouton rejected the declaratory character of the unilateral acts by arguing that no rights concerning a geographical formation could possibly exist before people became aware of its existence.[69] At the sixty-eigth meeting of the International Law Commission, Brierly deduced that if sovereignty over the continental shelf "belonged *ipso jure* to the littoral state, there was no necessity for the latter to make any claim or annexation." [70] Waldock, attempting to resolve the problem of the continental shelf by resorting to the law of territorial acquisition by occupation, viewed the unilateral acts of states as acts of annexation; they were therefore essential in giving rise to the exclusive rights of the coastal state annexing its shelf, yet without effect generally.[71] Lauterpacht, seeking a legal and rational explanation of the continental shelf doctrine in the fact of territorial contiguity and its economic and political aspects, considered the proclamations and enactments of the littoral states declaratory of their title to the submarine areas;[72] they were not "a source of title or a means of acquiring it," although they were necessary "in deference to an obvious proposition of order and orderliness." [73]

Yet, apart from the differences inherent in the varied theoretical approaches, students of the problem encountered still further difficulty of a

[69] Mouton, *op. cit.* (note 61), p. 269.
[70] U.N. International Law Commission, *Yearbook* 1950, vol. 1 (Summary Records of the Second Session, 68th Meeting, 14 July 1950), p. 227.
[71] Waldock, *op. cit.* (note 57) 115 ff.
[72] Lauterpacht, *op. cit.* (note 55) 431.
[73] *Ibid.* 418.

more technical nature. Legal experts of the United Nations Secretariat found that

> the value of these unilateral acts is one of the least studied questions in the technical field of international law. By comparison with the extraordinarily rich literature on bi- and multilateral legal acts one is struck by the poverty, both as to number and length, of works on unilateral legal acts.[74]

But they also asserted that "in point of fact, declarations like those of the President of the United States or later declarations are such as can have force of law in the international sphere." [75] Under these conditions, little agreement could be expected even among those on the positivistic side of the theoretical fence who had not accepted the declaratory character of the unilateral acts of states – that is, little agreement beyond a somewhat vague admission, such as Vallat's, that a unilateral declaration "may be regarded as providing the seed from which . . . rights and rules may grow";[76] or such as that of the United Nations legal experts who, concluding their study of the problem, admitted that the unilateral proclamations "may constitute the origin of a new law." [77] In Mouton's words, "A certain nucleus of a rule of law has certainly been created," around which a "condensation" may take place, but "we would not be able to say that the unilateral act creates at once a rule of law";[78] and Mouton then comes to "the provisional conclusion that the value of the unilateral acts is an initiative impulse to a new development in international law." [79]

The general uncertainty expressed by the various writers was also mirrored in a 1953 report by the Committee on Interior and Insular Affairs of the United States House of Representatives; the Committee would go no further than to state that the effect of the Truman Proclamation "was *to stake out a claim* to whatever natural resources exist in the Continental Shelf under the ocean" and that the legal effect of all the proclamations, some of them very broad in scope, "is not certain and a special committee of the United Nations is giving study to it at this time." [80] The International Law Com-

[74] U.N. Secretariat, *op. cit.* (note 53), p. 89.

[75] *Ibid.*, p. 90. The same view was expressed by Goldie who termed the Truman Proclamation a "juristic act" and stated: "It is generally agreed that the unilateral declarations of States relating to the continental shelf should have force in International Law, since they are not intended to be of a purely domestic nature . . ." L.F.E. Goldie, "Australia's Continental Shelf: Legislation and Proclamations," 3 *International and Comparative Law Quarterly* 558 (October 1954).

[76] Vallat, *op. cit.* (note 52) 337.

[77] U.N. Secretariat, *op. cit.* (note 53), p. 100.

[78] Mouton, *op. cit.* (note 61), pp. 264–265.

[79] *Ibid.*, p. 275.

[80] U.S. Congress . . . ., *op. cit.* (note 26), p. 17. Emphasis added.

mission, to which the report apparently referred, stated that in its opinion there could be no question of "giving authority of a legal rule to a unilateral practice resting solely upon the will of the States concerned" [81] and, searching for other valid reasons for recognizing the rights of the coastal state, found them particulary in the fact of territorial contiguity of the shelf and its implications.[82]

Thus there was only one – and a negative – point on which some agreement existed without significant objection: that the unilateral acts of states, *i.e.*, their various declarations and enactments, when considered as mere expressions of will and without further formal conditions or legal bases, could have no definite legal effect.[83] This view is clearly implied in the terms by which the legal experts of the United Nations Secretariat described one of their specific tasks in a study of the law of the sea: to ascertain "whether in international law there are rules by means of which, with suitable adaptation, unilateral declarations concerning the continental shelf may have the effect of law *erga omnes* and to what extent they can do so." [84]

The Formal Criteria of the Growth of Custom

The theoretical debate on the validity of the continental shelf doctrine was almost entirely focused on the emergence of a norm effective *erga omnes*; hence considerable attention was paid to the traditional requirements for the coming into existence of a new general rule of customary international law, such as the generality of the new practice, its duration, and the attendant *opinio juris*. But, however widely accepted in theory, none of these formal elements succeeded to live through the continental shelf debate unscathed.

The requirement of *the generality of practice, i.e.*, that it be actively pursued by a number of states and acquiesced in by other states, received differing measures of recognition. At this point it is worth noting that by 1950 nineteen states,[85] now including Venezuela as a party to the Treaty of the Gulf of Paria, acted to claim control over the adjacent submarine areas, and no protests were recorded by then. Geographically, the state activity was confined primarily to the Western Hemisphere and the Middle East, with

[81] U.N. International Law Commission, *Yearbook* 1956, vol. 2 (Documents of ILC, Eighth Session), p. 298.

[82] *Id.* Also, Sørensen, *op. cit.* (note 67) 227.

[83] For an opposite view, see Professor Yepes' statement, p. 32. It should also be noted that certain unilateral expressions by a state do have definite and immediate legal effect if they constitute contractual offers or an estoppel.

[84] U.N. Secretariat, *op. cit.* (note 53), pp. 90–91.

[85] For the sequence of national claims see p. 44.

the exception of the Philippines, and Pakistan. By 1957, six more states so acted: the Republic of Korea, the Dominican Republic, Israel, Australia, India and Cuba; still no protests were recorded.[86] The geographical spread was somewhat broadened by British action on behalf of North Borneo, Brunei, and Sarawak. Twenty-five states certainly do not represent anything even approaching a numerical majority. However, one must note that by February 1960 the number of formal national claims reached no more than thirty-five.[87] Under such circumstances it is indeed possible to entertain the notion that a number of states decided not to make a formal claim in the belief that the continental shelf belongs to the coastal state *ipso jure* and a proclamation or decree was thus unnecessary.[88]

Summed up, the views of writers create an impression that the generality of practice is a criterion of dubious value. As early as 1946, Vallat submitted his view that "general recognition and acceptance by states may perfect the rights claimed by the United States and establish new rules ... based on the doctrine of the continental shelf." [89] Lauterpacht, in 1950, spoke of "the practically unanimous practice of the coastal states concerned – a practice which has not been followed by protests by other interested states or by states in general." [90] In the same period, Mouton found the number of states which had generally accepted the new practice to be "considerable" [91] but not sufficient, in quantity or quality, to create a customary rule, while to O'Connell, writing in 1955, the national assertion of competence to extend the state's sovereignty over the continental shelf by "over twenty nations" was sufficient. However, O'Connell qualified the numerical requirement by stressing that among them were the major powers "with preponderant interest in both the freedom of the seas and the protection of coastal resources," [92] an aspect already emphasized by Lauterpacht

[86] Sometimes Japanese reaction to Australia's shelf policy is interpreted as a protest. In 1953 Japan asked Australia to agree on the submission to the International Court of Justice of their pearl fishery problem arising from the new continental shelf policies of Australia. In 1955, Japan forwarded to Australia a draft Special Agreement on the submission of the case. However, the case was not adjudicated. Brief reference to the Japanese moves in 1 *Japanese Annual of International Law* (1957) 78, 81. A fuller account of the Japanese-Australian controversy in Shigeru Oda, *International Control of Sea Resources* (Leyden: Sythoff, 1963), pp. 34–35.

[87] *Cf.*, U.N. Secretariat, *Supplement to Laws and Regulations on the Regime of the Territorial Sea* ... (U.N. Legislative Series), Doc. A/CONF.19/5 (10 February 1960) and addenda thereto.

[88] U.S. Naval War College, *International Law Studies* 1959–1960 (vol. LIII: The Law of the Sea; Some Recent Developments, by Carl M. Franklin), (Washington, D.C.: Government Printing Office, 1961), p. 9, note 6.

[89] Vallat, *op. cit.* (note 52) 337.

[90] Lauterpacht, *op. cit.*, (note 55) 392–393. To Lauterpacht, as already indicated above, the national claims to continental shelf were not of crucial importance as law-creating elements, as he considered them merely declaratory, though necessary and significant.

[91] Mouton, *op. cit.* (note 61), p. 265.

[92] O' Connell, *op. cit.* (note 49) 194–195.

who assessed the relative importance of states inaugurating the change as more important than the number participants.[93] Then, in 1956, Kunz considered that the practice of states, to be legally effective, "need not be universal; but it must have been applied by the overwhelming majority of states which have hitherto had an opportunity of applying it. This is not the case." [94] But Kunz did not attempt the impossible: to give an absolute or relative figure indicating what, in his view, would be "the overwhelming majority" or how one could reliably measure the opportunity of states to apply the continental shelf practice.

The second formal requirement – *the duration of the practice* over a considerable period of time – caused less difficulty, but as an objective criterion in determining the validity of the continental shelf rule, met with no great fortune. Many writers ignored it; those who did not, considered it as relative and unimportant. Three views may sufficiently illustrate the problem. Kunz admitted that "international law does not determine the length in time of a particular usage required to have legal effects; even a relatively short time may suffice." [95] Lauterpacht, in 1950, found that legally relevant international practice "need not be spread out over decades"; providing it is consistent and uniform, it "can be packed within a short space of years." [96] Mouton takes a somewhat closer look at the problem and finds the element of time significant since "customary law is the result of growth, and growth takes time." But he immediately conditions his own statement by reasoning that "the time required certainly depends on the amount of precedents" represented by the various unilateral acts of states.[97] And even when he applies the notion of prescription to the national continental shelf claims, he encounters considerable difficulty in determining the necessary lapse of time and, concluding this line of thought, limits himself to the statement that he

> would be inclined not to count for the calculation of whatever period may be taken as necessary, the first 3 years after the cessation of hostilities in World War II, because the Governments of most countries had quite different things to think about than the unilateral acts we are discussing.[98]

[93] Lauterpacht, *op. cit.* (note 55) 394, 395, 414, 431.
[94] Kunz, *op. cit.* (note 50) 830.
[95] *Ibid.*
[96] Lauterpacht, *op. cit.* (note 55) 393. Goldie expressed the same view when he stated that "the length of time is not, *per se*, important" since it is proportionate, among other conditions, "to the importance of the states adopting the new principle in the international practice." Goldie, *op. cit.* (note 75) 558.
[97] Mouton, *op. cit.* (note 61), p. 265.
[98] *Ibid.*, p. 269.

Next, such conditions as consistency and clarity of state practice require some attention. They refer particularly to the geographical as well as functional limits of national control claimed over the continental shelf. It is necessary to note at this juncture that throughout this chapter we are discussing the continental shelf as a geographical and legal concept comprising the seabed and its subsoil with their contents, but not the waters or air above it. But even in this sense, the geographical and functional limits of claimed continental shelf rights do not provide a picture of clarity, definiteness and consistency.

As to geographical limits, states used in their proclamations and enactments an endless variety of criteria:[99] to some, the continental shelf represented a geographical concept without the need of a further definition. Other states accepted and claimed the adjacent shelf to where the water above it reaches the depth of 200 meters or 100 fathoms, the average maximum depth of the sea above the shelf. Still others used as the limit the depth of water admitting of exploitation of shelf resources, while a group of countries claimed their continental shelf to a specified offshore distance often wholly unrelated to the actual geographical extent of the shelf.

The functional criteria, *i.e.*, the resources claimed on and in the shelf, showed less variety but greater vagueness. The widely used term "natural resources" which the various countries claimed as their actual or potential property contained in the continental shelf or on its surface was often meant to describe primarily mineral resources such as oil and related substances; in other cases, it was used to emphasize exclusive rights to sedentary forms of marine life found on the shelf.

This variety of criteria applied by individual states in their continental shelf claims necessarily led to criticism. Examining the substance of the various proclamations and enactments, Waldock described the state practice as "desultory and inconsistent" and as such incapable to provide "an adequate basis for a supposed new rule" which would need for its legal validity "the support of a general, unambiguous practice." [100] However, on the whole the variety and ambiguity did not unduly disturb the majority of

[99] Some indication of that variety is obvious from U.N. Secretariat, *Extent of Jurisdiction Claimed over the Territorial Sea, the Contiguous Zone and the Continental Shelf: Synoptical Table.* Doc. A/CONF.13/C.1/L.11/Rev. 1 (3 April 1958). The document is also reprinted in U.S. Naval War College, *op. cit.* (note 88), pp. 273–287.

[100] Waldock, *op. cit.* (note 57) 143, 144. Georges Scelle, *Plateau Coninental et Droit International* (Paris: A. Pedone, 1955), p. 38, raises the same argument: "Pour qu'il y ait évolution du Droit coutumier, il faut encore, selon nous, qu'il y ait non seulement multiplicité de précédents mais que le développement de l'éthique sociale soit 'unilinéaire,' que ces précédents aient le même contenu et la même portée. A cette condition seulement ils ont chance de réunir l'assentiment universel or, la situation est ici tout autre."

writers concentrating on the basic principle of the legal status of the continental shelf rather than on its geographical and functional fringes. Both Young[101] and Azcárraga[102] noted the "studied lack of precision" characterizing a number of national claims to the adjacent continental shelf. O'Connell also mentions it in connection with the Australian proclamation.[103] The requirement of consistency and clarity assumed more significant proportions[104] only in connection with the International Law Commission's attempts to define the limits of the continental shelf[105] – yet here we would already enter the twilight zone between codification and progressive development of international law and leave the area of a theoretical search for legal criteria determining the validity of a customary rule of that law.

The elusive problem of the so-called psychological element, the *opinio juris* or, as defined by Hudson, the "conception that the practice is required by, or consistent with, prevailing international law," created somewhat less difficulty in the theoretical discussions of the continental shelf doctrine than could have been expected. To Lauterpacht, the essential conception that the continental shelf practice is in conformity with the existing law was evident from the "unilateral declarations by traditionally law-abiding states, within a province which is particularly their own" and from the absence of protests against that practice on the part of other states which "may be fairly interpreted as meaning that they 'accepted [it] as law' – *i.e.* as being in conformity

[101] Young, *op. cit.* (note 52) 853.

[102] José Luis Azcárraga y Bustamante, "Los Derechos sobre la Plataforma Submarina," 2 *Revista Española de Derecho Internacional* 64 (1949).

[103] O'Connell, *op. cit.* (note 49) 193.

[104] *E.g.*, Richard Young, "The Geneva Convention on the Continental Shelf: A First Impression," 52 *American Journal of International Law* 735 (1958), criticized the Convention for setting the extent of the shelf as the outer limit of possible exploitation as introducing "a continuing uncertainty about the precise extent of offshore claims" and commented that "no rule which leaves offshore claims so hazy can be regarded as adequately stated." Earlier Kunz, *op. cit.* (note 50) 831, objected against the International Law Commission's draft articles which had described the shelf as beginning "outside of the area of the territorial sea" when he noted that "it is not possible to determine the beginning of the continental shelf, as long as there is no generally agreed norm concerning the maximum width of the territorial sea." Similar comments, particularly with regard to the outer shelf limits, were voiced and implied by Mouton, *op.cit.* (note 61) pp. 41–5, and in his *Recent Developments in the Technology of Exploiting the Mineral Resources of the Continental Shelf* (U.N. Conference on the Law of the Sea, Preparatory Doc. No. 20). Doc. A/CONF.13/15 (3 January 1958), pp. 3–4. The vagueness of proposed shelf limits was also criticized by a number of governments, *e.g.*, Norway (Doc. A/CONF. 13/5, p. 97), the Netherlands (*ibid.*, Add. 1, p. 110), and the Soviet Union (statement by Mr. Morozov at the 488th meeting of the Sixth Committee of the General Assembly on 3 December 1956, Doc. A/CONF. 13/19, p. 83).

[105] In its first draft of 1951, the International Law Commission defined the continental shelf simply by using the criterion of exploitability as its outer limit; in 1953, the Commission abandoned this concept in favor of a firm boundary of the shelf rights defined by the 200-meter depth-line of the superjacent waters; this concept survived, but in 1956 the criterion of exploitability was added to it and this combined form was retained in the resulting Geneva Convention. (UN Doc. A/1858, A/2456, A/3159.) *Cf.*, Mouton, *op. cit.* (note 104), pp. 3–4.

with the existing law." [106] O'Connell does not seem to have considered the requirement of the *opinio juris* too seriously when he commented that "protests have not been directed against the less exaggerated claims only because no state had had sufficient economic interests in the matter to challenge what might have been described as an intention to commit a wrong." [107] Kunz, discussing "the necessary requisite of the *opinio juris*," emphasized it as a primarily objective rather than a psychological element. One must infer from his writing that, to him, the crucial question seems to have been whether the practice of states relating to the continental shelf was required by law rather than being merely consistent with it; for immediately upon opening the problem of the *opinio juris*, Kunz inquires whether the national claims could possibly be based on a pre-existing norm or some established legal principle, and his answer is in the negative.[108]

The consistency of the continental shelf doctrine or, more loosely still, its compatibility with previously established rules of international law drew considerable attention of writers as an essential factor determining the possibility, the extent and the speed with which the doctrine would assume legal validity. The opinions expressed had a remarkably broad range. Waldock argued that the doctrine, operating "in a field where under the established law a State has no exclusive rights unless it can show an exceptional title by specific acts of occupation," consequently "is not merely novel but involves a reversal of existing customary law";[109] and it was in order to overcome this handicap when Waldock demanded more consistency and a heavier volume of state practice before he would admit the existence of a general customary rule of international law. However, Waldock was here concerned primarily with the modes of territorial acquisition rather than with the substantive compatibility of the self doctrine with existing rules. Lauterpacht held that the continental shelf practice of the United States, Great Britain and other states "did no violence to any established prohibition – or proposition – of international law" and that it "does not constitute a drastic change in the law" [110] which, in his view, again somewhat relieved the string-

[106] Lauterpacht, *op. cit.* (note 55) 395, 394.

[107] O'Connell, *op. cit.* (note 49) 194.

[108] Kunz, *op. cit.* (note 50) 830–831.

[109] Waldock, *op. cit.* (note 57) 143. Vallat, *op. cit.* (note 52) 335, also viewed the continental shelf doctrine as a reversal of existing customary law: "The principle of international law, at present generally accepted, that the seabed and subsoil outside the boundaries of territorial waters is *res nullius* over which sovereignty may be acquired by effective occupation . . ." was to Vallat a principle valid in 1946. However, he softened the harshness of that view by admitting that the principle may be inadequate to meet the new situation brought about by technological progress and economic needs in addition to being "a principle of rush and grab which may easily lead to disputes and inconvenient situations."

[110] Lauterpacht, *op. cit.* (note 55) 393, 394.

ency of such traditional requirements for the crystalization of custom as the duration of practice.[111] In fact, according to Lauterpacht, the authority and usefulness of the traditional conception of the freedom of the seas "can be safeguarded only if it is acted upon in accordance with its true purpose and the ever valid test of reasonableness.[112] Mouton, approaching the problem directly from the principle of the freedom of the high seas, and while not yet admitting the validity of the continental shelf rule, found that the right claimed by coastal states "can be housed comfortably under the uses made of the high seas and seabed on one side, and the eminent domain over the resources of the nearest subsoil on the other side." [113]

The Substantive Factors – Political and Economic

In general, however, the view was widespread among writers that the continental shelf doctrine did entail some modification of existing rules of international law, mainly those deriving from the principle of the freedom of the high seas. Modification may mean refinement; whether it does or not, it does mean change, marginal or substantial. Yet it appears from the writings of jurists that they generally did not consider such a change in the existing law a bar to the emergence of a new customary rule as long as the disturbance in the established order was of lesser impact than the public good derived from the change. Thus we come to the broadest possible requirement, considered by many writers important for the conversion of the continental shelf doctrine into a rule of law: that it create or serve higher public values than those it may eventually reduce or extinguish. The values most often mentioned were (1) fulfillment of public economic needs; (2) orderly exploitation of the shelf resources; and (3) prevention of international incidents which could occur should one nation consider its security compromised by another constructing continental shelf installations in the vicinity of the former's coast.

It is true that the theoretical treatment of these substantive factors differed from one writer to another. For some, they represented merely guiding points – or points of persuasion – in the policy of the law rather than a proof of the legal validity of the continental shelf doctrine. Others accepted their objective effectiveness in the emergence of a rule of law. In all cases, however, such theoretical discussions dealt with the administrative, economic,

[111] Goldie, *op. cit.* (note 75) 558, expressed the same view when he stated that the duration of practice required for the growth of custom is "proportionate to the degree of change to existing international law."

[112] Lauterpacht, *op. cit.* (note 55) 407.

[113] Mouton, *op. cit.* (note 61), p. 315.

and political values seen in the continental shelf doctrine as factors effecting the compatibility of the emerging continental shelf rule with other established rules of law – and the question whether or not, and to what extent, a new rule fits into the existing order cannot be legally irrelevant for the growth of custom.

To Lauterpacht, the three values of economic, administrative and political character were embodied in the fact of territorial contiguity of the continental shelf with the land mass – a fact providing the "legal basis of utility and reasonableness which is most consistent with the technical realities of the situation, with the security of states, and with the requirement of international stability." [114] Relying on the test of reasonableness, Lauterpacht argued that "The resources of the submarine areas adjacent to the coast of the state cannot be feasibly and reasonably utilized by all. They can be so utilized mainly by the adjacent coastal state." [115] As to the value of orderly administration of economic activities on the shelf, we have already seen that Vallat recognized the need as early as 1946 and contrasted it with a different alternative – a situation of "rush and grab" permitting each state to occupy and thus acquire submarine areas anywhere in the world.[116] Mouton, while demanding greater intensity of state practice to inject legal validity into the continental shelf doctrine,[117] considered the compatibility of the doctrine with the freedom of navigation on the high seas:

> Shipping should suffer *reasonable* sacrifices, because the oil company is just as well a user of the high seas and subsoil as the shipowner is, but shipping in general is an interest of a higher order. The situation would change . . . if oil supplies would necessitate drastic measures for a reasonable distribution. Oil production would then rise to the same level of world interest.[118]

Mouton thus seems to imply quite clearly that shifts in the hierarchy of values directly affect the scope and validity of customary rules .

Treating the question of the continental shelf as a problem of progressive development rather than codification of international law, the International Law Commission paid special attention to the compatibility of the proposed

[114] Lauterpacht, *op. cit.* (note 55) 431. Restated by Goldie, *op. cit.* (note 75) 566, the political, economic and administrative values were put into imperative terms: "Today the military security of the coastal State *demands* that it should control its adjacent and contigunous submarine areas. Furthermore, its economic security makes a *demand* no less pressing. Many of the natural resources of the continental shelf are intimately associated with the life of the littoral community. Improper use of offshore mineral resources may adversely affect the mineral resources of the contiguous land. It *becomes imperative* that a common authority should control both." Emphasis added.

[115] Lauterpacht, *op. cit.* (note 55) 407.

[116] See note 109.

[117] Mouton, *op. cit.* (note 61), pp. 265–266.

[118] *Ibid.*, p. 287.

continental shelf rules with other existing rules of law in its commentary to one of the draft articles it prepared. The Commission qualified the effective exploitation of natural resources of the shelf as "necessary to meet the needs of mankind"; it admitted that such activity "may affect the freedom of the seas," but considered that "nevertheless, this cannot be a sufficient reason for obstructing a development which . . . can be to the benefit of all mankind," with the reservation that the freedom of the seas "is of paramount importance to the international community." [119] In his Abu Dhabi Award, Lord Asquith of Bishopstone also considered the question of "not what is but what ought to be the rule" of the continental shelf; his answers, stressing the economic, administrative and political values of the shelf doctrine warrant quotation at some length:

(1) it is extremely desirable that someone, in what threatens to become an oil-starved world, should have the right to exploit the subsoil of the submarine area outside the territorial limit; (2) the contiguous coastal Power seems the most appropriate and convenient agency for this purpose. It is in the best position to exercise effective control, and the alternatives teem with disadvantages; (3) there is no reason in principle why the subsoil of the high seas should, like the high seas themselves, be incapable of being subject of exclusive rights in any one . . . The subsoil . . . of the submarine area is not a highway between nations and the installations necessary to exploit it . . . need hardly constitute an appreciable obstacle to free navigation; nor does the subsoil contain fish. (4) To treat this subsoil as *res nullius* – "fair game" for the first occupier – entails obvious and grave dangers so far as occupation is possible at all. It invites a perilous scramble . . . (I)t is difficult to imagine any arrangement more calculated to produce international friction than one which entitles nation A, it may be thousands of miles from nation B, to stake out claims in the Continental Shelf contiguous to nation B by "squatting" on B's doorstep – at some point just outside nation B's territorial water limit." [120]

A number of legal or material arguments or doubts could, of course, be raised against all these justifications of the continental shelf doctrine, and some were so raised. Without well founded evidence, the assumption that this is an almost "oil-starved world" is but an assumption[121] and one can agree with Waldock that "the needs of the world community cannot now be foretold." [122] Nor is it possible to measure reliably with Mouton how much

[119] U.N. International Law Commission, *Yearbook* 1956, vol. 2 (Documents of ILC, Eighth Session), p. 296.

[120] Award, U.S. Naval War College reprint (note 27), pp. 149–150.

[121] Addressing the Fuel Oil Distributors Association of New Jersey on April 30, 1948, R. M. Bartlett, Vice-President of the Gulf Oil Corporation, estimated the 1948 world production of crude oil at 8,650,000 barrels per day, and world consumption at 8,400,000 barrels per day. "Taken as a whole, these figures indicate that current consumption and output are almost identical – no opportunity for surplus to accumulate." Report, 128 (No. 3), *World Oil* 47 (July 1948).

[122] Waldock, *op. cit.* (note 57)140.

of its freedom shipping should sacrifice to the necessity of drilling for more oil, especially since it is mainly the oil-transporting tankers whose shipping routes cut through above the continental shelf oil fields. The Truman Proclamation of 1945 mentions self-protection as a compelling reason for the coastal nation to keep close watch over activities off its shores necessary for utilization of shelf resources: as we have seen, several writers considered the problem of security to be of real relevance. Yet like the Truman Proclamation they simultaneously accepted the technological argument that the effectiveness of utilization measures on the shelf depends upon cooperation and protection from the adjacent shore – an admission, in fact, that the danger of one state building installations off the shores of another is now insignificant if not unreal. On a different level, and accepting the international interest in greater oil production as a legal justification of national continental shelf claims, one may ask at least one question: Is then the coastal state obliged to search for and produce oil, and if oil deposits are non-existent, does its claim still hold?

There is no need to exhaust all the possible arguments and their variants in order to show their potential force of tainting with serious doubts the legal rationalizations of the continental shelf doctrine which were sometimes presented as an evidence of the doctrine's legal validity.

Synthesis and Projection

The high degree of inconclusiveness of the theoretical discussions concerning a legal regime of the continental shelf provokes a question: if men as qualified as the authors whose views we have surveyed should be unable to agree on the existence and the form of a continental shelf regime, could one really expect that governmental experts, whose objective valuations are necessarily conditioned by the diverse national interests they serve, would develop views sufficiently similar to lead to compatible national policies and an international practice free of disputes? The obvious answer is that it is not very likely – yet the fact remains that ever since 1945 the continuously spreading practice of a national coastal control over the seabed beneath the adjacent high seas has been remarkably peaceful.

The contrast between the conflict of theories and the tranquility of practice is, of course, artificial. The theoretical dispute was taking place in the realm of such generalizations and abstractions as almost to border on unreality – a disciplined and controlled unreality, but unreality nevertheless. For throughout the theoretical debate, as we have seen, writers and jurists concerned themselves with the question whether or not the continental shelves around the world were governed by a law valid *erga omnes*; in fact, it was as if they assumed that the legal relationship of, for instance, the United States and the United Kingdom, with reference to their respective continental shelves, was produced by the same forces and must necessarily be of the same quality as the corresponding relationship of India and Japan; or as that of India and the United States; or of Japan and Norway. But, to maintain this highly generalizing and abstract level of discussion and analysis, one must also use generalizing and abstract tools. Hence, applying the traditional requirement of the generality of practice, one avoids descending into the varied forms and consquences of national control over the continental shelf, and simply calculates how many states have in one way or another indicated their attitude toward such a control. The requirement of the duration of the practice is likewise deprived of its varied content, the question being whether a certain time elapsed since the inception of the practice and not what actually did and could transpire in that time in different bilateral or multilateral situations. Finally the requirement of the *opinio juris* must be, on the abstract level of generalization, either avoided or treated as a product of unexplained and, therefore, somewhat mysterious forces pervading the consciousness of governments.[123]

It is, of course, also possible to combine all these factors into clusters; during the debate the relative function of each element was said to depend on the presence or absence of various general conditions. The required volume and duration of state practice were qualified by the importance of the participating states (Lauterpacht, Goldie, O'Connell); the consistency and volume of practice were conditioned by its compatibility with the existing order (Waldock, Oda); further still, the required duration of practice was held dependent on general political conditions of the world (Mouton). There was a number of similar combinations, each of them perhaps basically sound, yet their sum was anything but a clear picture of the legal regime of the continental shelf and of its roots.

The abstract uses of the various criteria for the coming into existence of

132 The recurring and disturbing notion of some writers that legal rules – as if they had a life of their own – can secretly sneak into existence, may be illustrated by Franklin's statement elaborating on a simile used earlier by O'Connell: "Admittedly it is debatable as to when . . . [the] international doctrine and practice [with respect to the continental shelf] became established as a part of customary international law, just as it is difficult to know when a route across a commons acquires "the character of an acknowledged path." " But Franklin's very next sentence shows that the difficulty arises from a far too general and, therefore, superficial method of finding customary rules: "Although it is a matter of opinion as to exactly when the parade of proclamations on the continental shelf developed a path which was not only discernible, but well-defined and acknowledged, it seems clear and indisputable that the path has now been established . .. " Carl M. Franklin in U.S. Naval War College, *op. cit.* (note 88), p. 62.

a customary rule and the resulting inconclusiveness of the inquiries seem to have provided one of the impulses leading some of the writers to search for substantive factors that would justify their own conclusions. All these factors – administrative, political or economic – can be and have been characterized as giving the alleged legal regime a foundation of reasonableness; but the argument from reasonableness, used as an objective justification of a new law, must be treated with caution.

However reasonable may be the basis of all the rationalizations giving the shape to, or intended to justify, the continental shelf doctrine, there is always a three-fold problem:

First, reasonableness in itself is a highly subjective quality. What may seem eminently reasonable to one mind, another might reject as not sufficiently realistic, or as lacking in vision or foresight, or simply as unacceptable. Ultimately it is the power of the human intellect, the ability of man to reason persuasively on the basis of selected facts and of assumptions about the relationships of such facts, that determines the given degree of reasonableness.

Second, reasonableness is inherently a quality of the present. What may seem convincingly reasonable at one moment may prove completely untenable at the next when new facts emerge.

Third, one can hardly assert that states automatically fashion their policies and practices according to what may appear highly reasonable to a disinterested international jurist; their motivations are often different and one could probably put together a whole list of internationally valid rules and widespread usages that an internationally oriented mind would classify as unreasonable.

The argument that the continental shelf doctrine, ascribing to the coastal state exclusive shelf rights, is conducive to public order on the high seas appealed to a majority of participants in the continental shelf debate. However, in contrast to Lauterpacht, in whose opinion the doctrine met the crucial test of utility and reasonableness, Georges Scelle put forward a different view; while denying the legal existence of the continental shelf regime, he advocated the establishment of an international authority dealing with questions pertaining to the regime of the continental shelf and entitled, first, to set the conditions with which concessions on the continental shelf would have to comply and, second, to grant such concessions.[124] The International Law Commission rejected such proposals as unreasonable and impractical, saying that "such internationalization would meet with insurmountable practical difficulties, and would not ensure the effective exploitation of natural

[124] Scelle, *op. cit.* (note 100), p. 59.

resources necessary to meet the needs of mankind." [125] J. P. A. François as a special International Commission Rapporteur saw fit first to consider still further enlargement of Scelle's proposals until they would place under an international "maritime office" all questions of public law affecting the sea, and then rejected them *in toto* as "not yet feasible." [126]

It does indeed appear that the ascription of exclusive shelf rights to the coastal state was a reasonable solution of the problem as it existed in the 1940's and perhaps in the 1950's. But reasonableness is an unstable element; for instance, the practice of states may today be heading, under the impact of greatly improved technology of undersea exploitation and through the ever-present inclination of states to expand their spheres of control, toward defining the continental shelf as the seabottom as far as it is exploitable, and possibly toward a partitioning of the entire ocean floor. In addition, the responsiblity of the controlling state for the safety and rights of the users of the high seas above the shelf may give the controlling state certain rights of supervision and possibly jurisdiction over the movements and actions of such foreign users of the high seas. Most likely a majority of writers would consider such a development as undesirable and leading to an unreasonable situation – and seen from that perspective the "utopian" designs for some kind of an international shelf regime would in turn be characterized as more reasonable.

Projecting the lessons derived from the continental shelf debate into our own examination of the emergence and growth of a legal regime of the continental shelf, we shall:

a) Avoid accepting the continental shelf practice of the various states as a mere procession of declarations, decrees and utterances by governments. Rather, and even at the risk of getting somewhat deep into technical and

[125] *Op. cit.* (note 119).

[126] J. P. A. François, *Regime of the High Seas and Regime of the Territorial Sea*, UN Doc. A/CN.4/97, p. 8. During the 1958 Geneva Conference on the Law of the Sea, the idea of international control over the continental shelf found some support in the proposals and arguments of the representatives of the Federal Republic of Germany, Japan and Monaco. U.N. Conference on the Law of the Sea, 6 *Official Records* 7–8, 14, 18, and 125–126 (Doc. A/CONF.13/42). Also see Whiteman, *op. cit.* (note 67) 631, note 11. In the International Law Commission, Mr. Hsu (China) proposed to "entrust the development of the continental shelf to the international community" and suggested that an internationally controlled exploitation of the shelf resources be organized. U.N. International Law Commission, *Yearbook* 1950, vol. 1 (Summary Records of the Second Session, 66th Meeting, 12 July 1950), p. 215. Mouton, *op. cit.* (note 61), pp. 311–312, while admitting the difficulty of instituting a system of international exploitation of the shelf resources, proposed the establishment of an international body with a limited supervisory authority over the shelf operations. The idea of international control or supervision was also expressed during the Copenhagen conference of the International Law Association by Albert de La Pradelle, Tatiana Guldberg, and Paul de La Pradelle, and was discussed disapprovingly by Jonkheer P. R. Feith. International Law Association, *Report of the Forty-Fourth Conference*, Copenhagen 1950 (London: I.L.A., 1952), pp. 91–93, 102–103, 110–112'

chronological detail, we will attempt to see what the actual shelf practice entailed, what consequences it has had and what expectations it mav have aroused.

b) Avoid analyzing the continental shelf regime as a homogeneous body of rules, each of them uniformly applicable under any conditions anywhere and at all times.

c) Avoid applying the formal criteria determining the existence of a binding international custom mechanically and so as to justify our own theories; rather we shall attempt to see to what extent have they been actually present in different situations and what conditions affected their operation.

To proceed in this particular manner demands the use of what may be called the bilateral approach; a method of determining the existence, scope and intensity of customary rules comprising the legal regime of the continental shelf by analyzing their legal development in terms of state-to-state relations. We may not be able to state with conviction, as some writers variously did from 1950 on, that the continental shelf practice has become, *in toto,* a part of general customary law. But we may recapture at least some of the dynamism of a developing international custom and trace and identify some of the effective forces providing that complex movement of law and politics with speed and direction.

CHAPTER II

THE CONTINENTAL SHELF, ITS UTILIZATION AND CONTROL

The primary purpose of this chapter is to present an outline of the main political and economic facts accumulating on the continental shelves of the world by the postwar practice of states.

But even a mere description of facts presupposes an initial evaluation of the available data because, clearly, not all of them possibly can or should be included. And an evaluation of facts as to their relevance is a problem of deliberate choice. The criteria of the eventual selection of some data, and rejection of other, are to no small extent determined by the guiding concepts of the study; here primarily by the view that the customary rules comprising the legal regime of the continental shelf are largely a product of an unceasing interaction of political decisions and their political, economic and social consequences which, in turn, necessitate further state activity and decisions, and that this process of constant interaction, highly dynamic and cumulative, must be studied in terms of time movement rather than statically.

It is thus under the guidance of these and other concepts, as we have discussed them earlier, that the following descriptive sections emphasize the time element in the growth of state practice and national involvement on the continental shelf; and that considerably more attention than in other studies of the same subject is paid here to what are considered both the direct and indirect consequences of the initial state claims to exclusive shelf control, namely, the forms, depth and spread of industrial and economic involvement on the continental shelf.

THE CONTINENTAL SHELF AND ITS RICHES

As a geological formation, the continental shelf may be generally described as the submarine continuation of the land mass, extending under the sea to where the sea floor begins to fall off steeply into oceanic depths – *i.e.*, a submarine area lying between the coast and the first substantial fall-off on the seaward side.[1] But this underwater platform on which the continents seem to be sitting is highly irregular; conventionally, the seaward edge of the continental shelf and the beginning of the steep continental slope is taken to start at a water depth of 100 fathoms or 200 metres, but instances are known where the increase of slope begins at more than 200 fathoms or less than 65. Sometimes there is no identifiable slope at all; instead, what would ordinarily be the edge of the shelf is a sea floor torn into intersecting ridges, basins and elongated troughs.[3]

It is also possible to visualize the continental shelf as a ring around all continents, formed by a submarine area covered by relatively shallow waters; but it is a ring of very uneven width, varying from zero to more than 800 miles.[4] Its average width is 30 miles for the entire world, and its aggregate area is roughly 11 million square miles.[5] But it is probably more realistic to note that more than 50 per cent of the total continental shelf area lies within what Pratt describes as the great mediterranean regions of the earth:

> The Arctic Mediterranean, commonly designated as the Arctic Ocean, but in reality a shallow land-locked sea occupying the depression bounded by the continents of North America, Europe and Asia; the American Mediterranean, the waters of the Gulf of Mexico and the Caribbean Sea in the irregularly downwarped basin between the continents of North and South America; the Asiatic Mediterranean, the island-studded and essentially land-locked seas between the continents of Asia and Australia; and the mediterranean region of Europe and the Near and Middle East . . .[6]

Next to the Gulf of Mexico and the Caribbean Sea, the East Indian archipelago contains the greatest expanse of shallow seas in the world; the entire submerged area between the islands of Sumatra, Java and Borneo is covered

[1] Jacques Bourcart, *Géographie du Fond des Mers: Étude du Relief des Océans* (Paris: Payot, 1949), p. 130. Also, J. H. F. Umbgrove, "Origin of Continental Shelves," 30 *Bulletin of the American Association of Petroleum Geologists* 250 (1946).

[2] John B. H. Wiseman and Cameron D. Ovey, "Definitions of Features on the Deep-Sea Floor," 1 *Deep-Sea Research* 14 (October 1953).

[3] *Ibid. Cf.*, U.S. Naval War College, *International Law Studies* 1959–1960 (vol. LIII: The Law of the Sea; Some Recent Developments, by Carl M. Franklin), (Washington, D.C.: Government Printing Office, 1961), p. 14.

[4] Harald Ulrik Sverdrup, Martin W. Johnson, and Richard H. Fleming, *The Oceans, Their Physics, Chemistry and General Biology* (New York: Prentice-Hall, 1942), p. 21. The maximum width of the continental shelf is found in the North Polar Sea along the coast of Siberia. *Ibid.*

[5] Wallace E. Pratt, "Petroleum on Continental Shelves," 31 *Bulletin of the American Association of Petroleum Geologists* 658 (1947). As to the distribution of the shelves, Pratt states, *ibid.*: "Among the continents, Africa exhibits the least expanse of continental shelf. The eastern margins of North and South America have wide continental shelves, whereas their western coasts plunge with relative abruptness to oceanic depths. Similarly, the eastern edges of the continents of Asia and Australia, together with the intervening region of East Indies, are bathed by wide stretches of shallow, continental shelf water."

[6] *Ibid.* 659.

by water less than 300 feet deep.[7] The North Sea, all the way across from Germany, is less than 180 feet deep in most places, while the depth of Persian Gulf waters is 150 feet with occasional dips into 240 feet.[8] In the Gulf of Mexico itself, except for scattered local irregularities, the shelf off Louisiana and Texas deepens gulfward at the rate of 10 feet per mile and its width varies from 15 to 140 miles.[9]

Throughout the 19th century small areas of the continental shelves were exploited as grounds for sedentary fisheries, primarily pearl and chank fisheries.[10] During the same period, sporadic attempts were made to penetrate into the shelf subsoil by – primarily – coal mines leading from the shore.[11] Such mines were dug from the shores of England, Australia, Chile, Japan and Canada.[12] However, the world took a new look at its continental shelves in the general period of World War II when the need for petroleum pushed technology sufficiently ahead to bring oil and gas deposits under the bottom of the sea progressively within the reach of the oilman's drill. And it was primarily this mineral wealth which brought onto the shelves both Great Britain and the United States in 1942 and 1945 respectively, and afterwards a number of other states in a rapid sequence. Compared to the yield of sedentary fisheries,[13] the mineral wealth of the continental shelves is immense; according to one estimate, the continental shelves of the earth contain more than 1,000 billion barrels of oil or approximately 500 times the world's annual consumption of the late 1940's.[14] And in addition to petroleum, the shelves are known to contain a great variety of other minerals such as manganese, iron, copper, cobalt, and nickel, some of them "simply lying on the ocean floor waiting to be dredged up." [15] Other substances, more difficult to extract, are already being exploited.[16]

[7] T. R. Goedicke and Edgar R. Locke, "Worlds' Offshore Oil Areas," Part II, 5 (No. 4) *Offshore* 56 (December 1956).

[8] *Ibid.* 55.

[9] O. W. Noland and Roy M. Huffington, "Development and Outlook for the Continental helf of Texas and Louisiana," 1 (No. 5) *Offshore Operations* 9 (January 1955). According to Parks of Humble Oil and Refining Co., one of the firms heavily involved in continental shelf operations, the maximum width of the continental shelf adjacent to Texas and Louisiana is 175 miles. Mercer H. Parks and James C. Posgate, "Drilling and Producing Operations on the Continental Shelf," American Petroleum Institute 28th Annual Meeting, *Proceedings* (Chicago, November 1948), Section IV – Production, p. 86.

[10] *Cf.*, U.S. Naval War College, *op. cit.* (note 3), pp. 30 ff.

[11] *Ibid.*, pp. 32–33.

[12] Gilbert Gidel, *Le Droit International Public de la Mer*, vol. 1 (Chateauroux: Imprime par les Etablissements Mellottee, 1932), p. 510.

[13] *Cf.*, Richard Young, "Sedentary Fisheries and the Convention on the Continental Shelf," 55 *American Journal of International Law* 359, fn. 2 (1961).

[14] Pratt, *op. cit.* (note 5) 669.

[15] John L. Mero, "Minerals on the Ocean Floor," 203 (No. 6) *Scientific American* 64 (2 December 1960).

[16] *E.g.*, sulphur in great quantities is being recovered from the shelf subsoil off Louisiana coast

It was the knowledge that these riches are hidden in the sea bottom, and the growing technical ability to tap this source of wealth, that made many states shortly after World War II to take the crucial step onto the continental shelf – and into the "mysteries" of international custom.

NATIONAL SHELF POLICIES

The United States Proclamation 2667 of 28 September 1945, issued by President Truman, may be taken as the event giving rise to the doctrine of the continental shelf and expressing its essence.[17] In its operative part, it proclaimed the policy of the United States to regard "the natural resources of the subsoil and sea bed of the continental shelf beneath the high seas but contiguous to the coasts of the United States as appertaining to the United States, subject to its jurisdiction and control," while recognizing and preserving the "character as high seas of the waters above the continental shelf and the right to their free and unimpeded navigation."

The Truman Proclamation was followed, in a rather rapid sequence, by declarations, decrees and various legislative instruments on the same subject by a number of states. All these acts, although representing but a small part of the general practice of states regarding the continental shelf, often played a central role in the various legal studies of the doctrine. The sequence of the verbal acts of the states claiming exclusive rights on the adjacent continental shelves is shown by the following table.[18]

As we have noted in the preceding chapter, most of the theoretical considerations of the legal validity of the continental shelf doctrine were based on the various unilateral, formal acts of states – proclamations, decrees,

by drilling from a huge platform constructed at the cost of some $30,000,000. News report, 8 (No. 4) *Offshore* 26 (July 1958). – An application for a lease to exploit phosphate deposits 40 miles off Southern California coast was being processed by the United States Department of the Interior in early 1961. U.S. Department of the Interior, Office of the Solicitor, Memorandum of 5 May 1961 to the Director of the Bureau of Land Management. (Kindly supplied to the writer by the Department.) Doc. 94127–61, M–36615.

[17] Text in 10 *Federal Register* 12303; 13 *Department of State Bulletin* 485 (1945); 40 *American Journal of International Law* 45 (Suppl. 1946). – The text of the draft proclamation was tentatively approved by President Truman in May 1945 and, prior to its formal issuance, was used by the Department of State in informal consultations with representatives of Canada, Cuba, Denmark, France, Great Britain, Iceland, Mexico, Netherlands, Norway, Portugal, and the Soviet Union. None of the governments consulted expressed opposition to the proposal. Cf., Gabriel Steele, "The Development of Law on the Continental Shelf." (M.L. thesis, Columbia University, 1966), p. 40.

[18] Unless otherwise indicated, information shown in the table is derived from: U.N. Office of Legal Affairs. *Laws and Regulations on the Regime of the High Seas.* Vol. 1 of *U.N. Legislative Series* (1951), Doc. ST/LEG/SER.B/1; U.N. Office of Legal Affairs. *Supplement to Laws and Regulations . . .* VOl. 8, *U.N. Legislative Series* (1959), Doc. ST/LEG/SER.B/8; U.S. Naval War College, *International Law Situation and Documents* 1956 (Washington, D.C.: Government Printing Office, 1957).

TABLE I

Continental Shelf: National Claims 1945–1958

date	*country*	*type of action*	*characteristics*
Sept. 1945	United States	Presidential Proclamation	mineral resources; extent not stated
Oct. 1945	Mexico	Presidential Proclamation	all resources; geographical limits of shelf
Mar. 1946	Panama	Constitution	vague
Oct. 1946	Argentina	Presidential Decree [a]	sovereignty claimed; unclear
June 1947	Chile [b]	Presidential Proclamation	undefined limits
Aug. 1947	Peru [b]	Presidential Decree	undefined limits
Oct. 1947	Guatemala	Petroleum Law & other acts	resources up to geographical limits
Jan. 1948	Nicaragua	Constitution	general geographical limits
July 1948	Costa Rica	Decree Law	200 miles offshore distance; ambiguous [c]
Nov. 1948	United Kingdom for Bahamas & Jamaica [d]	Order-in-Council	"alteration of boundaries"; shelf undefined
May 1949	Iran	Bill before the Majlis [e]	sovereignty claimed; shelf undefined
May 1949	Saudi Arabia	Royal Pronouncement	follows U.S. Proclamation; unclear
June 1949	(United Kingdom) for nine Arab Sheikdoms	Proclamations	reliance on established practice; shelf undefined
June 1949	Philippines	Petroleum Act	shelf resources; ambiguously defined
Mar. 1950	Honduras	Constitutional Amendment	sovereignty; limits unclear
Mar. 1950	Pakistan	Declaration	annexation; geographical limit
Sept. 1950	El Salvador	Constitution	200 sea miles offshore claimed
Nov. 1950	Ecuador	Congressional Decree	shelf claimed as property; 200 meters depth limit
Nov. 1950	Brazil	Presidential Decree	dominion claimed; shelf not defined
Jan. 1952	Republic of Korea	Presidential Declarations	sovereignty claimed; no limits accepted
July 1952	Dominican Republic	Legislative Act	vague; natural resources claimed
Aug. 1952	Israel	Governmental Proclamation	limits by exploitability
Sept. 1953	Australia	Proclamation	seabed and subsoil; no limits stated [f]
June 1955	Cuba	Legislative Decree	vague in all respects
Aug. 1955	India	Presidential Proclamation	sovereign rights; restricted to shelf resources
Mar. 1956	Portugal	Law	seabed and subsoil claimed as property

See notes page 45.

legislative acts and executive orders – claiming exclusive coastal controls over the outer submarine areas. The controls were claimed for a wide range of different purposes, and over submarine areas variously defined. But the formal acts represent no more than a segment of the actual practice of states. The countries claiming their adjacent shelves were not interested in simply asserting on the shelf some abstract legal rights. They aimed at creating a system of order which would permit them to utilize the shelf, and to control its utilization. Thus it is necessary to review in some detail such activities on the outer continental shelves as may be reasonably regarded as consequences of the governmental claims and, therefore, as a part of international practice within the meaning of the doctrine of the shelf. And, since we are also concerned with the historical growth of the legal regime of the continental shelf, it is of importance to survey the gradual thickening of that practice in a broad chronological perspective.

INDUSTRIAL INVOLVEMENT ON THE SHELF

Although states did claim and exercise exclusive rights of control and regulation over areas of the continental shelf long before 1945, the earlier legal evaluations of such activity are neither numerous nor extensive;[19]

[19] Young, *op. cit.* (note 13) 360–362; U.S. Naval War College, *op. cit.* (note 3), pp. 30–37. C. John Colombos, *The International Law of the Sea*, 4th rev. edition. (London: Longmans, 1959), p. 61; Edwin Borchard, "Resources of the Continental Shelf," 40 *American Journal of International Law* 57–59 (1946); Gilbert Gidel, *Le Droit International Public de la Mer*, vol. 1 (Chateauroux: Imprimé par les Établissements Mellotteé, 1932), pp. 488–501, 507–514; Philip C. Jessup, *The Law of Territorial Waters and Maritime Jurisdiction* (New York: G. A. Jennings Company., 1927), pp. 13–16; Cecil Hurst, "Whose Is the Bed of the Sea? Sedentary Fisheries outside the Three-mile Limit," 4 *British Year Book of International Law* 34–43 (1923–1924); Thomas Wemyss Fulton, *The Sovereignty of the Sea* (London: Blackwood, 1911), pp. 697–698; Sir Travers Twiss, *The Law of Nations*, 2nd revised edition. (Oxford: Claredon Press, 1884), pp. 311–313.

Notes page 44.

[a] On 24 January 1944 Argentina declared by a decree that "... zones of the epicontinental sea of Argentina shall be deemed to be temporary zones of mineral reserves."

[b] In 1952, Chile and Peru were joined by Ecuador in a tripartite Declaration on the Maritime Zone with the claim of national sovereignty over the seabed and the waters above to an offshore distance of no less than 200 nautical miles.

[c] Modified by Decree Law of 2 November 1949.

[d] The United Kingdom later took similar action with respect to British Honduras, the Falkland Islands, Sarawak, North Borneo, British Guiana, and Brunei. Earlier (1942), the United Kingdom annexed the outer submarine areas of the Gulf of Paria on behalf of Trinidad and Tobago.

[e] 5 *Revue Egyptienne de Droit International* 347 (1949). The bill became a law only in 1956.

[f] 100-fathom depth line as a limit is claimed only in the Australian Pearl Fisheries Act 1952–1953, not in the Proclamation.

their volume and scope seem commensurate with the sparsity of such practice and its relatively insignificant territorial extent. In general terms, the practice was confined to sedentary fisheries in specific areas of the continental shelf beneath the high seas in the vicinity of the countries exercising control and jurisdiction or, later, consisted in excavation of tunnels and mines leading from the shore under the seabed in search of minerals. The legal nature of the exclusive rights exercised over areas yielding harvestable marine life was considered to be of a prescriptive character, with one variation of no great significance: at a certain point legal emphasis shifted from basic prescriptive elements – unchallenged usage of long duration – to those derived from the law of territorial acquisition by occupation; acts of appropriation and subsequent actual control were considered legally effective to give rise to the exclusive rights.[20]

However legally interesting in itself, the early practice of states to claim and exercise exclusive rights on the continental shelf adjacent to their coasts probably lacked the character or proportions of a general usage likely to mature into a major and general rule of law. Writers did not consider it as such;[21] governments displayed no awareness of it[22] and no inclination to base on it some more general claims predicated on full reciprocity.

The early practice of some states to exercise exclusive control over specific sedentary fisheries on the outer continental shelf can in no sense be considered as providing an impulse for the postwar emergence of the doc-

20 Richard Young, *op. cit.* (note 13) 361–362.

21 Among writers referred to above p. 23, (note 65), one may find disagreement concerning the existence and the legal foundations of a particular rule based on prescription or occupation, but no doctrinal dispute as to whether the practice itself did or did not grow into a general customary rule. The one dissenting voice is that of Carl M. Franklin who argued that several desirable results might have ensued if "the United States proclamation had been predicated essentially upon established sources of international law, particularly upon customary international law which has long recognized the right of coastal states to exercise sovereignty over submarine subsoil resources beyond coastal waters to the extent of existing technology, and over sea bed resources (sedentary fisheries) under a custom going back many centuries . . ." U.S. Naval War College, *op. cit.* (note 3), p. 41.

22 The United States Department of State considered in 1918 that the United States had "no jurisdiction over the ocean bottom of the Gulf of Mexico beyond the territorial waters adjacent to the coast." This statement was contained in a letter by which the Department of State answered an inquiry by a United States citizen who had claimed that he had discovered oil on a Gulf of Mexico shoal some 40 miles from land, and wished to obtain a leasehold to have his rights protected. Reacting to the possibility that the inquirer may erect an artificial island, the Department further stated that, possibly, the United States "would assume some sort of control over the island if erected, and inhabited and controlled by United States citizens in the name of the United States." G. H. Hackworth, *Digest of International Law*, vol. 2 (Washington, D.C.: Government Printing Office, 1941), pp. 679–680. Off the north-east coast of the Island of Ceram in the Netherlands Indies, exploration and exploitation rights for petroleum and allied substances were granted by a law in 1930 for sea areas within the 3-mile territorial sea. In 1937, petroleum exploitation rights along the east coast of Sumatra had their outer limits defined by the boundary of the territorial waters. J. P. R. Feith, "Rights to the Sea Bed and its Subsoil," International Law Association, *Report of the Forty-Third Conference*, Brussels, 1948, p. 184.

trine of the continental shelf. Technical advances in the methods of harvesting the sedentary species of marine life did not occasion an increase of this type of exploitation large enough to require a special system of intensive administration and control; nor were the various instruments used for the harvesting of such species of a type and size[23] likely to arouse, on the part of the coastal state, a serious concern that, should they be used off its coasts by foreign fishermen, the security of the state would be jeopardized. It will be also noted that, when we now proceed to survey such industrial and state activity on the outer continental shelves as may be reasonably regarded to have been undertaken in response to the postwar continental shelf claims, we shall deal almost exclusively with exploration and exploitation of petroleum and related mineral deposits of the shelf subsoil. This, however, has not been a matter of our choice; a search through industrial journals and other literature dealing with sedentary fisheries has yielded no evidence that any specific activity related to sedentary fisheries has taken place on the outer continental shelves as a consequence of or by way of implementing the postwar continental shelf claims.

The technological progress in the exploitation of offshore mineral resources, and the economic and commercial interest in that exploitation, obviously compelled the governments to take political action with respect to the shelf. One can easily agree with Scelle that the governments acted mainly to satisfy the "economic appetite" of the petroleum companies,[24] and also, undoubtedly, to satisfy an even hungrier appetite of their own. Yet it seems just as obvious that the industries of the mineral-extraction field deemed a political action necessary before they would venture onto the shelf. They were seeking there conditions of relative order and stability providing a reasonable assurance to the investors that their funds sunk into the bottom of the sea would not rust away and disintegrate while political and legal storms blew above.

Admittedly, one cannot prove that without the many assertions of national jurisdiction and control over the continental shelf, the petroleum industry – the principal exploiter of the shelf riches – would have been less active at the bottom of the sea. To say that prior to the 1945 Truman Proclamation no attempts were made to produce oil from wells drilled beyond the

[23] For a description of the various harvesting instruments, see U.N. Conference on the Law of the Sea, 1 *Official Records* 176 (Doc. A/CONF.13/37). The following statement made by the Japanese delegate in Committee IV of the 1958 Geneva Conference may be taken as a statement of fact: "Sedentary fisheries . . . had since time immemorial been subject to their own regime and the technical advances that had been made gave rise to no serious practical difficulties in that regard." U.N. Conference on the Law of the Sea, 6 *Official Records* 56 (Doc. A/CONF.13/42).

[24] Georges Scelle, *Plateau Continental et Droit International* (Paris: Pedone, 1955), p. 35.

3-mile limit[25] actually means very little. Not only did World War II keep the oil industry in general busy on the active land fields and away from difficult, time-consuming and costly offshore exploration; understandably, also the technology of offshore drilling was at a relatively low level.[26]

But even in the absence of material evidence one can argue with some degree of persuasiveness that without governmental acts the petroleum industry would be much more cautious and slower in pushing its pursuit of the shelf resources out under the high seas. Obviously the petroleum industry would labor under serious uncertainty should the United States and other countries fail to assert their control over the shelf. If the governments ignored the shelf completely, or chose to view it as *res communis* open to all, the absence of an effective authority would either lead to national and international industrial disputes or, rather, the prospect of such disputes and possible losses would discourage the petroleum industry from heavy and widespread continental shelf investment.[27]

Should the governments adopt the concept of the continental shelf as *res nullius* open to acquisition by individual states, the industrial risks would be somewhat lessened in shelf areas over which a state would effectively assert

[25] The first well beyond the three-mile limit – 11 miles offshore in 17 feet of water – was completed in 1947 by Kerr-McGee Oil Industries, Inc. on the continental shelf of the Gulf of Mexico in Block 32 in the Ship Shoal area off Terrebonne Parish, Louisiana. J. E. Kastrop, "56 Years Of Gulf Coast Oil," 130 (No. 7) *World Oil* 59 (June 1950). In 1946 Manolia Petroleum Company carried out the first deep test on one of its five large blocks leased from the State of Louisiana, approximately five miles from Point Au Fer, the nearest land, about 37 miles of Morgan City. The operation was then described as "the first carried on at such a distance from the shore." News report, 42 (No. 26) *Oil and Gas Journal* 62 (2 November 1946). The drilling did not lead to production.

[26] In November 1942 a special drilling equipment designed for offshore oil operations was proposed to the United States Department of Commerce, prompted by the urgent war-time need for higher oil production. Named "Shrewsbury Sub-Sea Well Drilling Column," the equipment was designed for water depths of 1,000 feet or more. It does not seem to have been put to work as yet. In 1945, many details of the equipment were reported to have been still "in formulative stage." R. D. Shrewsbury, "Deep Sea Drilling," 120 (No. 2) *The Oil Weekly* 33–36 (10 December 1945).

[27] An indication of the size of this problem, and the oil industry's need of a stable and effective authority established over the shelf, is illustrated by some investment figures in Table II, p. 52 below. The need for a recognized jurisdiction over the shelf resources is also clearly reflected in a memorandum of 19 January 1945, prepared presumably in the Department of State and now, unpublished, deposited in the files of the Department of Justice. The memorandum, intended to justify the proposed United States proclamation on the continental shelf, also states: "... the utilization and development of natural resources ... cannot proceed with assurance, however, in the absence of recognized jurisdiction over such resources. As a result, these resources will not in fact be put to practical use until a definite governmental policy with respect to the jurisdiction under which operations will be carried out has been made known. There is a natural reluctance to make the necessary investments and to install the expensive structures and machinery required for wells or mines, until there is reasonable assurance of title to the resultant products and of necessary governmental protection. In certain places off the coast of the United States, the beginning of operations awaits only this step. ..." Quoted in Gabriel Steele, *op. cit.* (note 17), p. 37.

its control with a view to acquiring the shelf by occupation. However, the petroleum industry would gain but a limited measure of hope for undisturbed operation. In theory, the question of effective occupation with regard to such areas as the bottom of the sea may not be difficult to resolve in the light of the minimal acts of occupation accepted in the cases of *Eastern Greenland* and *Clipperton Island*. But the states as well as the oil industry would have to ponder over a number of unwieldy questions of the following type: Should something more than a mere *animus occupandi* be required for effective occupation – such as properly licensed and publicly regulated industrial activity on the shelf – how far over the shelf would such acts radiate their legal effects? In the case of the United States, would such regulatory and industrial activity carried on in the Gulf of Mexico represent an effective occupation of the continental shelf off Maine? – off Alaska? – off Hawaii? Should the Soviet Union proceed to regulate exploratory and oil-extracting activity[28] on the continental shelf in the Bering Straits between its own coasts and Alaska, would it establish its rights for the entire shelf area[29] up to twelve or even three miles off the Alaskan coast?

The United States oil industry demonstrated its sensitivity to legal undertainties in 1950-1953, when the title controversy between the Federal Government and some of the states came to a head in the case of the United States *v*. Texas.[30] Of course, the uncertainties generated by the federal-state dispute are not truly comparable to those likely to emerge from full-fledged

28 The Soviet Union had both the technical knowledge and the industrial potential as well as the naval organization necessary to carry out such an operation. In 1946, Soviet offshore drilling in the Caspian Sea near Baku was reported increasing rapidly; new oil fields were opened and hundreds of producing wells were expected to be brought in. Report date-lined Moscow, 44 (No. 52) *Oil and Gas Journal* 61 (4 May 1946). Marine oil operations carried on by Soviet industry off Baku were reported in 1945 to have had a history of many years. Shrewsbury, *op. cit.* (note 26) 36.

29 Along the Alaska coastline the shelf extends several hundred miles under the Bering Sea. *Cf.*, U.S. Interior Department, *Annual Report of the Secretary of the Interior* [for fiscal year ended 30 June 1945] (Washington, D.C.: Government Printing Office, 1945), p. ix. Indications of the existence of oil-bearing strata off Alaska were reported in 1945. 44 (No. 24) *Oil and Gas Journal* 94 (20 October 1945). The continental shelf area south and west off Alaska is described as having approximately 460,000 square miles, of which 140,000 square miles are to the west, toward the Soviet territory. On both sides geological sedimentation and deformation is similar and corresponds to that of the adjacent oil-bearing land areas. The Bering Sea shelf is described as "intercontinental shelf area." George Gryc, *et. al.*, "Alaska" [part of a survey of "Possible Future Petroleum Provinces of North America"], 35 *Bulletin of the American Association of Petroleum Geologists* 168 (1951). A map of Alaska and adjoining continental shelf showing possible petroleum provinces, prepared in 1940 by U.S. Department of the Interior, Geological Survey, shows a dividing line running between Alaska and Siberia through the Bering Straits, but not representing a continuation of the 100-fathom contour line shown in the Pacific area to the south. *Ibid.*, pp. 152–153. A chart in Harald Ulrik Sverdrup, Martin W. Johnson, and Richard H. Fleming, *The Oceans, Their Physics, Chemistry, and General Biology* (New York: Prentice Hall, 1942), p. 30, shows the depth of the Bering Straits as not exceeding 200 meters, and a table in *ibid.*, p. 37, gives the water depth in the Straits as 55 meters.

30 339 U.S. 707 (1950). Preceded by two other submerged land cases: United States *v*. California, 332 U.S. 19 (1947), and United States *v*. Louisiana, 339 U.S. 699 (1950).

international controversies; during the American title controversy, turning primarily on the distinction between, and separability of, sovereign and proprietary rights in the continental shelf under the territorial sea,[31] but not so much on the territorial extent of such rights, the United States oil companies could be certain that the shelf resources would be available to them either under federal or state leases. The only basic uncertainty was the amount of royalties they would pay to one or the other landlord,[32] and the length of time over which the controversy might be dragged out. Yet, as a result, there was a general curtailment of all offshore activity – geophysical, leasing, and drilling – on the United States shelf[33] between March 1950 and August 1953 when the Outer Continental Shelf Act[34] was passed.

Also indicative of the effects of legal uncertainties on the petroleum industry and its offshore exploits are two comments on the possibility of oil exploration and exploration in the Gulf of Mexico, one made in 1935, another in 1962. A petroleum engineer, concerned in 1935 with Gulf oil deposits within the three-mile limit, admitted the possibility that in some distant future oil exploitation and development may extend beyond that line, but he saw three kinds of obstacles to such a venture: engineering practicability, economic viability and, also, "outside the territorial waters complications would arise over exploitation and development rights and ownership claims." [35] In 1962, Walter Sullivan reported in *The New York Times* on

[31] For an able discussion of this problem, presented from the point of view of Texas, see Price Daniel [Attorney General of Texas], "Sovereignty and Ownership in the Marginal Sea and Their Relation to Problems of the Continental Shelf," [a paper prepared and delivered at the 44th Conference of the International Law Association, Copenhagen,30 August 1950] 3 *Baylor Law Review* 241–266 (1951).

[32] *Cf.*, U.S. Congress. Senate. Committee on Interior and Insular Affairs. *Submerged Lands Act.* Report [from the Committee rto accompany S.J. Res. 13, 23 March 1953], 83 Cong. 1st Sess., S. Rep. 133, p. 8. – If the leases to the 350,000 acres of submerged lands, sold by Texas for $7,000,000 prior to the suit of United States *v.* Texas, had been let under the Federal Mineral Leasing Act, they would have cost the oil companies about $87,000. *Cf.*, James Wm. Moore, "Expropriation of the Texas 'Tidelands' by Judicial Fiat," 3 *Baylor Law Review* 135 (1951).

[33] O. W. Noland and Roy M. Huffington, "Development and Outlook for the Continental Shelf of Texas and Louisiana," 1 (No. 5) *Offshore Operations* 9 (January 1955). Also, it was reported that "Legal uncertainties caused by the federal-state controversy over continental shelf leases are slowing offshore oil and gas development and even threaten to halt all new exploratory work." Henry Ozanne, "Federal-State Dispute Slows Continental Shelf Development," 131 (No. 4) *World Oil* 49 (September 1950). Walter S. Hallanan, president of the Plymouth Oil Co., stated before a Senate committee: "At one time a total of 23 rigs were drilling in the Gulf area. Last month there were 14 ... Not a single well is being drilled today off the coast of Texas. There is reason to fear that, unless the existing confused situation is in some manner clarified by congressional action, operations may continue to decline until they are at a complete standstill." U.S. Congress. Senate. Committee on Interior and Insular Affairs. *Submerged Lands.* Hearing on S.J. Res. 195, 14–19 August 1950 (81st Cong., 2d Sess), p. 55.

[34] 67 Stat. 462. This was an Act "To Provide for the Jurisdiction of the United States over the Submerged Lands of the Outer Continental Shelf and to Authorize the Secretary of the Interior to Lease Such Lands for Certain Purposes."

[35] Neil Williams, "Exploration for Oil Out in the Gulf Is Within Engineering Possibilities," 34 (No. 8) *Oil and Gas Journal* 42 (11 July 1935).

evidence, uncovered by three Columbia University scientists, of salt domes buried in sea bottom sediments in the center of the Gulf of Mexico and indicative of a possibly large oil field some 2.5 miles under the surface of the high seas. The newspaper report also states: "However, so far oil companies that have heard of the discovery have been hesitant. Because the region is in international waters, it lies beyond the jurisdiction of various tax laws, but it also lies beyond the protection of American law." [36]

It thus seems safe to assume that the upsurge of industrial offshore interest and activity after 1945 was not simply a natural consequence of peace; that, in fact, such interest as the industry took in the continental shelf was also directly caused by the initial governmental action seeking to establish over the shelf a definite and recognized legal regime. In other words, the continental shelf declarations and enactments of the various states, unopposed by other countries, seem to have created a general expectation of order and stability on the continental shelf and thus set off a rapid growth of deep industrial involvement in the seabed and subsoil.

But this involvement itself, seen from the international perspective, would further reinforce and refine the proclaimed policies by being an implementation of them. As such, it has an undeniable communicative value: the initial verbal communications – such as the Truman Proclamation – are shown, when implemented, to be serious expressions of stable policies, with the stability in each instance increasing with every increase in the material, political and psychological involvement of the nation in the claimed submarine area.

To measure in detail the dynamics of the postwar industrial involvement on the continental shelves around the world would mean to go far beyond the scope and purpose of this study. However, an illustrative glimpse at some indices of the process of the deepening involvement is essential.

[36] Walter Sullivan, "Large Oil Field in Sea Indicated," *The New York Times*, 7 July 1962, p. 19, col. 1. While there is no reason to doubt the accuracy of the report regarding the hesitancy of oil industries being caused by legal uncertainties, the character of those doubts seems to be described incorrectly. The problem does not arise from the region being "in international waters," since the status of international waters above the continental shelves is no bar to the appropriation of the shelf itself and its subsoil. Rather it seems uncertain whether the region is not actually closer to the Mexican continental shelf than to the United States shelf; according to a map accompanying the news report, such would appear to be the case. Consequently, under the two principles assumed as affecting the validity of national continental shelf claims – those of contiguity and of exploitability of resources – the wealth of the discovered region, if and when exploitable, could be claimed by Mexico.

Industry and the U.S. Continental Shelf

The value of submerged oil lands in the Gulf of Mexico and contiguous to the United States, estimated at more than $ 50 billion, was understandably a powerful magnet for an enterprising and well-developed petroleum industry whose feeling of legal and political uncertainties beyond the limits of territorial waters had been relieved by the Truman Proclamation.

The quest for the immense submerged areas of the Gulf of Mexico, with their promise of oil, gas and sulphur, started in earnest only after the

TABLE II

Industrial Activity on Outer U.S. Continental Shelf, Gulf of Mexico, 1945–1960
Miscellaneous Indices

	Exploration & Leasing [a]	*Drilling & Production*	*Investment*
1945	129,000 acres leased [b]		per acre aver. $ 5.12 (for lease)
1946	560,000 acres leased [b] 2 exploration crews active		
1947	380,000 acres leased [b] 18 exploration crews active	1 oil well completed	per acre aver. $ 19.01
1948	30 exploration crews of 20 oil companies active	26 wells drilled	$ 29 million invested since 1945 in exploration alone
1949	40 oil companies exploring	53 oil & gas wells drilled 20 completed & producing	monthly rate of investment in exploration & drilling – $ 5.25 million
1950		120 oil & gas wells drilled 60 completed & producing	total industrial investment since 1945: $ 234 million total revenues: $ 6.3 million
1951–1953			per acre aver. $ 78.46 total investment since 1945 – $ 650 million
1954	525,000 acres leased	oil produced since 1945: 40 million barrels major sulphur mine active	per acre aver. $ 347.85
1955	670,000 acres leased		
1956–1957		135 drilling units active	
1958–1960	850,000 acres leased	oil since 1945: cca 200 mil.bb 1,054 active oil & gas wells	

[a] Part of acreage within the 3-mile limit.
[b] State leases, Louisiana and Texas; other data for federal leases only.

settlement of the federal-state dispute in 1953. But, as can be seen from Table II, representing a chronological survey of various indicators of industrial activity[37] on the continental shelf in the Gulf of Mexico adjacent to U.S. coasts, the oil and gas companies began to reach out for the submarine riches as soon as the United States policy was known.

Of course, an industrial development of such great scope, novelty and rapidity does not rest on the efforts of one industrial branch alone. It requires support from other fields of human endeavor, and thereby generates an ever-widening involvement of numerous specialized strata of the national community. Designers and engineers solved many problems for the marine drillers, and anticipated their needs.[38] Electronic industry contributed by perfecting even such seemingly marginal devices as underwater closed-circuit television enabling the drillers to observe their drilling operations in waters 600 feet deep. Shipyards and aircraft industry were involved in bringing out new types and heavier volumes of special, fast boats and helicopters for transportation of crews and trouble-shooting experts from land to the sea installations; from 1947 on, the various oil industry journals abound in reports and advertisements on such transportation means. In a still wider circle of activities related to continental shelf operations, a number of physical sciences were called upon to join in the effort, among them meteorology (effect of winds on shelf structures), chemistry (problems of corrosion), and oceanography (effects of the oceanic environment such as waves, tides, and currents on over-water operations).

Shelves around the World

Up to now we have been discussing the scope of industrial involvement on the continental shelf of the United States. Since 1945, the American industry led the world in the scope and magnitude of offshore operations

[37] Unless otherwise indicated, all data used in this section were obtained through a detailed examination of the following industrial journals published between 1945 and 1962: *Offshore* (formerly *Offshore Operations*), *Oil and Gas Journal*, *World Oil* (formerly *The Oil Weekly*), *Petroleum News Service*, *Petroleum Times*, and *World Petroleum*; and, further, from the pertinent records of the Committee on Interior and Insular Affairs of the U.S. House of Representatives as listed in the bibliography.

[38] One indication of the sudden surge of technical interest is provided by Emory N. Kemler and Edward W. Rosencrants, *Offshore Summary* (Spring Park, Minn.: Summary Reports, 1954; mimeographed), pp. 1.A.1 –16.A.3.Their bibliography lists 384 articles and papers dealing with general problems of offshore oil operations, and 158 additional articles on different technical problems of offshore structures and drilling barges. A detailed inspection of Kemler-Rosencrants bibliography discloses that well over 80 percent of the material listed was published after 1945. *Offshore Summary* also shows that in 1945–1953, the U.S. Patent Office registered 81 patents for various devices intended for use in the exploitation of continental shelf resources.

as well as in the development and perfection of the great variety of the necessary tools. But the basic pattern of the industrial involvement which we have followed with reference to the United States shelf was, in general, repeated on the continental shelves off the coasts of other countries; while different geographical and geological conditions may have required different methods of work and types of tools, the petroleum industry had to follow the same processes beginning with the initial recognition that shelf operations would not represent an international legal risk, and from then on through the entire sequence of surveying, leasing, exploring and drilling.

The scope of continental shelf operations off the coasts of countries other than the United States should not be thought of as insignificant. By the end of 1957, only about one-fourth of the world's marine drilling rigs operated on the United States shelf.[39] The other three-fourths were distributed among all the continents with the exception of Antarctica, but their distribution was unequal: most of the industrial activity was concentrated in the three major mediterranean areas, the American, Middle-Eastern and Asiatic. The following table illustrates the general trends[40] in the spread of continental shelf activity around the world.

The indication is clear that the industrial involvement on the world's continental shelves was a direct consequence[41] of unilateral governmental acts embodying the essence of the continental shelf doctrine: the right of the littoral state to assume and exercise jurisdiction and control over the resources of the adjacent continental shelf. This concept, when asserted by many and in principle denied by none, created on the part of the oil industry an expectation that the proclaimed order is stable and reasonable enough to permit a long-term, costly involvement in the exploration and exploitation of continental shelf riches. In a material sense, it is possible to say that the

[39] Editorial, 7 (No. 1) *Offshore* 18 (September 1957). In July 1957, 448 marine drilling rigs and 102 drill tenders were active or about to start operations on the continental shelves around the world – an increase of 37 percent over 1956. Report, 6 (No. 6) *Offshore* 79 (August 1957). During the next twelve months till July 1958 a further increase of 7.4 percent was recorded. Report, 9 (No. 1) *Offshore* 19 (August 1958).

[40] The survey of industrial activity on the continental shelves of the world, presented inTable III, is undoubtedly incomplete and could be enriched by many details; however, a search through industrial magazines cited for Table II above, and author's correspondence with oil companies active or known to be interested in offshore operations, indicate that the data included in Table III fairly represent the actual world-wide trends in the exploration and exploitation of continental shelves.

[41] There is, of course, the ever-present question of cause and consequence. As we have seen, industrial shelf activity was most intensive on those shelves over which the littoral states had declared their control while it was non-existent, limited or hesitant elsewhere, *e.g.*, off West German, Belgian, Dutch or Japanese coasts. But it is also true that the presence or promise of exploitable shelf resources was, to the governments, an impulse to claim the adjacent shelves. One can do little to resolve the question except simply to note that in practically all instances the industrial shelf activity followed the governmental proclamations and enactments.

TABLE III

Industrial Activity (Starts) on World Continental Shelves (U.S. Excluded)
1945–1958

Year	*Country or area*	*Type of activity*	*Characteristics*
1945	Bahamas	surveys, licencing	small scale, low intensity
1946–1947	Trinidad	exploration	limited; focused on drilling from shore
	Bahamas	exploration; no drilling	two oil companies engaged
1948–1950	Persian Gulf	exploration	extensive; several companies active
	Mexico	exploration	small scale
1951	Persian Gulf	oil test drilling	one of world's largest oil fields found
1952–1954	Egypt, Libya	exploration	intensified following major oil find in 1956
1955	Cuba	exploration	large scale; foreign companies; drilling 1957
	Brit. Guiana	licencing; test drilling	
	Senegal	exploration	off Dakar, up to 60 miles offshore
	Australia	exploration	limited area off Shark Bay, W. Australia
1956	Brunei		
	Argentina	test drilling	
	Brazil		
	Pakistan		concessions issued
	Japan	intensive exploration	
1957	Dutch Guiana	leases & concessions	in offshore belt up to 55 miles wide
	Guatemala	leases & concessions	foreign companies; 40-year leases
	Honduras	leases & concessions	up to 150 miles offshore
	Nicaragua	oil test drilling	
	Port. Guinea	surveyed; concessions	11 million acres on- and offshore
	Nigeria	oil test drilling	off Niger delta; after 14 months of surveys
1958	Mexico	test drilling; no production	program started 1949
	Sarawak; N. Borneo	oil test drilling	
	Gabon	exploration	still continued 1960–61

unilateral acts led a wide industrial sector not only to spend billions of dollars on the continental shelves, but in fact channelled a considerable amount of human resources into a new pattern of previously nonexistent activities and endeavors. The spreading of the industrial shelf activity, when traced from 1945, clearly shows the sequence; governmental acts invariably preceded industrial and economic development of the continental shelf. By 1950, eighteen governments had made their continental shelf claims; at that time, however, only the United States and, to a lesser extent, the British sectors of the Gulf of Mexico shelf had an industrial development of a real consequence. Industrially, the continental shelf doctrine has been applied fully and generally only after 1950.

THE SHELF AND THE STATE

The industrial involvement on the continental shelf is certainly the most conspicuous, clearly visible part of the entire process through which the continental shelf doctrine has been implemented in practice. The size and intensity of that involvement are not legally irrelevant to the growth of the eventual customary rule; but the involvement of the state is undoubtedly still more significant.

By state involvement on the continental shelf we do not mean the initial governmental declaration of a specific continental shelf policy. The term is rather used to describe the consequences of such declarations, the steps leading from a policy statement to its practical implementation. To clarify the meaning still further, one may consider the following contrast:

If, during the 1945-1958 period, all governments issued declarations asserting national control over the adjacent continental shelves, but if there were no leasing, exploratory and industrial activity on the shelves and therefore no actual need for governmental regulation, a customary rule of international law taking the form of a tacit agreement, could still be said to have emerged as a result of such declarations – one, in fact, closely akin to a treaty rule but for its form and the lack of precision and firmness. But it would have been a relatively unstable rule resting on nothing more than policy declarations. A reversal of continental shelf policy by a group of states, for instance a shift to a policy claiming that the continental shelves under the high seas belong to the international community, could be possibly opposed on the theoretical grounds of inconsistency with the earlier stand but, beyond that, on nothing truly tangible. Such a reversal could not be reasonably opposed by claiming that it represented an instance of bad faith causing a loss to those who had relied on the original policy line and acted accordingly, as no action and no loss could be shown. This is not to imply that such a change would be easy to bring about; in the relations of states the psychological attachment of a nation to a piece of unused and uninhabited territory or to an unexercised right is often as strong or stronger than the economic or political import of that territory or right on the life of the state. But a psychological attachment, while politically effective and often decisive, is too feeble to become a sole foundation of an international legal right of a state when that claimed right is disputed or denied by others. Besides, it is difficult to show persuasively that a psychological attachment existed when it had not been consummated in practice. In this study then, the term "state involvement" signifies the practical consummation by a state of a right asserted by the initial continental shelf proclamation or enactment.

In general terms the state involvement on the continental shelves falls into two closely related categories – economic and political. The economic involvement is measurable in terms of the share contributed by the use of the continental shelf to the overall economic life of the state. That share may consist of the direct state income represented by bonuses, rentals, royalties and taxes or, in case of countries with nationalized industries, by the net value of resources extracted from the shelf. But the share also includes the contribution of the continental shelf activity to the enlargement of the national industrial base, the diversification of secondary industries supporting the continental shelf operations, the higher level of employment and its effect on the general living standard and, possibly, the changed dependence of a nation on the import from other countries of products previously not available domestically or in short supply and now obtainable from the continental shelf.

The economic involvement of a state on the continental shelf, permitted by national policy and international acceptance of it or silence following its declaration and implementation, does of course vary considerably from state to state. It is quite possible that such shelf activity as there might now be off the coasts of Gabon represents a greater share in the economic life of that state than the intensive and highly developed oil and gas production from the seabed of the northern Gulf of Mexico does in the United States economy. To obtain a realistic picture of the world-wide state involvement on the continental shelves, one would have to study in all requisite detail the shelf activity off every single country – a task certainly much beyond the scope of the present inquiry.

As our primary purpose here is to illustrate the way and scope in which a state may become economically involved on the continental shelf, it might suffice to consider the industrial shelf expenditures flowing directly to the state in the form of lease bonuses, royalties and other fees;[42] to consider the amounts and value of minerals extracted and the taxes payable on them; and to consider further the added benefits to the national finances arising

[42] For some indication see Table II at p. 52 above.

from the attending income taxes and the national income increased by the work on the continental shelf.

It is one of our provisional conclusions that the following questions would not only be legally relevant, but also unavoidable, if one should determine the effects of unilateral governmental declarations regarding the continental shelf and the effects of international acceptance of them by commission of omission: Did the international acts or omissions lead states and industries to become economically involved on the continental shelves? If so, to what extent? How deeply would be the economic life of one or more states affected by a denial of the continental shelf rule? It is submitted that, in the case of the continental shelf, the legal effects of acts and omissions such as unilateral governmental acts and governmental failure to protest are to a degree directly proportionate to the consequential and underlying economic movements, changes and developments.

But it remains also to consider the political involvement of states on the continental shelf. Same as on the economic side of the picture, it also varies greatly from state to state and is determined by a multitude of conditions. Varying degrees of industrial activity on the shelf require varying intensity of regulatory functions performed by the state. Dredging of minerals from the seabed may demand controls less stringent than those required for seismic exploration or oil and sulphur extraction by means of permanent and sizeable platforms. Further, the scope and intensity of state control is likewise determined by the degree to which the sea areas involved are vitally important to the fisherman, and by the volume of shipping on the superjacent waters.

Here, as elsewhere in this paper, a detailed state to state study of the regulatory activities performed by the governments would be impractical. But again an illustrative glimpse may be obtained by a closer look at the variety of functions in which the United States Government has become involved subsequent to its continental shelf proclamation.

Some of the functions performed by the United States in implementing its continental shelf policy were basically of an economic rather than regulatory nature. For instance, in 1948 the United States Navy carried out exploratory work in the Gulf of Mexico some 75 miles from land to discover possible oil reserves, and subsequently reported the presence of salt domes in the area surveyed.[43] The implementation of the Truman Proclamation also resulted in enlarging by some 750,000 square miles of the continental shelf the area over which the Geological Survey within the Mineral

[43] 128 (no. 3) *World Oil* 39 (July 1948).

Resources section of the United States Department of the Interior has its specific jurisdiction and duties to perform.[44]

The government had two primary regulatory tasks to perform: first, to provide for orderly coexistence of the companies exploring the shelf and exploiting its natural resources; second, to provide for orderly coexistence between the companies active on the continental shelf and the users of the high seas covering the shelf, especially those engaged in navigation and fishing.

The first task of placing the industrial shelf activity onto an orderly basis has been accomplished by the system of leases. The Outer Continental Shelf Lands Act of 1953[45] stipulated that an oil and gas lease shall cover a compact area not exceeding 5,760 acres.[46] To provide for as much precision as possible in defining the leased blocks of shelf area, the Bureau of Land Management issues official leasing maps and distributes them to the industry.[47] But long before 1953-1954 when the Act and the regulations implementing it were promulgated, the states of Texas and Louisiana had their own systems of leasing established and applied, based on lease blocks of 5,760 acres (3 square miles) and 5,000 acres respectively.[48] Apart from exactly defining the shelf areas leased to the industry, the federal regulations contain numerous and detailed provisions determining the mode of industrial coexistence on the shelf – *e.g.*, provisions governing easements, rights of way and rights of use in the leased areas to permit the working of adjoining lands or leases.[49]

[44] The activities of the Geological Survey, established by the Act of 3 March 1879 (20 Stat. 394; 43 U.S.C. 31), are described as the classification of federal lands as to water storage, water power, and mineral value; supervision of mining and oil and gas leases on federally controlled lands; making geological surveys and investigations to determine and appraise the mineral and mineral fuels resources and to determine the geologic structure of the United States and its territories, and for this purpose to engage in geologic mapping, physical exploration when necessary, as well as the development of new prospecting techniques. *United States Government Organization Manual 1962–63* (Washington, D.C.: Office of the Federal Register, 1962), pp. 236–237.

[45] 67 Stat. 462. Public Law 212, 83rd Congress, 1st Sess., H.R. 5134.

[46] *Ibid.*, Sec. 8.

[47] 43 *Code of Federal Regulations* 201. 3.

[48] U.S. Department of the Interior, *Leasing and Operating Regulations for the Submerged Lands of the Outer Continental Shelf* (a booklet issued by the Department to put into one volume the basic law and the leasing and operating regulations concerning mineral development of the continental shelf areas beyond the 3-mile limit of the territorial sea, marked as Int.-Dup. Sec., No. 61031), p. 33.

[49] 43 *Code of Federal Regulations* 201. 121; 30 *Code of Federal Regulations* 250. 18. Many other regulations seeking to provide for orderly shelf activities – including the solution of problems arising from Federal-State jurisdiction controversies involving the industry – are contained in the Interior Secretary's notice "Oil and Gas Operations in the Submerged Coastal Lands of the Gulf of Mexico" issued on 11 December 1950 (16 *Federal Register*), and its amendments and supplements listed in Sec. 7 of the Outer Continental Shelf Lands Act of 1953.

The problem of reconciling the oil industry's interests in shelf operations with those of shipping and fishing has been much more cumbersome. It is indeed possible that even without any regulatory supervision by the government the oil companies operating on the shelf would eventually find some modus vivendi among themselves; it is more difficult to imagine that serious conflicts between oilmen, shippers and fishermen would be avoided or settled without governmental regulations and the consequent administration of justice in cases of disputes or conflicts.

With respect to navigation and shipping the United States Government had in fact a dual function when regulating the industrial shelf activity. Such laws and regulations as it issued were designed to protect the narrower national interest in assuring the domestic shipping industry and the local fishermen of their continued profitable use of the high seas – restricted perhaps, but orderly. And at the same time the governmental regulations were protecting the broader international interest in continued freedom of navigation on the high seas and the freedom of high sea fishing.

Mouton observed in 1952 that structures built on the continental shelf may represent a danger "for other users" of the seas, and proposed that "an international body should be empowered to decide whether installations should be built in certain places where hindrance to shipping may occur." [50] However, the realities of the continental shelf operations show that the proposal, sound in principle and laudable as an attempt to enlarge the area of international cooperation and organization, would be somewhat insufficient in practice. For the problem is not merely to determine where installations should or should not be built; it consists to a much greater degree in regulating and supervising the constructions and their equipment, in enforcing the necessary rules and in modifying them on a continuing basis according to new needs. The United States Outer Continental Shelf Lands Act of 1953 authorizes the Coast Guard to promulgate and enforce all regulations needed with respect to lights and other warning devices on the shelf structures, safety equipment, and other matters relating to the promotion of safety of life and property, and to install such equipment on the structures at the cost of the operator who failed to have done so himself.[51] But even during the years before the Act various governmental authorities were fulfilling the regulatory functions with respect to offshore drilling. Before an oil company could start preparations for drilling, it had to secure a permission from adjacent county or parish authorities, a permit from the state

[50] M. W. Mouton, *The Continental Shelf* (The Hague: Nijhoff, 1952), p. 314.
[51] 67 Stat. 463.

oil-and-gas regulatory body[52] and, under Section 10 of the River and Harbor Act of 3 March 1899, an authorization from the Army Chief of Engineers for building operating structures.[53] Before an oil company started a survey of the shelf areas, it had to notify the United States Coast Guard and then subject itself to such regulations as existed at the time, such as rules pertaining to handling of explosives, requirements covering the vessels used in the shelf operations, and regulations concerning lights and signals on offshore structures and similar appurtenances.[54] The fact that as early as November 1948 the United States Coast Guard appointed a special board to study the need for additional personnel, equipment and regulations concerning continental shelf operations[55] reflects both the increasing tempo of offshore activity and the intensity of governmental supervision over it. The clash of interests between the shipping and oil industries off the United States coasts appears to have assumed more serious proportions only after 1953-1954 with the growing speed of offshore drilling following the passage of the Outer Continental Shelf Lands Act. In March 1955 the oil industry, intent on constructing permanent platforms off California's Long Beach, met with the objections of the United States Navy maintaining that the man-made islands are becoming "a menace to navigation and may ruin one of the finest harbors in the world.[56] As stated in 1956 by Captain J. C. Wendland, United States Coast Guard Marine Inspection Officer, Eighth Coast Guard District at New Orleans:

> All vessel operators, and especially the large oceangoing ship operators, have more than a passing interest in these fixed and mobile platforms. It has long since ceased to be a novelty to see these oil wells at sea. The ships operating in the Gulf of Mexico have been aware of and are concerned with their movement seaward.[57]

The seaward movement of the oil wells actually meant that ships had to stay for continuously longer mileage within designated fairways when ap-

[52] R. G. Watts, "Regulations Covering Drilling Activities in Coastal Waters," American Petroleum Institute, 28th Annual Meeting, *Proceedings* (Chicago, November 1948), Section IV – Production, pp. 77–78.

[53] 30 Stat. 1151; 33 U.S.C. 403.

[54] Admiral Joseph F. Farley (Commandant, U.S. Coast Guard), contribution to a discussion of regulations covering offshore drilling, American Petroleum Institute, *op. cit.* (note 52), pp. 80–82.

[55] "Coast Guard May Assign More Men to Gulf Area," 47 (No.29) *Oil and Gas Journal* 64 (18 November 1948). The article also quotes Admiral Joseph F. Farley: "From the shipmaster's viewpoint, the oil-drilling structures, erected in navigable waters, constitute obstructions to navigation which must be adequately lighted and provided with suitable fog warning signals. Regulations dealing with such requirements are in effect, Coast Guard facilities will have to be augmented to meet the responsibility of enforcement. Channels through congested regions must be properly buoyed for regular marine traffic."

[56] Editorial, 1 (No. 7) *Offshore Operations* 7 (March 1955).

[57] Quoted in 4 (No. 2 *Offshore* 15 (April 1956).

proaching or leaving United States coasts.[58] The shippers were interested in short and unobstructed routes between ports, while the oil companies saw under the fairways the most promising oil prospects.[59] It was, of course, impossible to find an ideal solution which would allow both the exploitation of shelf areas under the fairways and at the same time improve navigation, as an oil company's executive demanded.[60] However, the Coast Guard in the New Orleans District, apart from its regulatory, supervisory and enforcement activity, established a special Panel of Advisers to the Coast Guard Commander under the chairmanship of a Coast Guard officer, the members representing the various interests co-existing in the Gulf of Mexico, and eventually did succeed in effecting a harmonious relationship between the Coast Guard and the oil and affiliated industries in the area while maintaining high standards of marine safety.[61]

The coexistence of the fishing and oil interests presented another series of problems to governmental regulation of offshore activity. As early as February 1945, the Louisiana state government had a study made of the effect on marine life by offshore seismic exploration for oil and gas;[62] the resulting report,[63] while mentioning considerable resistance of shrimp to heavy undersea detonations, was generally inconclusive with further tests planned. However, the report was reprinted in one of oil industry journals under the hopeful – and misleading – title "Shrimp Don't Mind Dynamite; Louisiana Experiments Pave Way for Expanded Marine Oil Research,[64] and with the equally hopeful commentary that search for oil may now be speeded up without any conflict with the industries depending upon fish, oysters and shrimp.

Of course, conflict followed and bred new regulations and methods of control. Complaints of fishermen that large quantities of fish are being killed by increasing geophysical shooting in the waters of the Gulf of Mexico brought about in September 1947 public hearings before the Texas School

[58] Official leasing maps as well as their various reprints from the different periods after 1945 clearly show the seaward movement of leased blocks of continental shelf area in the northern Gulf of Mexico. *E.g.*, Offshore Chart, State of Louisiana, prepared by Douglas Maginnis, published by *Offshore*, 1959.

[59] Report, 5 (No. 5)*Offshore* 56 (January 1957).

[60] Report, 5 (No. 2) *Offshore* 26 (October 1956).

[61] Captain E. R. Vorenkamp, Chairman of the Panel of Advisors to the Commander, Eighth Coast Guard District, *ibid.* 25.

[62] Seismic crews working in the Gulf of Mexico were increasingly using a shock-wave technique known as refraction and involving the detonation of dynamite charges of up to 800 pounds and sometimes even heavier.

[63] James Nelson Gowanloch, "Report of the Chief Biologist," State of Louisiana, Department of Wildlife and Fisheries, *First Biennial Report* 1944–1945, pp. 142–148.

[64] 116 (No. 12) *The Oil Weekly* 48–51 (19 February 1945).

Board, the chief beneficiary of submarine operations off Texas shores.[65] The purpose of the hearing was to determine what regulations would reduce dangers to fish life. Eventually a committee was named to draw up a control plan for consideration; from testimony presented at the hearing the following regulations appeared probable: suspension of explosive charges above the ocean floor; limitation of charges; prohibition against leaving in the sea obstructions or lighted buoys; prohibition of shooting within a specified distance from a fishing boat already in the area.[66] By 1948, both Texas and Louisiana were issuing to exploration parties permits allowing detonation charges up to 50 pounds, *i.e.,* sixteen-times smaller than the 800-pound standard considered practical by the oil companies.[67]

Apart from the state governments, the United States Fish and Wildlife Service was conducting its own studies of the effects on marine life of continental shelf exploration and exploitation; state-hired biologists were assigned to serve in an advisory capacity with operating seismic crews and at the oil company's expense; yet in spite of all these efforts, in 1948 law suits involving many million dollars were threatened against several of the major oil companies by the fishing interests.[68] Only in the middle 1950's some mode of a more peaceful coexistence between the oil and fishing interests seems to have been achieved judging by the greater rarity of reports on conflicts in the various industrial journals. The 1953 Outer Continental Shelf Lands Act did, of course, provide that it ". . . shall be construed in such manner that the character as high seas of the waters above the outer Continental Shelf and the right to navigation and fishing therein shall not be affected." [69] However, the regulations issued by the Department of the Interior's Geological Survey, implementing the Act, come closer to reality when they bind the continental shelf operators to ". . . take all reasonable precautions to prevent damage or waste of any natural resource or injury to life or property or the aquatic life of the seas." [70]

All these illustrations of United States governmental regulatory activity related to an orderly relationship among continental shelf operators, fishermen and shipping companies do not actually show the full depth of state involvement on the continental shelf. The requirements of order have brought onto the United States shelf – in addition to the Department of the Interior

65 At the time, Texas was exercising its control over continental shelf operations up to a 27-mile distance from the shore and claimed more. *Cf.*, note 38.

66 Report, 127 (No. 6) *World Oil* 46 (October 1947).

67 Watts, *op. cit.* (note 52), p. 77.

68 C. C. Bates and A. H. Glenn, "Oceanography in the Offshore Drilling Campaign," 127 (No. 13) *World Oil* 114–126 (April 1948).

69 Sec. 3 (b), 67 Stat. 462.

70 30 *Code of Federal Regulations* 250. 30.

and its several offices and bureaus, the Coast Guard, and the Army Corps of Engineers – also the United States Public Health Service and the United States Customs Service; altogether, according to a survey made by a major oil company, some sixty governmental agencies were involved in continental shelf operations off United States coasts in 1948,[71] and there are no indications that their number and the depth of their involvement have decreased in the following years.

The United States example of governmental economic and regulatory activity with respect to the continental shelf obviously is not a typical one. The volume of governmental supervision is inevitably determined by a number of factors: the intensity of industrial operations on the continental shelf adjacent to the state territory; the volume of shipping on the high seas over the exploited shelf areas; the amount of high sea fishing carried on in the superjacent waters; and, undoubtedly, by the complexity of the governmental system as well as by the state's standards in maintaining public order.

However, the United States example also leads to a different set of observations. The industrial activity on the continental shelf requires a certain minimal amount of continuous administrative and executive supervision if the participants in the activity are to coexist in an orderly manner and if other interests affected by the shelf operations are to be effectively protected. Not only does the coastal state seem best equipped to judge the amount of regulation required to maintain order in the adjacent shelf areas and to enforce its laws and regulations pertaining to it; in many cases the national and international interests in orderly shelf exploitation coincide. By securing to ships safe freeways above the continental shelf the state also protects its ports and their prosperity. By enforcing regulations prohibiting the use of excessive seismic charges or of industrial equipment and practices conducive to oil pollution of the seas the state protects not only international fishing interests and rights but mainly its own.[72] In a majority of cases fishermen from the coastal state are the primary users of fishing grounds immediately beyond the limits of territorial waters; besides, seismic explosions and oil pollution in the adjacent high seas are no respecters of the limits of territorial waters and affect their marine life as well.

[71] Mercer H. Parks (of Humble Oil and Refining Co.) during a discussion of Watts, *op. cit.* (note 52), p. 85.

[72] Thus, for instance, the Government of Morocco ordered in 1963 on the continental shelf off Sati a suspension of seismic soundings carried on under a prospecting permit by a French oil exploration firm. The order was issued in response to complaints by local sardine fishermen. *The Christian Science Monitor*, 20 March 1963.

POLITICAL AND INDUSTRIAL LIMITS OF THE SHELF

What is still needed is a working definition of those parts of the seabed and subsoil on which industries and states were actually active until 1958. First of all one must distinguish between two phases of state activity; one, when the government lays down a claim to a certain submarine area or professes to control it in accordance with international law, and defines that area so as to best serve its own interests; and second, when the state actually permits or encourages the industry to start the shelf exploitation and proceeds to control it and to regulate the activities of other users of the high seas above the shelf.

The first phase of the state practice involves the national community primarily psychologically and politically, the second engages it economically and organizationally. And it is contended that these two phases are different in their legal effects. But before we analyze that contention and attempt to defend its relevance for the growth of some customary rules of international law, a closer look at the difference between state claims and state activity with respect to the continental shelf seems in order. It can be done by reviewing and summarizing some earlier findings in this study with certain new material added.

Political Concepts of the Continental Shelf

As we have already noted in various connections above, the states defined their submarine areas adjacent to their coasts and purported to fall under their jurisdiction, control or sovereignty in a number of ways. In their official proclamations and enactments, some states simply used the term "continental shelf" and defined it no further, creating the impression that they conceived it as a geographically definable part of the seabed and its subsoil.[73] Others were more specific by using the conventionally accepted average of water depth at which the shelf falls off into oceanic depths, the 200-meter[74] or 100-fathom[75] line. Another variant of the geographical concept was to use the term "continental shelf" with an express addition "at whatever depth it may be found," [76] possibly a reflection of the fact that in some cases the continental slope begins only at a depth much greater than 200 fathoms. Further there were governmental claims in which the geographical term

[73] *E.g.*, the United States in the 1945 Truman Proclamation, Guatemala and Australia.
[74] *E.g.*, Mexico, Nicaragua, Ecuador.
[75] *E.g.*, Pakistan, Falkland Islands; and Australia, in the Pearl Fisheries Act.
[76] *E.g.*, Honduras and Costa Rica.

"continental shelf" was avoided, the submarine areas in question being simply described as the seabed and subsoil adjacent to the coasts;[77] still other claims where the states chose to ignore the geographical realities of the shelf completely and sought to set their jurisdiction and control over the seabed and subsoil up to a 200-mile distance from the shore line;[78] and finally claims attempting to erase any geographical seaward limits of the continental shelf by introducing the "test of exploitability" concept[79] – the right of national jurisdiction and control continuously to follow the driller and the dredger out under the sea as far as he may be able to go. And it was this last definition of the continental shelf limits by the elastic double standard of water depth and the test of exploitability which finally found its way into article 1 of the Convention on the Continental Shelf, adopted by the United Nations Conference on the Law of the Sea held in 1958 in Geneva.

Taken as a whole, these definitions of the continental shelf provide but little guidance as to what are the seaward limits of the submarine areas claimed by the various states – unless, of course, one should choose to take article 1 of the Convention on the Continental Shelf as a culmination and a meeting point of all previously divergent claims, a choice of a doubtful value indeed.

The Shelf Utilized and Controlled

The practice of industrial exploitation of continental shelf resources from 1945 till 1958, and of state regulation and control over such activity, reflects none of the divergence displayed by the political concepts of the seaward limits of the shelf. An extensive search through industrial magazines, scientific journals, governmental documents and special papers written by experts commissioned by international organizations reveals no evidence that, until 1958, any concept of the continental shelf defined by any terms other than geographical would have a practical significance.

A rather interesting picture is obtained by systematically arranging the steps which men and their national communities have taken to reach for and appropriate the continental shelf resources.

The most far-reaching is the political step already discussed – the claim of states to the right of exclusive control and use of shelf resources in submarine areas contiguous to the national coasts and stretching as far seaward

[77] *E.g.*, Saudi Arabia and the British-protected Arab Sheikhdoms.
[78] *E.g.*, Peru, Chile, Ecuador, Costa Rica, El Salvador.
[79] *E.g.*, Israel, the "Resolution of Ciudad Trujillo" of 1959, Egypt.

as the technology of submarine exploitation would go. In theory this might mean that the entire ocean floor all around the world would in time be parcelled out among the various states.

Leaving this aside, one may look at the many other steps taken: (1) Technological advances in *reaching* the seabed and subsoil resources under progressively increasing water depths; (2) Engineering advances in constructing industrial equipment *technically capable to extract* useful materials from the seabed and subsoil under greater water depths; (3) Commercial advances in *actual exploitation* of shelf resources at increasing depths.

Ad (1): As to *technological advances*, in 1957 methods were found and proven for drilling core tests to gather geological information from the seabed and its subsoil under waters up to 1,500 feet deep.[80] However, drilling is not the only method of discovering sea bottom riches. It is needed to reach materials deep in the subsoil, such as oil, gas, and sulphur. But minerals such as manganese, iron, copper, cobalt, nickel and phosphorite, some of them lying freely on the ocean floor, are easier to reach. Those lying closer to the shore in relatively shallow water are now being dredged out. But the methods of dredging under great depths are a wide-open field of technological advances. For over one hundred years scientists have used the dredging method to obtain samples from ocean floor under waters as deep as 30,000 feet; and now designs have been described for commercial dredging from the seabed in depths up to 14,000 feet.[81] While technology has thus reached far out beyond the geographical limits of the continental shelf, this must be noted: that until 1958 neither the drilling of core tests nor dredging on sea bottom beyond the continental shelf and slope were accompanied by actual manifestations of national control over the submarine areas so used. On the whole, such technological tests were sporadic and of short duration.

Ad (2): *Engineering progress* in construction of equipment technically capable to extract natural resources from the seabed and subsoil was until 1958 much more modest. As we have seen, the engineers for many years had their eyes set on the 600-foot depth mark. Bus as late as September 1957, the maximum depth at which the best drilling equipment in the Gulf of Mexico was capable of operating – but was not acutally operating – was 180 feet.[82]

[80] Developed and patented by the CUSS group consisting of Continental Oil, Union Oil, Shell Oil and the Superior Oil companies, and tested off California coasts; cf., 145 (No. 6) *World Oil* 130 (Nov. 1957).

[81] John L. Mero, "Minerals on the Ocean Floor," 203 (No. 6) *Scientific American* 70–71 (2 December 1960).

[82] Report, 7 (No. 1) *Offshore* 53–57 (September 1957). Only three years later, in September 1960, three out of one hundred and seventeen drilling units operating in the Gulf of Mexico were reported *to have the capacity* to drill under the maximum depth of 600 feet of water. 13 (No. 4) *Offshore* 23–28 (September 1960).

There is a marked difference between this fact and the following opinion with which a leading oil industry journal welcomed in 1957 the news of the forthcoming United Nations Conference on the Law of the Sea:

With the advancements in drilling techniques that have already been made and those that are on the drawing board, 600 feet is no longer the water depth limit for drilling . . .[83]

Ad (3): *Actual exploitation* of continental shelf resources advanced into greater depths of water at a still slower pace. In June 1948 an oil industry journal published a map of the northern Gulf of Mexico accompanying an article on oil exploration on continental shelves; the map showed the outline of the shelf only to the 250-foot water depth.[84] But it was still a very generously drafted outline, for only in 1957 was the 100-foot water-depth barrier actually broken, followed by a new record of 137 feet reached in April 1958,[85] during the period of the Geneva United Nations Conference on the Law of the Sea. If these records are unimpressive compared to the larger vistas sought by and opening before the eyes of the engineers, scientists, and governments, they are still but records and therefore exceptions. In August 1957, a great majority of the 448 marine drilling rigs and 102 drill tenders around the world was reported working in water depths from 10 to 50 feet.[86] And reports dated four and a half years later show that there was no sudden surge into greater depths in the intervening period; in the Gulf of Mexico, where the most advanced methods of commercial drilling have been employed and several records set, submarine areas beyond the 20-fathom or 120-foot depth range were reported too deep for most drilling units.[87]

Governmental leasing of submarine areas for industrial exploitation, as an actual manifestation of effective state control over the continental shelf, did of course maintain an edge over the drillers. In 1955, the United States Government offered for leasing continental shelf areas in the Gulf of Mexico under waters not deeper than 100 feet,[88] next year, tracts of submerged acreage offered for lease by the United States Department of the Interior covered a depth range from 20 to 140 feet,[89] but only in 1962 did federally

[83] Editorial, 7 (No. 3) *Offshore* 34 (November 1957).
[84] 45 (No. 6) *Oil and Gas Journal* 98 (15 June 1946).
[85] The record-breaking drilling of a well under 200 feet of water off the Louisiana coast in South Timbalier section was reported one and a half years later. 11 (No. 1) *Offshore* 20 (August 1959). The greatest depth of water through which commercial drilling was done from a fixed platform, 207 feet, was claimed by the Gulf Oil Company. 15 (No. 7) *The Orange Disc* 34 (July–August 1962).
[86] Report, 6 (No. 6) *Offshore* 79 (August 1957).
[87] Report, 16 (No. 5) *Offshore* 13 (March 1962).
[88] Report, 2 (No. 4) *Offshore* 26 (June 1955).
[89] Report, 4 (No. 2) *Offshore* 31 (April 1956).

leased tracts in the Gulf of Mexico involve acreage lying, in some isolated instances, under 400 to 600 feet of water.[90]

To summarize the findings of this chapter, the following might be stated:

(a) From 1945 to 1958 governmental declarations and enactments, whether unilateral or multilateral, were aimed at establishing a regime of national jurisdiction and control over the adjacent continental shelves in most areas of the world; while in the earlier years of the period the continental shelves were conceived of as a geological formation, after 1950 the concept has changed into a political one, with outer limits of the politically defined shelf far beyond its geographical boundaries.

(b) The governmental actions, however divergent, nevertheless met with no effective protests and in general created an expectation on the part of states and industry that it is legally permissible, politically prudent and economically safe to start exploiting shelf resources under the national control of the adjacent states.

(c) Industrial and state involvement on the continental shelves deepened rapidly after 1945 and particularly from 1950 to 1958; nationally controlled shelf activity was continually spreading seaward, but throughout the 1945-1958 period in no known case did it leave the geographical limits of the continental shelf.

(d) Only the *over-water* exploration and exploitation of *mineral* resources of the outer continental shelves can be considered as a direct consequence of the postwar shelf claims by the coastal states.

[90] *Business Week*, No. 1699, 24 March 1962, p. 31. The only instance known to this writer of leasing submarine areas beyond the 600-foot depth limit by a state other than the United States dates from 1960, when Libya issued an industrial concession for a huge tract of submerged land with water depths exceeding 900 feet. 13 (No. 6) *Offshore* 17–18 (Nov. 1960).

CHAPTER III

POLITICAL AND LEGAL PROBLEMS OF THE CONTINENTAL SHELF: AN OUTLINE

Against the background of state practice in the exercise of exclusive coastal rights over the adjacent outer continental shelf one can project the political and legal problems that developed between 1945, the year when the doctrine of the shelf was formulated, and 1958, the time when the United Nations Conference on the Law of the Sea was convened to draft, among others, the Convention on the Continental Shelf.

But there was more than a thirteen year gap between the two dates. While the mineral resources of the outer continental shelf were gradually more and more utilized under the exclusive control of the respective coastal states, an increasingly more complex pattern of political and legal problems was enveloping the status of the outer submarine areas. The inconclusive theoretical debate of writers and jurists reviewed above was but one reflection of that complexity. The strenuous efforts between 1951 and 1956 of legal experts on the United Nations International Law Commission to codify and develop the law of the continental shelf[1] provided further evidence how the political and legal problems of the continental shelf multiplied in course of time.

In this chapter, we examine the main legal and political problems arising from the continental shelf doctrine as it was formulated in the 1945 Truman Proclamation, and as they were reflected in the attitudes of states later and primarily in the discussions of state representatives at the 1958 Geneva Conference.

The purpose of that examination is twofold. First, it should indicate what are the main component parts of a legal regime of the continental shelf that are in need of definition and regarding which there has been some

[1] In this study we often refer to, but do not undertake a systematic study of, the International Law Commission's work on the law of the continental shelf. By its own admission, the International Law Commission was codifying as well as developing that law, and found it impossible to draw a dividing line between those provisions of its drafts that were intended to reflect the existing legal situation, and others representing proposals *de lege ferenda* to be accepted by the states in their practice or as provisions of a treaty.

measurable volume of state practice. It obviously does not suffice to recognize that the continental shelf doctrine ascribes to the coastal state exclusive rights over its adjacent outer continental shelf; it is also necessary to consider the geographical limits within which such rights may be exercised, and the functional limits of such rights in terms of the purposes served. Secondly, since we are concerned with the customary law of the continental shelf, the examination should assist us in defining what the states participating in the 1958 Geneva Conference did or did not consider to have been a settled law of the continental shelf. It is, of course, true that the purpose of the Conference regarding the continental shelf was not to embody in a treaty the previously unwritten but settled rules comprising the legal regime of the shelf. The delegates' task was to negotiate a treaty and not to codify a body of established rules. But the Conference itself provided a forum for the fullest possible expression and confrontation of official views on the subject. Of the eighty-six participating delegations, over sixty used their opportunity, primarily in Committee IV dealing with the continental shelf problems, to state the views of their governments. One thus expects to find in the Geneva discussions some evidence not only of what the participating states wanted the law of the continental shelf to be under the Convention, but also what they considered the law had been prior to the Conference and, as it was, almost thirteen years after the doctrine of the continental shelf had been formulated by the United States.

POLITICAL AND LEGAL ASPECTS OF THE DOCTRINE: 1945

The survey in the preceding chapter of industrial and state activity on the outer continental shelves provides further evidence, in addition to the reciprocal policies underlying that activity and expressed in the doctrine of the shelf,[2] that the postwar problems of the continental shelf had no direct connection with the earlier isolated instances of exclusive coastal control exercised over some outlying but limited sedentary fisheries.[3]

But the continental shelf doctrine, as it emerged shortly after World War II, was not only an entirely new development; it was a break, in law as well as in fact, with a past characterized by sporadic claims and acts of exclusive state control over specific areas of adjacent continental shelf, and not a continuation of that past.[4] However, the break was not altogether sudden; the

[2] The question of reciprocity as an essential element of the continental shelf doctrine is examined below in this chapter.
[3] P. 42.
[4] *Id.*

1942 United Kingdom-Venezuela Treaty of the Gulf of Paria and and the subsequent British Order in Council[5] represent a significant stepping stone from the prewar to the postwar practice of states regarding the adjacent continental shelves.

The Gulf of Paria separating Venezuela and Trinidad is a relatively narrow expanse of sea which, in the 1940's, held a big promise of containing accessible pools of petroleum and related substances in its seabed and subsoil.

The Treaty of the Gulf of Paria, signed by the United Kingdom and Venezuela on 26 February 1942, was obviously intended to allow orderly petroleum exploration and exploitation on the Gulf of Paria continental shelf. Articles 5 to 8 of the Treaty refer to permanent installations on the shelf in connection with the safety of navigation, and to measures designed to prevent harmful pollution of sea waters by oil.

However, petroleum as the material object of the Treaty is not the only point making the Treaty into a forerunner of the postwar shelf practice which also concentrated, at least at first, on the mineral resources of the shelf. It contains several other principles which separate it distinctly from the past. The Treaty provides (Articles 6 and 8) that nothing in it shall be held to affect in any way the status of the waters of the Gulf of Paria or any rights of passage or navigation on the surface of the seas outside the territorial waters. This contrasts sharply with the practice established by the British Colonial Act of 1811 which asserted dominion over Ceylonese pearl banks far beyond the three-mile limit and authorized the seizure and condemnation of any boat found within the limits of the banks.[6] Similarly, the legal obligation of the parties to the Treaty to prevent oil pollution of superjacent waters (Articles 7 and 8) is a modern concept, although the Treaty does not express it in general terms; each Party obligates itself not to permit oil pollution of the other's territorial waters or the foreshore. Significantly perhaps, the Treaty does not provide for non-interference with general fishing rights in the high seas of the Gulf of Paria.

On balance, however, the Treaty does not constitute the beginning from which the modern continental shelf doctrine and the rule could emerge. It is a bilateral treaty obligating each party not to assert "any claim to sovereignty or control" over certain submarine areas adjacent to the coast of the other;

[5] Texts of both documents, the Treaty and the Submarine Areas of the Gulf of Paria (Annexation) Order in Council of 6 August 1942 in 144 *British and Foreign State Papers* (1940–1942) 1067 and 971. Also in 1 *U.N. Legislative Series* 44–47.

[6] Legislative Enactments, Ceylon, 1707–1879, Regulation No. 3 of 1811 for the protection of H.M. pearl banks of Ceylon. *Cf.*, U. S. Naval War College, *International Law Studies* 1959–1960 (vol. LIII: The Law of the Sea: Some Recent Developments, by Carl M. Franklin), (Washington, D.C.: Government Printing Office, 1961), p. 30.

the area assigned to each is well defined by a dividing line (Article 3) running through the Gulf. Nothing in the Treaty indicates the expectation of the United Kingdom or Venezuela that other countries could deduce some general principles from the Treaty upon which to base their own claims to the continental shelves adjacent to their coasts. No such principles are stated. No claim by either party to sovereignty over the submarine areas as against other states is made. One may say with Vallat that the Treaty was a fact of which third parties could in practice be expected to take notice but no more than that.[7]

This general evaluation of the legal significance of the Treaty of the Gulf of Paria is only partially disturbed by the subsequent Submarine Areas of the Gulf of Paria (Annexation) Order in Council of 6 August 1942. In its material elements it corresponds to the Treaty. As an act of annexation, of course, it is of more general significance; it claims an exclusive right *vis a vis* the community of states in a manner similar to that of the 1811 British Colonial Act asserting dominion over Ceylonese pearl banks. Thus taken together, the Treaty and the Order in Council may represent the beginnings of an exclusive right that could eventually mature either as a prescriptive right or as a title obtained by the legal process of territorial aquisition. Yet in either case the basic concept of general and full reciprocity essential for the emergence of a customary rule of a wider application is missing. And in either case something more than a mere *animus occupandi* would be required for the full effectiveness of the exclusive right claimed.

One may of course reflect that in fact the stage was perfectly fitted to an unobstructed emergence of the exclusive right claimed. Even if we disregard the three remaining war years, no countries other than Venezuela or the United Kingdom had either an active interest in, or the full technical capability of, exploiting the shelf resources in the Gulf of Paria. The possible historical growth of a prescriptive title or title by occupation was of course affected by and submerged in the developments initiated by the 1945 Truman Proclamation, and it is needless to speculate how much time, and how intensive practice, would be required for the isolated Gulf of Paria rights to mature. It is of no more than historical interest now to consider that for almost thirteen years after the Treaty and the Order in Council there was no over-water drilling operation undertaken off the Trinidad coasts. Some exploratory work had been done,[8] but all wells reaching into the subsoil of

[7] F. A. Vallat, "The Continental Shelf," 23 *British Year Book of International Law* 336 (1946).

[8] In 1946, geophysical work in the Gulf of Paria was in progress with three seismic groups and one gravity-meter party working. Private companies had received exploration permits and oil experts expected actual marine drilling to start during the first quarter of 1947. By the end of 1946 it was reported that "actually no marine licenses have yet been granted by the Government [of

the continental shelf were drilled from the shores. Only in the early months of 1955 the drilling of a well designated as High Seas No. 1 was started from a drilling platform six miles out in the Gulf of Paria in forty feet of water.[9]

The Truman Proclamation of 1945

The British practice regarding the Gulf of Paria shelf did not significantly change the legal status of the continental shelf in general. It did not seek to bring about any such change. Furthermore, it went relatively unnoticed partly because of its very limited scope, but mainly by having been drowned by the tidal wave of World War II. The legal situation remained unchanged at least until 28 September 1945, when President Truman issued the Proclamation by which the doctrine as well as the practice of the continental shelf were initiated.

In form, the Proclamation was a statement of a forthcoming United States policy justified by reference to (a) the long range worldwide need for new sources of petroleum and other minerals; (b) the progress of technology beginning to permit the utilization of such resources; (c) the need of a recognized jurisdiction over such resources to assure that their utilization and conservation would be orderly; (d) the practicability of exploitation directed and supported from the adjacent land; (e) the geographical and geological unity of the land mass with the adjacent continental shelf; and (f) the interests of the coastal state in having its security undisturbed by prolonged and intensive foreign activities close to its shores.

In its political intent, the Truman Proclamation was an act of international persuasion; as a Presidential Proclamation, it was bound to be noticed by other governments. Every state with a sea coast could use the general bases of the Truman Proclamation and place upon them its own claim.

The economic-political aim of the Truman Proclamation is likewise clear from its text. The obvious desired effect was to create a climate of stability favorable to heavy investment necessary for oil and gas exploitation.

The legal aim and technique of the Truman Proclamation were a subject of some controversy. Rather than to enter its thicket it suffices to note Waldock's view:

Trinidad], but it is understood that authorities are pretty well committed on approval of applications for much of the acreage on which applications have been received." Report, "Expansion in Trinidad on Conservative Scale; Offshore Drilling Soon," 124 (No. 1) *The Oil Weekly* 13–14 (2 December 1946).

[9] Report 2 (No. 2) *Offshore Operations* 18 (April 1955).

. . . it seems to me significant that the [United States] shelf Proclamation, unlike the fishery Proclamation, does not undertake reciprocally to recognise the right of other States to assert a similar right. International legislation taking the rudimentary forms which it does, the undertaking of reciprocal treatment in the fishery Proclamation suggests to an international lawyer an invitation to other States to join in a deliberate and legislative development of customary law. The absence of any similar undertaking in the shelf Proclamation, issued on the same date, can hardly be accidental and does rather indicate that the United States did not consider recognition by other States in any way necessary to give legal propriety to its claim to the resources of the shelf.[10]

Yet if one is permitted to draw conclusions as to the legal intent and technique of the shelf Proclamation by reference to an entirely different statement of policy, it is doubly appropriate to seek guidance from the text of the Proclamation itself. And the text, on three counts at the least, does suggest that the Truman Proclamation might have had the function of initiating a deliberate development of customary law. First and generally, as noted above, the proclaimed United States policy was based on facts and goals of a general character, not applicable exclusively to the United States; in the last paragraph of the preamble, the United States Government states its view "that the exercise of jurisdiction . . . by *the contiguous nation* is reasonable and just . . ." [11] and nowhere indicates that it views it as such only for the United States. Second, when speaking of mineral resources of the continental shelf off the United States coasts, the Proclamation invokes the need of a "*recognized* jurisdiction over these resources . . ." [12] Third, in its operative part the Proclamation proposes the use of "equitable principles" as a method of determining the outer limits of its continental shelf in cases where the shelf "extends to the shores of *another State,* or is *shared with* an adjacent State . . .;" [13] thus, at least implicitly, the Truman Proclamation does recognize the right of other states to adopt a corresponding policy, and in fact welcomes the exercise of that right.

The legal significance of the Truman Proclamation lies in its spirit of reciprocity. By justifying its proclaimed policy by general goals, interests and facts, such as public order, satisfaction of world economic needs, security requirements of coastal states, and territorial contiguity, the United States was not merely claiming a right to exercise jurisdiction and control over the natural resources of its adjacent 750,000 square miles of the continental

[10] C. H. M. Waldock, "The Legal Basis of Claims to the Continental Shelf," 36 *Transactions of the Grotius Society* 138–139 (1950).
[11] Emphasis added.
[12] Emphasis added.
[13] Emphasis added.

shelf.[14] To have that right recognized by others, the United States was, implicitly yet clearly, denying itself an opportunity to assert for itself or its national industries free access to the resources hidden in about ten million square miles of the continental shelves off foreign coasts.[15]

One may ask, of course, whether the reciprocal spirit of the Truman Proclamation was not more apparent than real, *i.e.*, whether the United States was really denying itself anything in return for the recognition by others of the claimed exclusive jurisdiction and control over the resources of the continental shelf adjacent to its coasts. The answer seems to lie in (a) possible alternative courses the United States could adopt, and (b) in the United States' technological, economic and political capabilities then existing.

As to policy alternatives, only two warrant closer attention. Instead of issuing the Proclamation in the form of a statement of a general continental shelf doctrine, the United States could rely on the law of territorial acquisition by occupation if the continental shelf were to be considered *res nullius*; or on the rights of the first user it the shelf were looked upon as *res communis*. Such alternative policies, however, would be realistic only if their adoption by the United States could be implemented in practice. And available evidence suggests that in the early postwar years the United States was in a favorable position, by virtue of its technology, its economic strength and its general power, to launch and sustain a policy of occupying or using the continental shelf adjacent to its coasts as well as shelf areas contiguous to the coasts of others.

As to the shelf areas around the United States, the United States Department of the Interior had in 1945 everything ready to start an intensive and extensive geological survey of the submerged lands.[16] On the level of private enterprise, American oil companies were already pushing their exploratory work out into the sea primarily in the Gulf of Mexico. In 1944, Magnolia Company conducted geophysical work off the Louisiana coast, and in 1945,

[14] This extent of the United States continental shelf was given in a press release accompanying the Truman Proclamation. 13 *State Department Bulletin* 484 (1945). Harold L. Ickes, the Secretary of the Interior, employed the figure of "about 760,000 square miles" in U.S. Department of the Interior, *Annual Report of the Secretary of the Interior* [fiscal year ended 30 June 1945], (Washington, D. C.:Government Printing Office, 1945), p. vi. However, some estimates of the area of the United States continental shelf run as high as one million square miles, *e.g.*, W. E. Pratt, "Petroleum on Continental Shelves," 31 *Bulletin of the American Association of Petroleum Geologists* 658 (April 1947).

[15] Pratt, *ibid.*, estimates the aggregate area of the continental shelves as "roughly 11 million square miles." However, due to different geographical concepts, the data vary considerably. According to J. H. F. Umbgrove, "Origin of Continental Shelves," 30 *Bulletin of the American Association of Petroleum Geologists* 250 (1946), the shallow shelf seas up to the approximate depth of 200 meters cover an area of only 10 million square kilometers, *i.e.*, about 4½ million square miles.

[16] Ickes in U.S. Department of the Interior, *op. cit.* (note 14), p. x.

when the State of Louisiana held its first offshore lease sale, Magnolia leased 129,000 acres of the shelf, some of the area well beyond the three-mile limit of the territorial sea.[17] In 1945, Secretary of the Interior Ickes mentioned but did not identify an oil company which had "explored the waters of the Gulf of Mexico for oil up to 26 miles off the Louisiana coast." [18] In the field of exploration and exploitation of shelf resources, the United States oil industry already had amassed considerable experience; the Creole Oil Field off Cameron Parish, Louisiana, was discovered in March 1938 as a result of exploitation of onshore or shallow water anomalies.[19] The first drilling there – in open waters of the Gulf of Mexico – started on 6 October 1938 as a joint operation of the Superior Oil Company and the Pure Oil Company, 6,000 feet offshore in 14 feet of water.[20]

When one combines the technological progress with the size and wealth of the United States oil industry, it is difficult to imagine that its activity on the continental shelf adjacent to the United States coasts would be seriously curtailed by the activity of foreign oil companies, private or nationalized. As far as drilling for oil and gas is concerned, operations on the continental shelf in 1945 heavily depended on support and cooperation from the nearest shore, something which the competitive foreign companies would have some difficulty in obtaining on United States soil even if they had all other technical and financial means to venture onto the continental shelf around the United States. One may thus assume that even without the Truman Proclamation and the doctrine it expressed, the petroleum resources of the United States continental shelf would be exploited primarily by United States industry. The United States Government could then proceed to protect and regulate that activity and construct upon it a claim of territorial acquisition or to let it continue and protect it merely as a legal use, by the first user, of a *res communis* to which all have a right even if not the means to exercise that right.

In addition, the United States could secure some advantages for itself and its national companies on the continental shelves elsewhere. If, instead of

[17] O. W. Noland and Roy M. Huffington, "Development and Outlook for the Continental Shelf of Texas and Louisiana," 1 (No. 5) *Offshore Operations* 9 (January 1955). In December 1946, Magnolia was reported drilling a well in 25 feet of water in the open sea five miles off Louisiana. Report 124 (No. 4) *The Oil Weekly* 27 (23 December 1946).

[18] Ickes in U.S. Department of the Interior, *op. cit.* (note 14), p. x. The reference was possibly to Magnolia Oil Co.

[19] Noland and Huffington, *op. cit.* (note 17) 9.

[20] I. W. Alcorn, "The Pure Oil Company's Tideland Development," 129 (No. 1) *World Oil* 115 (May 1949). List of test wells drilled off Texas and Louisiana as early as 1938 and all of them very close to the shore is given by James S. Critz, "Oil Possibilities on the Gulf Coast Continental Shelf," 124 (No. 6) *The Oil Weekly* 21 (6 January 1947). In the Elwood field off California, piers were built in approximately 40-ft. water depth and several wells drilled directionally from each pier. R. D. Shrewsbury, "Deep Sea Drilling," 120 (No. 2) *The Oil Weekly* 36 (10 December 1945).

issuing the Truman Proclamation, the United States Government adopted a policy which would seek to protect internationally competitive activity on the continental shelves everywhere, American interests would have been in a favorable position. In this sense the continental shelf activities of The Superior Oil Company of California provide an outstanding illustration.

In 1944, the company won considerable recognition for developing and using successful offshore seismic-survey techniques and, toward the end of 1945, dispatched its seismic fleet from Cameron, Louisiana, to explore a continental shelf area of many thousand square miles on the Bahama banks west of Andros Island to the Keys east of Florida Straits.[21] As early as 1948-1949, The Superior Oil Company acting through a wholly-owned subsidiary, negotiated with Sheikh Shakhbut of Abu Dhabi to obtain oil rights on the outer submarine areas of Abu Dhabi.[22] This in itself indicates that The Superior Oil Company had the necessary experience, scientific and technological knowledge as well as the financial means to start the costly seismic survey on the continental shelf under the high seas off Abu Dhabi. In the absence of the Truman Proclamation, and of the corresponding acts by Great Britain on behalf of the Arab Sheikhdoms, the company would have been materially as well as legally able to undertake offshore activities in the Persian Gulf without any leases as long as it could secure the necessary shore support and cooperation.

Under these circumstances, the United States could view the continental shelf as either *res nullius* or *res communis* and extend its full protection to the company's installations accordingly. Under the *res nullius* viewpoint, the United States Government could regulate the company's operations and, to use the terms employed by the United States Department of State in 1918 with reference to a proposed construction of a permanent platform some 40 miles out in the Gulf of Mexico, could "assume some sort of control" over the installations "if erected, and inhabited and controlled by United States citizens in the name of the United States." [23] And in 1945 the United States certainly had the necessary naval power effectively to carry out perhaps a limited yet significant administrative and regulatory activity in various areas of the world. Thus a claim of territorial acquisition by occupation could be progressively built up over specific areas of continental shelves several thousand miles from the United States.

[21] E. H. Short, Jr., "Seismic Fleet Departs on 1,500 Mile Journey to Bahamas," 44 (No. 32) *Oil and Gas Journal* 82 (15 December 1945).

[22] These negotiations, and Sheikh Shakhbut's decision to lease to the company the outer submarine areas off Abu Dhabi, led in 1951 to the arbitration between Abu Dhabi and the Petroleum Development (Trucial Coast) Ltd. with Lord Asquith of Bishopstone as umpire. The arbitration award is discussed at pp. 135 – 138.

[23] See p. 46, footnote 22.

As another variant under the same policy, it is not difficult to visualize a United States company obtaining protection from the United States Government for its installations it might have erected north of central Cuba and in an area now falling, under the legal regime of the continental shelf, under foreign jurisdiction.[24] The sea there is extremely shallow, with depths varying from as little as 6 to 33 feet,[25] to make the area inviting to the industry. And it would be accessible to it as the distance from the United States land is not such as would permanently bar exploitation dependent on shore support.

Under the *res communis* viewpoint, the role of the United States Government could be confined to an effective protection of United States oil companies operating on the continental shelves under the high seas anywhere. Assimilated to the high seas, the continental shelves and their resources would be open to all. However, an oil field discovered through several stages of costly seismic surveys and experimental drilling and with the wells finally opened up could no longer reasonably belong to all just as a whale, killed, marked and left floating for a later recovery by a factory ship, may no longer be taken by anyone who may happen to come upon it, but only by those who originally captured it.

Summing up, the element of reciprocity contained in the Truman Proclamation of 1945 was more than a legal fiction. Notified of the proclaimed United States policy – the policy of a state well-endowed with the industrial potential, scientific knowledge, financial means, and sufficient power to protect its interests on a world-wide scale – other coastal countries could start with greater confidence to plan and implement their own national or private industry programs of exploring and exploiting the resources of the continental shelves adjacent to their respective coasts. And they could do so with a justified expectation that they or their industries would not waste energy and funds through unsuccessful race against a superior competitor, for the potentially strongest one publicly and formally declared itself out of the race.

We may thus say that by creating a set of justified expectations on the part of other states and, on a lower level, among the managers of the petroleum industry, the Truman Proclamation had the basic characteristics of an estoppel. Indeed, its initial legal significance was very much limited. The United States Government had unilaterally proclaimed its continental shelf policy and surely could unilaterally change it. But until it should have done so, its

[24] On legal problems affecting the area, see p. 113.

[25] John L. Rich, "Submarine Sedimentary Features on Bahama Banks and Their Bearing on Distribution Patterns of Lenticular Oil Sands," 32 *Bulletin of the American Association of Petroleum Geologists* 767 (1948).

Proclamation was bound to continue affecting the policies and acts of other states. In other words, the Truman Proclamation had the potential to cause other states to plan and implement shelf policies which , without the Proclamation, they might not consider and undertake. Summarizing the foregoing examination, the weight of expectations created on the part of other states by the Truman Proclamation was closely dependent on the following factors:

a) The policy was announced by the United States President in a formal document and as such was bound to be noticed by other governments.

b) Both the form and the contents of the document indicated that the policy proclaimed had been seriously studied and, therefore, was not likely to be changed from day to day.

c) The Proclamation clearly implied the intention of the United States not to claim any rights on the continental shelves adjacent to foreign coasts.

d) The effectiveness of the element of reciprocity depended on the actual potential of the United States to adopt and implement a different policy whereby the United States could possibly obtain some rights which it denied itself by the Proclamation; *i.e.*, such factors as the United States economic, technological and financial potential as well as its relative power status were of considerable importance.

By contrast, one may take the text of the Truman Proclamation and imagine, without changing its contents, that it were issued by some small, perhaps newly established, economically weak country with a short coastline and without a navy. The proclamation would still embody the continental shelf doctrine and could, by the persuasiveness of its argument, result in an adoption of that doctrine by other states. However, it is more difficult to imagine that other countries would, as a consequence of that proclamation alone, seriously consider an adjustment of their own policies, since the proclaimed policy of a small and weak country would give them no cause to expect that their own adjusted policies would have a reasonable chance to mature and become fruitful without a serious and perhaps overwhelming challenge.

To the same extent as the relative weight of the United States increased the effects of the Truman Proclamation among other countries, it also tended progressively to limit the freedom of the United States to change its shelf policy. Aware of its country's relative weight, the United States Government had to consider that the Truman Proclamation would create a set of reasonable expectations on the part of other states, and that in time these states might act on the basis of such expectations. *I.e.*, in time the United States might find itself legally estopped from changing its policy and seeking rights on foreign continental shelves if, by any such change, it would also seek to compel others to modify, to their detriment, their own shelf policies and activities adopted in response to the expectations created by the Truman Proclamation.

Before concluding this section, it is necessary to define with greater precision the actual technical scope of the expectations the Truman Proclamation was bound or likely to create.

The Proclamation makes no attempt to define the continental shelf, its seabed and subsoil; but, by stating in the preamble that the shelf "may be regarded as an extension of the land-mass of the coastal nation and thus naturally appurtenant to it" and that the shelf resources "frequently form a seaward extension of a pool or deposit lying within the territory," the continental shelf of the Truman Proclamation is obviously a geographical concept and its limits could be determined by geographical measurements.

This impression is strengthened by the press release accompanying the Proclamation and published simultaneously in the United States *Department of State Bulletin.*[26] The press release indicates that the geographical measurement of the shelf is indeed the method of defining its limits, for it states the shelf area of the United States to be 750,000 square miles; and it also refers to the shelf by describing it as an area generally covered by no more than 100 fathoms (600 feet) of water, another broad geographical concept.[27]

The press release itself was taken as a means of interpreting the Proclamation, and thus was not without effect on the nature and scope of the expectations the Proclamation was bound to create. The Division for the Development and Codification of International Law of the United Nations Secretariat's Legal Department included the text of the press release in the *U. N. Legislative Series,*[28] and added some quotes from the *Annual Report of the Secretary of the Interior* for 1945 (Harold L. Ickes), which also defined the continental shelf in geographical terms when stating that, "approximately described," it is an area "covered by no more than 600 feet of water." [29] Both

26 13 *State Department Bulletin* 484 (1945).

27 The International Committee on the Nomenclature of Ocean Bottom Features of the International Union of Geodesy and Geophysics defined the continental shelf, shelf edge and shelf borderland as "the zone around the continent, extending from the low-water line to the depth at which there is a marked increase of slope to greater depth. Where this increase occurs, the term shelf edge is appropriate. Conventionally its edge is taken at 100 fathoms (or 200 metres) but instances are known where the increase of slope occurs at more than 200 or less than 65 fathoms." John D. H. Wiseman and Cameron D. Ovey, "Definitions of Features on the Deep-Sea Floor," 1 *Deep-Sea Research* 14 (1953). A group of experts called by the UNESCO at the request of the U.N. Secretariat, while trying to determine the elements that could lead to a definition of the continental shelf by the 1958 Geneva Conference on the Law of the Sea, also stresses that "the average slope is much steeper beyond 200 metres [depth] than nearer shore." UNESCO Secretariat, "Scientific Considerations Relating to the Continental Shelf," U.N. Doc. A/CONF.13/2, in U.N. Conference on the Law of the Sea, *Official Records*, v. 1, p. 40. Umbgrove, *op. cit.* (note 15) 250, uses the 200 metre depth line as a basis for determining the area of the continental shelf.

28 1 *U.N. Legislative Series* 39 (1951).

29 Ickes in U.S. Department of the Interior, *op. cit.* (note 14), p. ix.

the press release and the Report are described in the *U. N. Legislative Series* as "official comments." [30] It appears that these comments did influence the policies of other governments as well as the notions of private industry interested in the continental shelf operations. The 200-meter water depth line, although representing but an approximation almost nowhere exactly corresponding to actual geographical facts,[31] was used by Mexico in 1945 to describe the seaward limit of the continental shelf.[32] The oil industry also accepted the average 600-foot or 200-meter water depth as an official limit of the shelf.[33]

But the Truman Proclamation did not pertain to the entire geographical area of the shelf. In its operative part, it proclaimed a specific United States policy to regard only certain resources of the continental shelf as subject to United States jurisdiction and control. Explicitly, the Truman Proclamation speaks of "the natural resources of the subsoil and sea bed of the continental shelf." In fact, however, it defines them with greater precision. Analyzed in detail, the Proclamation is clearly focused on and covers almost exclusively mineral resources and, among them, especially such substances as petroleum and its derivatives, sulphur and possibly other minerals whose extraction demands extensive installations

Being reciprocal in character, the Proclamation, as soon as it was communicated to other governments, had an initial effect of a political as well as legal character. By proclaiming a specific continental shelf policy, the United States Government compelled itself not to reverse it without an equally full announcement or notification, for it had to consider that by publicizing its

[30] 1 *U.N. Legislative Series* 39 (1951)

[31] *Cf.* note 27 above. Irregularities in the depth of the superjacent waters are not unimportant even when the difference from the average depth is no greater than 10%, *i.e.*, 60 feet. In areas where the shelf slopes gently ,as in the Gulf of Mexico, the 60-foot difference in depth represents a surface distance of six miles. *Cf.*, Noland and Huffington ,*op. cit.* (note 17) 9, for statement that the shelf off the United States coast deepens into the Gulf of Mexico at the rate of 10 feet per mile.

[32] Presidential Declaration of 29 October 1945. English translation in 1 *U. N. Legislative Series* 13 (1951).

[33] Reporting on the Truman Proclamation, one of the leading United States oil industry journals stated that "the continental shelf is defined as extending out to where the water is 100 fathoms (600 feet) in depth." 44 (No. 22) *Oil and Gas Journal* 72 (6 October 1945). A news report in 124 (No. 4) *The Oil Weekly* 27 (23 December 1946) speaks of the "600-foot limit claimed in the President's proclamation." During a discussion at an annual meeting of the American Petroleum Institute in 1948, a question was asked whether the 600-foot depth limit of the shelf is but a "practical" limit or one used as a definition of the shelf by President Truman. The author of the paper then under discussion replied: "It has been so long since I looked at the proclamation that I could not answer with certainty, but I feel fairly sure he mentioned 600 feet in it . . ." Parks, during the discussion of Mercer H. Parks and James C. Posgate, "Drilling and Producing Operations on the Continental Shelf," American Petroleum Institute, 28th Annual Meeting, *Proceedings* (Chicago, November 1948), Section IV – Production, p. 106. As late as 1955, an oil-industry executive described the water depth of 600 feet as "the official edge of the continental shelf." Ira H. Cram, "Review and Appraisal of Offshore Operations," 2 (No. 2) *Offshore Operations* 11 (April 1955).

continental shelf policies, and due to its relative weight and potential, it may have caused other governments to plan and act in a corresponding manner. The obligation thus assumed by the United States is admittedly one of a political character but not without legal significance; for the United States Government had to consider that by making the Proclamation and by failing to revoke it, its future legal discretion to act with respect to the continental shelf may be considerably limited solely through the concurrent or subsequent action of other states. Indeed, there is nothing as yet to indicate that the Truman Proclamation of 1945 directly created even a semblance of a general customary rule of international law. Of course, it immediately started a process by which political discretion transforms itself into a specific legal relationship; by itself, however, the Proclamation embodied only a doctrine outlining and rationalizing the proposed future contours of a legal regime of the continental shelf. The chief component parts of the doctrine formulated by the Truman Proclamation appear to be the following: (a) every coastal state should have the right to exercise exclusive control and jurisdiction over the continental shelf under the high seas adjacent to its territorial waters; (b) the right to exercise such exclusive control and jurisdiction should only be a right over the exploration and exploitation of those mineral resources of the shelf whose extraction requires or allows the use of relatively permanent and sizeable installations in or above the waters covering the shelf; (c) the seaward limits for the exercise of such exclusive rights should be defined by reference to geographical and geological criteria.

CONCEPTUAL ENLARGEMENT OF THE SHELF DOCTRINE: 1945–1958

We have seen in the preceding chapter that such industrial and state activity as actually took place between 1945 and 1958 on the outer continental shelves as a consequence of the various governmental claims to exclusive shelf rights was in fact so limited that it almost exactly corresponded to the essence of the shelf doctrine expressed by the Truman Proclamation: the coastal state's exclusive control was exercised over industrial activity confined to the exploration and exploitation of petroleum and its related substances within the geographical limits of the continental shelf.

But, while undiluted in its practical application on the continental shelves, the doctrine was subjected to political and conceptual modifications and enlargement almost as soon as it was formulated in the Truman Proclamation. Responding to the combined claim-and-proposal of the United States, several states attempted, not unsuccessfully, to expand two of the main component parts of the shelf doctrine. The first component is represented by the functional limits of the coastal rights, that is, the range of the uses of the shelf falling under exclusive coastal control. The functional limits were claimed by some states to include everything from the proposed right to explore and exploit certain mineral resources of the shelf up to the full coastal sovereignty – a term presumably meaning that the coastal state may use the adjacent shelf in any way it sees fit as long as it does not encroach on previously established rights of other countries. The second component part of the doctrine, that is, the territorial limits of the coastal rights, was for some time after 1945 relatively firm; but, particularly in the 1950's, it was also subjected to political and conceptual expansion. While in the earlier years most of the states had seemed satisfied in their individual claims with a studied vagueness as to the geographical criteria by which their shelves should have been measured, in the 1950's some of them abandoned the geographical and geological criteria altogether. The continental shelf was to be defined as those submarine areas, adjacent to national coasts, whose natural resources are accessible for exploitation. The epithet "adjacent" or, sometimes, "contiguous," was the only remaining link preserving some semblance between the politically and the geographically defined continental shelf.

Of course, the narrow functional limits of the exclusive coastal rights, restricted in the Truman Proclamation to the exploration and exploitation of those mineral resources whose extraction from the shelf requires installations, do – and undoubtedly did in 1945 already – provoke certain questions. Were sedentary fisheries to be completely excluded from the scope of the Proclamation? Would extraction of minerals by dredging from ships and without any installations on the shelf be outside the United States jurisdiction and control as defined by the Proclamation? If the United States claimed no more than an exclusive right to control the exploitation of certain mineral resources, would other uses of the shelf be outside its exclusive control – such as, for instance, the construction of submerged storage facilities on the ocean floor? [34]

Accompanying the text of the Truman Proclamation in the *Department of State Bulletin* was a statement that "The territorial limits of the United

[34] The feasibility of using the shelf in this manner has already been demonstrated. In the Gulf of Mexico, some 35 miles off the coast of Louisiana, mobile underwater storage unit was installed capable of holding 20,000 barrels of crude oil 25 feet below the surface. J. T. Hendrickson and C. E. Young, "Offshore Production Facilities," 8 (No. 1) *Offshore* 23 (March 1958). Also, report in 13 (No. 5) *Offshore* 21 (Oct. 1960). Federal regulations issued by the U.S. Department of the Interior to implement the 1953 Outer Continental Shelf Lands Act (67 Stat. 462) provide that the Secretary of the Interior "may authorize the subsurface storage of oil and gas in the lands of the outer Continental Shelf, whether or not produced from the outer Continental Shelf." 43 *Code of Federal Regulations* 201. 13.

States are precisely the same as before September 28, 1945, namely, three marine miles seaward from the coast..." [35] – a statement reinforcing our conclusion that the United States shelf policy as formulated in the Proclamation sought much less than to extend national sovereignty over the outer continental shelf. But one must also note that the concurrent press release spoke of United States "jurisdiction over the continental shelf" as well as "over the mineral resources of the continental shelf" as if these terms were synonymous. Of still greater interest are some statements made by the Secretary of the Interior in his official annual report for 1945 where he asserted that "We have acquired jurisdiction over the Continental Shelf" [36] but, after comparing the shelf to United States territorial acquisitions such as Alaska, the Danish West Indies and the Louisiana Purchase, stated that "The Continental Shelf cost only the forethought that was required to assert our sovereignty over it." [37]

Thus the problem of "limited but exclusive jurisdiction and control v. sovereignty," widely studied by legal scholars with a variety of conclusions reached,[38] arose almost simultaneously with the emergence of the doctrine of the shelf. And it has never completely disappeared. Many governments demonstrating their interest in the continental shelf after 1945, and whose unilateral acts had, in relation to the Truman Proclamation, the character of a response,[39] claimed sovereign rights over the adjacent shelves. Also the early oil exploration licenses issued by the British Government of the Bahamas to the Bahamas Oil Co. reserved to the Governor of the Colony full power to grant or demise to anyone liberty to undertake, on the licensed continental shelf areas, any activity other than that for which the license was granted, and this in itself testifies to the intention of the British Government

[35] 13 *State Department Bulletin* 484 (1945).

[36] Ickes in U.S. Department of the Interior, *op. cit.* (Note 14).

[37] *Ibid.*, p. x.

[38] Legal experts of the United Nations Secretariat, like Young and Hurst, viewed the Truman Proclamation as making no claim to national sovereignty over the continental shelf. *Cf.*, respectively, U.N. Secretariat *Memorandum of the Regime of the High Seas.* Doc. A/CN.4/32 (14 July 1950), p. 81; Richard Young, "Recent Developments with Respect to the Continental Shelf," 42 *American Journal of International Law* 849–850 (1948); Cecil J. B. Hurst, "The Continental Shelf" 34 *Transactions of the Grotius Society* 149 (1949). Lauterpacht, Brierly, Mouton, Waldock, and Vallat considered jurisdiction and control as claimed by the United States to be equivalent to sovereignty. *Cf.*, respectively, Hersch Lauterpacht, "Sovereignty over Submarine Areas," 27 *British Year Book of International Law* 389 (1950); J. L. Brierly, statement during the 68th meeting of the United Nations International Law Commission, Doc. A/CN.4/SR.68 (14 July 1950), p. 8; M. W. Mouton, *The Continental Shelf* (The Hague: Martinus Nijhoff, 1952), p. 278; Waldock, *op. cit.* (note 10) 128; Vallat, *op. cit.* (note 7) 336. For a fuller discussion of these and other views and their variants, *cf.*, U.S. Naval War College, *op. cit.* (note 6), pp. 44–49.

[39] The British practice in the Gulf of Paria and in the application of the Bahamas Petroleum Act 1945 makes the only significant exception. Not only does it seem to have developed independently of United States continental shelf policy; possibly it may have provided an impulse to the United States to lay out its policy in the Truman Proclamation.

to assert over the continental shelf full and exclusive authority.[40] In the following years, actions taken by the British Government on behalf of its colonies, and recommended to its Arab protectorates, invariably and directly confirm this intention.[41]

The scope of the continental shelf claims made between 1945-1950 by Panama, Nicaragua, Iran, Saudi Arabia, Pakistan and Brazil[42] corresponded to that of the British claims in the sense that the adjacent shelves were declared to form parts of the respective national territories. Although this was much more than the text of the Truman Proclamation implied, none of the claims mentioned met with a United States protest. Only in four outstanding instances the United States Government did send notes of protest – to Argentina, Chile, Peru, and El Salvador. The United States protest notes to the first three, all dated 2 July 1948, are identical[43] and state that the principles declared by each of the three countries "differ in large measure from those of the United States Proclamations[44] and appear to be at variance with the generally accepted principles of international law." Specifically, in its protest to Chile the United States Government noted

> that (1) the Chilean Declaration confirms and proclaims the national sovereignty of Chile over the continental shelf and over the seas adjacent to the coast of Chile outside the generally accepted limits of territorial waters, and (2) the Declaration fails, with respect to fishing, to accord appropriate and adequate recognition to the rights and interests of the United States in the high seas of the coast of Chile.

The crucial terms are, of course, under (1) in the above quotation; the sentence may create the first impression that the United States also protested the extension of Argentine, Chilean and Peruvian sovereignty over the continental shelf. However, the official United States statements mentioned above

[40] Bahamas (Alteration of Boundaries) Order in Council, and Jamaica (Alteration of Boundaries) Order in Council, both of 26 November 1948, seek to legalize a practice initiated by the issuance of licenses in 1945. Texts of both orders in 1 *U.N. Legislative Series* 31, 33 (1950).

[41] Texts of these proclamations, *ibid.*, 23–30. The Bahamas and Jamaica policy was followed in 1949 by action with respect to the nine Arab Sheikhdoms under British protection; in cases of Abu Dhabi, Ajman, Dubai, Quatar, Ras al Khaimah, Sharjah, and Umm al Quaiwain, the terminology was identical: the contiguous seabed and subsoil were proclaimed to "appertain to the land of ..... and are subject to its exclusive jurisdiction and control;" the Bahrain document proclaimed the contiguous seabed and subsoil to "belong to the country of Bahrain ... subject to the sphere of its absolute jurisdiction and its absolute authority." Kuwait proclaimed the seabed and subsoil to be "part of the principality of Kuwait and ... subject to its administration and authority." British actions with respect to British Honduras and the Falkland Islands likewise claim sovereign territorial rights on the continental shelves rather than rights to specific exclusive uses. The British Honduras and Falkland Islands Orders in Council in *ibid.*, pp. 304, 305.

[42] The texts of the appropriate documents of the six countries appear in *ibid.* arranged alphabetically except for Brazil (p. 299) and Pakistan (p. 303).

[43] Full texts of United States notes, *ibid.* 5, 7, 17.

[44] The note refers to both Proclamations issued by President Truman on 28 September 1945, one on the continental shelf, the second on fisheries.

and the absence of any United States protests against the British, Panamanian, Nicaraguan, Iranian, Saudi Arabian, Pakistani and Brazilian acts – all of them claiming sovereignty over the adjacent shelves – suggest that point (1) of the protest note could reasonably be read as follows:

that (1) the Chilean Declaration confirms and proclaims the national sovereignty of Chile *not only* over the continental shelf *but, beyond* and *above it,* over the seas adjacent to the coast of Chile outside the generally accepted limits of territorial waters.[45]

The validity of some such construction seems confirmed by the United States note of 12 December 1950 protesting against Article 7 of the El Salvador's Political Constitution of 7 September 1950.[46] The relevant paragraph of the Constitution's Article 7 reads:

The territory of the Republic within its present boundaries is irreducible. It includes the adjacent seas to a distance of two hundred sea miles from low water line and the corresponding air space, subsoil and continental shelf.

The United States note, brief and crisp, leaves no doubt about its meaning. The continental shelf and subsoil are not even mentioned or indirectly referred to. Full attention is focused on those provisions of Article 7 which, in the opinion of the United States, would

bring within the exclusive jurisdiction and control of El Salvador wide ocean areas which have hitherto been considered high seas by all nations. It would in these extensive waters and in the air spaces above supplant the free and untrammelled navigation of foreign vessels and aircraft by such controls as El Salvador, in the exercise of the sovereignty claimed, might apply.

The political and conceptual enlargement of the territorial limits of the exclusive coastal rights on the adjacent continental shelf was a much slower process. After analyzing the various governmental acts, it is possible to say that until the end of 1950, and with the exception of El Salvador, the various states claiming the adjacent continental shelf considered it as representing primarily a geographical, not a legal concept.[47] Even those countries which went far beyond the shelf proper and in sweeping claims sought to embrace in their national sovereignty wide expanses of the high seas, such as Costa

[45] Added words are emphasized.

[46] Both the El Salvadorean and the United States text in 1 *U.N. Legislative Series* 300–301 (1950).

[47] It is also of interest to note that the International Law Commission, while drafting its continental shelf articles, rejected the term "submarine areas" because this term used alone would give no indication of the nature of the submarine areas in question. International Law Commission, *Report of the Third Sessionn*, Dec A/CN.4/48 (30 July 1951).

Rica, Peru and Chile,[48] seem to have adopted a geographically defined concept of the shelf. A careful reading of the respective documents shows that in none of the three cases named did the claims clearly sweep all submerged land under the 200-mile extent of the sea over which sovereignty or exclusive protection was sought. In each case, the acts spoke of the adjacent continental or insular shelf whatever may be its depth under the sea;[49] but in each case again, the 200 mile extension of national sovereignty, stimulated primarily by a desire to enlarge the national control over all fisheries and whaling activities, included the seabed and, presumably, its subsoil only as a secondary and incidental claim and as if to make the primary 200-mile sweep of the high seas more secure and definite on all sides. The Peruvian Presidential Decree defined the continental shelf as forming "one entire morphological and geological unit with the continent."

After 1950 the political push seaward was fully under way. In several cases the 200-mile seaward distance from the national shores was claimed as the outer limit of the submarine areas under the exclusive coastal control,[50] only to be progressively overshadowed by the more elastic and expansive limit of possible exploitation. But a more comprehensive picture of the various political concepts of a legal regime of the continental shelf is provided by the records of the United Nations Conference on the Law of the Sea held in 1958 at Geneva to which we now turn.

[48] Costa Rican Decree Law of 1948, 1 *U.N. Legislative Series* 9–10 (1950); Peruvian Presidential Decree of 1947, *ibid.* 16–17; Chilean Presidential Proclamation of 1947, *ibid.* 6–7.

[49] *Cf.*, Organization of American States, Inter-American Specialized Conference on "Conservation of Natural Resources: The Continental Shelf and Marine Waters," *Background Material on the Juridical Aspects of the Continental Shelf and Marine Waters* (Ciudad Trujillo, Doc. 2, SG-2, 3 March 1956), p. 3.

[50] After 1950 some of the Latin American countries made the further step to define the limits of the claimed continental shelf by the 200-mile parallel. In a 1952 agreement between Chile, Ecuador, and Peru, and later adhered to by Costa Rica, also known as the "Declaration on the Maritime Zone," the geographical term "continental shelf" is no longer used. In clause II of that agreement the parties proclaim "as a principle of their international maritime policy that each of them possesses sole sovereignty and jurisdiction over the area of sea adjacent to the coast of its own country and extending not less than 200 nautical miles from the said coast." And by Clause III, their sole jurisdiction and sovereignty "over the zone thus described includes sole sovereignty and jurisdiction over the sea floor and subsoil thereof." U.S. Naval War College, *op. cit.* (note 23), p. 70, note 19, pp. 265–267. For an analysis of the legal characteristics of the 200-mile maritime zone as defined in the Santiago Declaration, and of the subsequent interpretations of the clause by its adherents, cf., García-Amador, F. V., *The Exploitation and Conservation of the Resources of the Sea* (Leyden: Sijthoff, 1959), pp. 76–79.

THE 1958 CONFERENCE ON THE LAW OF THE SEA

Analyzing the records[51] of the 1958 Geneva Conference, we shall concentrate on the three crucial aspects of the regime of the continental shelf: the exclusivity of coastal rights, their territorial limits, and their functional scope. In the Convention on the Continental Shelf adopted at the Conference, these three component parts of the negotiated treaty regime of the continental shelf are covered primarily in the three first articles:[52]

Article 1

For the purpose of these articles, the term "continental shelf" is used as referring (a) to the seabed and subsoil of the submarine areas adjacent to the coast but outside the area of the territorial sea, to a depth of 200 metres or, beyond that limit, to where the depth of the superjacent waters admits of the exploitation of the natural resources of the said areas; (b) to the seabed and subsoil of similar submarine areas adjacent to the coasts of islands.

Article 2

1. The coastal state exercises over the continental shelf sovereign rights for the purpose of exploring it and exploiting its natural resources.
2. The rights referred to in paragraph 1 of this article are exclusive in the sense that if the coastal state does not explore the continental shelf or exploit its natural resources, no one may undertake these activities, or make a claim to the continental shelf, without the express consent of the coastal state.
3. The rights of the coastal state over the continental shelf do not depend on occupation, effective or notional, or on any express proclamation.
4. The natural resources referred to in these articles consist of the mineral and other non-living resources of the seabed and subsoil together with living organisms belonging to sedentary species, that is to say, organisms which, at the harvestable stage, either are immobile on or under the seabed or are unable to move except in constant physical contact with the seabed or the subsoil.

Article 3

The rights of the coastal state over the continental shelf do not affect the legal status of the superjacent waters as high seas, or that of the airspace above those waters.

[51] The Conference records have been published in seven volumes, the first of which contains preparatory materials and documents. Throughout the remainder of this chapter, and following the first full citation of one of the volumes, the records of the Conference will be cited only as *Official Records*, preceded by appropriate volume number and followed by page number.

[52] For the full text of the Convention see U.N. Doc. A/CONF.13/L.55 reprinted as an annex in U.N. Conference on the Law of the Sea, 2 *Official Records* 142, Doc. A/CONF.13/38; also in 52 *American Journal of International Law* 858 (1958). The Convention, by art. 13/1, permits no reservations to the first three articles quoted above.

However, analyzing the Conference discussions which led to the final drafting and adoption of the Convention, we shall no longer aim merely to present a complete mosaic of the various political concepts of a legal regime of the continental shelf as they emerged during the Conference from the statements and proposals of the various participating delegations. While the political concepts shall inevitably appear in the course of the examination, our primary purpose now is to see whether the debates at Geneva provided any evidence of the conviction of states that there had been customary legal rules governing the shelf. One would indeed expect to find some such evidence. First, it would have been only natural if, in an effort to persuade others of the soundness of their views, the various delegations would try to show that in their arguments they actually relied on rules already in existence. Second, it is perhaps significant that the Convention on the Continental Shelf eventually received considerable support at the Conference as well as afterwards. Its text was adopted by 57 votes to 3 with 8 abstentions;[53] before 31 October 1958 the Convention was signed by 46 states,[54] and by the summer of 1964 the twenty-two states needed to bring the Convention into force ratified it or acceded to it.[55]

The Core Rule of the Legal Regime of the Shelf

The inner core of the legal regime of the continental shelf is represented by the right of a state to control exclusively some of the uses of the continental shelf under the high seas adjacent to that state's territorial waters. This definition is, advisedly, very coarse; it says nothing about the extent and limits of the seabed and subsoil described as "continental shelf," about the uses of such areas, and equally nothing about the fullness of the coastal state's control over them. It simply means that states other than the coastal state are excluded from utilizing and controlling the adjacent outer submarine areas for such purposes as might fall under the jurisdiction of the adjacent country. Did the attitudes of the various delegations participating in the 1958 Geneva

[53] 2 *Official Records* 57.

[54] List of signatories in U.N. Secretariat, *Status of Multilateral Conventions of which the Secretary-General Acts as Depositary*, pp. xxxi. 21–xi. 23, Doc. ST/LEG/3./Rev. 1.

[55] The first 22 states to ratify or accede to the Convention are listed in the order of the depositing of their instruments: Cambodia, Haiti, Soviet Union, Federation of Malaya, Ukrainian S.S.R., Byelorussian S.S.R., United States, Senegal, Venezuela, Czechoslovakia, Israel, Guatemala, Rumania, Colombia, Poland, Madagascar, Bulgaria, Portugal, Union of South Africa, Denmark, Australia, United Kingdom. Later, and until August 1967, ratification or accession instruments were deposited by: Albania, Dominican Republic, Finland, France, Jamaica, Malawi, Malta, Mexico, Netherlands, New Zealand, Sierra Leone, Sweden, Switzerland, Uganda, Yugoslavia.

Conference reliably indicate a conviction of states that there had been such a rule of customary law prior to their meeting?

On the whole, the picture obtained from a detailed analysis of the discussions in Committee IV (Continental Shelf) of the Conference[56] is interesting but unenlightening as to any general consensus concerning the rule in question. Of the 55 delegations which actively participated in the debates, 23 failed altogether to state their views of the existence or non-existence, prior to the Conference, of the core rule of the continental shelf; they concentrated their attention fully on their task to negotiate a treaty regime of the shelf. Among the others the divergence of views was remarkable. While 20 of them asserted, with varying degrees of emphasis and conviction, that the core rule of the shelf had become an established rule of customary law, 12 delegations clearly denied its existence and stressed the fully legislative task of the Conference.

Of those delegates asserting the previous existence of a customary rule, not one clearly defined the roots from which the rule might have grown. The Yugoslav delegate stated that a "new international practice" was created by the publication by "some thirty States" of "unilateral declarations extending their sovereignty to submarine areas beyond the limits of the territorial sea," and that the substance of this practice "was not contested"; his delegation therefore "did not oppose the formal and collective recognition of what was already an established legal institution . . ." [57] One single statement out of the generous contribution to the debates in Committee IV by the United Kingdom delegation also suggested that governmental claims regarding the exclusive coastal rights on the outer continental shelves were to be seen as the main basis of legal rules: "The rules of international law on the continental shelf were mainly the results of unilateral declarations, such as President Truman's proclamation of 1945." [58] The Australian delegation also indirectly stressed the role of governmental declarations and decrees when it cited conclusions reached by H. Lauterpacht in 1950 as to the legal validity of the core rule of the continental shelf created by "custom initiated by the leading maritime powers and acquiesced in by the generality of States." [59] The representative of Argentine expressed similar views:

[56] At the Conference most of the work on the envisaged treaty regime of the continental shelf was done in Committee IV. In the plenary meetings only brief discussions took place and minor changes were written into the drafted Convention on the Continental Shelf. The summary records of the plenary meetings provide but very little information beyond that obtained from the records of Committee IV.

[57] 6 *Official Records* 11.

[58] *Ibid.* 109.

[59] *Ibid.* 28. For Lauterpacht's views, see pp. 21, 24.

It was true that the affirmation of rights over the continental shelf took the form of unilateral acts by States, but that was not a valid reason for not recognizing the full rights of the State. International law was based on custom, and every custom originated in specific acts of States which by repetition acquired the force of a general and binding rule. ... The principal instrument affecting the continental shelf, President Truman's proclamation of 1945, and its acceptance by other States had given rise to a practice which, though based on unilateral acts, had acquired the validity of a principle of international law.[60]

The delegations of Ceylon and Cuba added their voices to those emphasizing the role of unilateral statements and other formal acts of states.[61] Only the observations offered by the Israeli delegate contained a somewhat fuller exposition of views of the bases of the alleged customary rule. According to the records of Committee IV ninth meeting, the delegate of Israel

disagreed with the view that there existed no customary international law which could provide the legal criteria for regulating the problems of the continental shelf. Considering the rapid development of modern science and technology, time should not be given an exaggerated importance as a creative element in the development of customary law. Although the United States proclamation of 1945, the first to introduce the concept of the continental shelf into international law, was of relatively recent date, the matter could reasonably be regarded as fully governed by international law. The existence of a sufficient body of State practice, the widespread acquiescence in that State practice, the large volume of authoritative literature and the work done by the International Law Commission and the General Assembly on the subject all supported that view.[62]

The statements of the other thirteen state delegations counted in as asserting the existence of a customary rule of law providing for exclusive coastal rights were even more distinguished by their brevity, generality, or even serious contradictions. The United States delegate simply stated in a carefully worded sentence that "Prior to very recent years, the legal status of the continental shelf, outside the recognized territorial sea was, in considerable measure, undefined." [63] To Uruguay, the "sovereignty of the coastal State over the continental shelf was a consequence of the progress of

[60] 6 *Official Records* 3.

[61] The Ceylonese delegate, having referred to "immemorial usage and uninterrupted ownership "as the basis of Ceylon's rights over its pearl fisheries, stated that the concept of the continental shelf "was based on the practice of a large number of States following the Truman declaration of 1945." *Ibid.* 13. The delegate of Cuba, after remarking that "the modern political, economic and legal realities" lay at the basis of a recognition of the exclusive coastal rights, said that "The national claims to the continental shelf made since 1942 had been acquiesced in by other States, and had thus become accepted international practice." *Ibid.* 25.

[62] *Ibid.* 17.

[63] Marjorie M. Whiteman (the United States delegate in Committee IV), "Conference on the Law of the Sea: Convention on the Continental Shelf," 52 *American Journal of International Law* 632 (1958).

science," [64] while in the view of the Philippine delegate "the sovereign rights of the coastal State" were "inherent in the sovereignty which the coastal State exercised over the adjacent land territory" and were not derived "from any specific provision of international law." [65] A similar view of the continental shelf falling under an exclusive coastal control because it was "an integral part of the mainland" – *i.e.*, the contiguity principle – was expressed by Mexico,[66] suggested by Portugal,[67] and accepted by Venezuela.[68] Statements by the delegates of Peru,[69] Lebanon,[70] Pakistan,[71] Indonesia[72] and Iceland,[73] also recognizing either directly or by clear implication the legal existence of exclusive coastal rights on the continental shelf, were generally vague as to the bases of such rights, while those of Chile and El Salvador contained serious contradictions[74] although, of course, the position of both these countries has been well known.

Statements by the twelve delegations denying the previous existence of a customary rule giving the coastal state exclusive rights on the adjacent continental shelf were perhaps clearer but not more fully reasoned. The delegation of the Federal Republic of Germany, while proposing the establishment of an international regime of the continental shelf, held that "according to the international law in force, the coastal State has no rights over the continental shelf beyond the outer limit of its territorial sea," [75] but in defense of that view relied only on unnamed "authorities," and on its own opinion that "Unilateral decisions and measures in the matter could hardly be said to take into account the common interests of all nations." [76] The French delegation did not even go that far and simply stated that

64 6 *Official Records* 5.
65 *Ibid.* 9.
66 *Ibid.* 15.
67 *Id.*
68 *Ibid.* 15.
69 *Ibid.* 10.
70 *Ibid.* 14.
71 *Ibid.* 19.
72 *Ibid.* 26.
73 *Ibid.* 28.
74 The Chilean delegate stated that his country "maintained the position it had taken in 1952 that sovereignty over the continental shelf belonged *ipso jure* to the coastal State . . ." (6 *Official Records* 16) and then said that "The Conference was legislating in the true sense of the word, since it was trying to reach agreement where no agreement had existed previously." *Ibid.* The delegate of El Salvador, before reciting from his country's 1950 constitution declaring national sovereignty over the continental shelf, stated that "if the Conference succeeded in reaching agreement on the rules referred to the Fourth Committee, it might go down in history as having given legal sanction to the new concept of the continental shelf." *Ibid.* 24.
75 Memorandum of the Federal Republic of Germany submitted as Doc. A/CONF.13/C.4/L. 1, printed as an annex in 6 *Official Records* 126–127.
76 *Ibid.* 31.

The articles of the continental shelf drafted by the International Law Commission did not constitute positive international law, but related to a new legal institution submitted to the Conference for incorporation in positive law.[77]

Corresponding views were expressed by the delegates of Sweden,[78] Norway,[79] Spain,[80] Japan,[81] and the Republic of Viet-Nam,[82] and were indicated, although less clearly, by the Soviet Union.[83] The four remaining delegations were somewhat more specific at least in their references to the unilateral declarations of states claiming exclusive shelf rights. As stated by the Turkish delegate, the concept of the continental shelf was "embodied only in unilateral declarations," and its alleged legality was "invalidated by well known arbitration decisions." [84] The delegate of Italy held that "The standing in international law of the many unilateral declarations of rights over the continental shelf by coastal States was an open question, for the Conference to decide." [85] Only two official statements had more substance and warrant fuller quotations. The delegate of Monaco

said that the question of the continental shelf fell under article 15 of the statute of the International Law Commission (General Assembly resolution 174 (II)), which spoke of the "preparation of draft conventions on subjects which have not yet been regulated by international law." With the exception of a few regional agreements, the concept of the continental shelf was so far embodied only in unilateral declarations. It could not be claimed that the rights of the coastal State over the seabed and subsoil of the sea in the proximity of its coast were already recognized, whether directly or implicitly, by international law.
The view that the continental shelf was subject to State sovereignty was not substantiated by the criteria of territorial sovereignty or by the general principles of international law; neither was it correct to argue that State practice in that respect fulfilled the conditions of a customary rule of international law.[86]

And the Greek delegate, after classifying the concept of the continental shelf as one that did not belong to existing international law but rather to the realm of theory, stated that

The Greek delegation did not consider that the institution of the continental shelf was regulated by customary rules of international law. Some ten years' practice

[77] *Ibid.* 1 and 22.
[78] *Ibid.* 3 and 50.
[79] *Ibid.* 4.
[80] *Ibid.* 7.
[81] *Ibid.* 14.
[82] *Ibid.* 24.
[83] *Ibid.* 99 and 112.
[84] *Ibid.* 12. The "arbitration decisions" probably refer to the 1951 Abu Dhabi arbitration under Lord Asquith of Bishopstone, and the earlier Quatar arbitation under Lord Radcliffe, neither of which was a case of international adjudication.
[85] *Ibid.* 64.
[86] *Ibid.* 18.

– which might, moreover, be described as inconsistent or even casual – could not be thought to constitute the long usage which was one of the prerequisites of the existence of an international customary rule; and other factors, including the opposition of certain major States to the concept of the continental shelf, had prevented the formation of such a rule based on general acceptance.[87]

The treatment by Committee IV of one specific paragraph of the 1958 Convention on the Continental Shelf would seem to promise a more substantial presentation of official views. Adopted as paragraph 3 of article 2, and brief enough to be quoted again – "The rights of the coastal state over the continental shelf do not depend on occupation, effective or notional, or on any express proclamation" – the sentence seems to open the way for a truly substantive discussion of the problem whether there was or was not a settled rule of customary international law on the subject. Proposed as a new article by the Cuban delegation,[88] the sentence was adopted in Committee IV by 41 votes to 7 with 12 abstentions,[89] and by the plenary meeting without any further discussion together with the rest of draft article 68, later to become Convention article 2.

Yet – in the first place – what validity did that sentence have, as a part of the Convention, before the Convention was ratified and in force? It does seem, to use the words of M. W. Mouton, representing the Netherlands, that the substance of the additional paragraph was redundant; it might have had a meaning

at the time when there still existed doubt whether these rights belonged to the coastal State *ipso jure*; it did not arise once these rights were clearly defined and embodied in an international convention.[90]

Second, one runs again into the ever-recurring question whether the inclusion of the stipulation did not in fact mirror the delegates' conviction that, in the absence of a customary rule, it was useful to have that provision.

Finally, Committee IV itself adopted article 2/3 after a brief debate; in its course the sentence was characterized as "unnecessary" and "superfluous" by those who had denied the existence of a customary rule governing the continental shelf,[91] while delegates of countries whose policies testified to a contrary opinion termed it "essential" and "logical and valuable" [92] and providing a "safeguard" [93] or even a "guarantee" without which "the whole

87 *Ibid.* 5–6.
88 6 *Official Records* 139, as Doc. A/CONF.13/C.4/L.45.
89 *Ibid.* 75.
90 *Ibid.* 74.
91 Federal Republic of Germany and Greece, *ibid.* 74.
92 Mexico and the Philippines, *ibid.*
93 Ghana, *ibid.* 75.

work of the Conference might prove unsuccessful." [94] The Cuban delegate himself, sponsoring the paragraph, admitted that it "might not be absolutely essential," and furnished the following explanation: the provision disclaiming the need for occupation or proclamation would provide for the eventuality that "another State" might be unaware, observing no acts of shelf occupation on the part of a treaty-meber lacking the technical means to exploit the shelf beyond the 200-meter depth, of the "sovereign nature of the rights of the coastal State" for the purposes stated in the Convention.[95]

It may thus be said that the Conference debates concerning the question of the legal existence or non-existence of exclusive coastal rights on the outer continental shelf were characterized not so much by a consensus as by a wide divergence of views. Such statements as were made were often genuinely unconcerned with the problem of an existing rule, an attitude, perhaps, not inappropriate at a treaty-making conference; however, views and assertions directed at the problem were often regrettably vague and studded with sweeping generalities as well as imprecisions of both language and thought. On the whole, the records of the 1958 Geneva Conference, used as a source of evidence showing the extent to which the generality of states did or did not accept the existence of a customary rule providing for exclusive coastal rights on the outer continental shelf, are in themselves as inconclusive as was the theoretical discussion of the problem in the 1950's.

Territorial and Functional Limits of Exclusive Coastal Rights

An examination of official views expressed by state delegations at Geneva as to the existence of customary rules determining the territorial and functional limits of exclusive coastal rights on the outer continental shelves is even less fruitful than the analysis concerning the core rule of the regime of the shelf. No awareness is detectable on the part of the state representatives that, as far as territorial limits of the coastal rights were concerned, they were building a conventional rule in an area where a customary rule had been established. And the legal hollowness of arguments advanced in support of the various political aims of states regarding the definition of the functional limits was but imperceptibly alleviated by the concept, on which

[94] Indonesia, *ibid.* 74. It appears that several delegations saw in the paragraph a reinforcement of what they considered a weak spot: the term "exclusive" rather than "sovereign" as a description, in draft article 68/1, of the nature of the coastal state's qualified rights in the adjacent shelf. The plenary meeting later restored the term "sovereign" in what was to become Convention article 2/1, but retained article 2/3 as well.

[95] *Ibid.* 74–75.

some delegations relied, of full state sovereignty extending *ipso jure* over the adjacent continental shelf. That sovereignty was said to arise from the fact of geographical and geological contiguity of the continental shelf and the land mass; yet those very delegations invoking that concept at the Conference also, at the same time, denied it. The denial was twofold; it was implied, first, by the insistence that the sovereign coastal rights extended over the living resources of the shelf and in its vicinity, *i.e.,* resources manifestly not falling within the facts of geological contiguity with the land; and secondly, by the refusal to define the shelf by those very geographical and geological criteria on which reliance was placed for the concept of contiguity.[96]

But the records of the Conference not only fail to provide any substantive evidence as to the existence of customary rules determining the territorial and functional limits of the exclusive coastal rights on the continental shelf. The notion of defining the territorial limits by the criterion of possible exploitation, the attempts to subsume living organisms under the shelf resources exclusively controlled by the coastal state, and the separate and often confused treatment of these two problems, all these factors jointly contribute to the suspicion that continuing and deep legal uncertainties will cloud even the treaty law of the shelf binding the parties to the Convention on the Continental Shelf; and that, therefore, its value as an evidence of state practice instrumental in the creation of customary rules would be severely limited.

The suspicion is engendered by the fact that the articles of the Convention adopted at Geneva are not sufficiently detailed to be self-interpreting. For instance, and mainly, the definition of the continental in article 1 by "a depth of 200 metres or, beyond that limit, to where the depth of the superjacent waters admits of the exploitation of the natural resources of the said areas," to have any practical meaning, would require a more exacting definition of the natural resources than that offered in article 2/4. Second, one would have to know how to measure and ascertain the actual maximum limit of exploitation achieved in practice. Third, when measured and ascertained at any specific time, would that limit apply – however fleetingly – as the maximum outer shelf boundary of all treaty members? Fourth, the Convention does not clarify whether unrestricted *exploration* of the natural resources of the shelf beyond the exploitation limit would be open to all and at all times. Answers to these and possibly many other relevant ques-

96 This problem was reflected in the statements of delegations representing the following states (names of countries are followed by page number of 6 *Official Records*): Argentina, 2–3; Philippines, 8; Colombia, 10, 40–41; Peru, 11; Mexico, 14–15; Chile, 16, 57–58; El Salvador, 24–25.

tions would have to be sought in the Conference debates, but a search for such answers in the Conference records is not overly productive.

Aspects of the Treaty Criterion of Exploitability

1. SHELF RESOURCES AND THEIR EXPLOITABILITY. To this question the text of the Convention seems to provide a clear and unequivocal answer. It defines the shelf as extending "to a depth of 200 metres or, beyond that limit, to where the depth of the superjacent waters admits of the exploitation of the natural resources," and also defines the natural resources as "mineral and other non-living resources . . . together with living organisms belonging to sedentary species."

But the Conference records show that these two definitions were arrived at through separate and even mutually incompatible processes of thought on the part of the participating delegations.

When article 67 of the International Law Commission's draft, later to become – slightly amended – article 1 of the Convention, was being discussed in Committee IV, the primary issue was whether the territorial extent of national shelf rights should be defined by firm, static limits, or by the dynamic criterion of exploitability. Several alternatives of defining the static limits were advocated: by the simple description of the submarine areas in question as a physical formation definable by geological and geographical criteria;[97] by the 200-meter,[98] 550-meter[99] or even 1,000-meter[100] depth of the superjacent waters; by a uniform seaward distance from the shores;[101] by a depth-and-distance combination,[102] and by a combined geographical-and-depth criterion.[103] All these suggestions and proposals were, of course, eventually abandoned, withdrawn or voted down, and the criterion of exploitability, in addition to the 200-meter depth limit, was retained by 51 votes to 9 with 10 abstentions in Committee IV;[104] in the plenary meet-

[97] Advocated, for example, by Panama, with the proviso that both the continental shelf and slope should be included in a comprehensive phrase "the continental base." *Ibid.* 5, 32–33.

[98] Also advocated, in the earlier stages of the Conference, by the United States representative in Committee IV, *ibid.* 19; and by, for instance, Tunisia, *ibid.* 21; Viet-Nam, *ibid.* 24; United Arab Republic, *ibid.* 27.

[99] Proposed, for example, by the Netherlands (*ibid.* 6, 37) and United Kingdom (*ibid.* 35–36) individually as well as in their joint proposal issued as Doc. A/CONF.13/C.4/L.32, *ibid.* 135.

[100] Proposed by India, Doc. A/CONF.13/C.4/L.29, later revised by replacing the 1,000-meter depth by 550 meters, *ibid.* 134–135.

[101] Advocated in Committee IV by Norway (*ibid.* 4–5) and proposed in the plenary meetings by Yugoslavia, Doc. A/CONF.13/L.14, in 2 *Official Records* 93.

[102] Proposed by Yugoslavia, Doc. A/CONF.13/C.4/L.12, in 6 *Official Records* 129.

[103] Proposed by Canada, *ibid.* 29–30, and Doc. A/CONF.13/C.4/L.30, *ibid.* 135.

[104] *Ibid.* 47.

ings, the words embodying the criterion of exploitability were voted on separately and adopted by 48 votes to 20 with 2 abstentions, while the article as a whole received 51 votes to 5 with 10 abstentions.[105]

However, during the debates of the territorial extent of exclusive shelf rights, delegates were thinking primarily in terms of *mineral exploitation by means of drilling into the subsoil of the shelf,* that is, mostly in terms of oil, gas and possibly sulphur extraction. Thus the Canadian delegate, while discussing the territorial extent of exclusive coastal rights on the shelf, referred to a "recent successful drilling [for petroleum] in 500 metres of water" as suggesting that the treaty limit of the coastal rights "might well be more than 200 metres" so as "to meet foreseeable" practical requirements of exploitation."[106]

Similarly, the United States delegate, while reversing her earlier position[107] and accepting in principle the criterion of exploitability,

> doubted whether, in an age of rapid scientific progress, it would be wise to liimit the area of exploitation . . . [by a definite depth of superjacent waters]. Only a few years previously exploitation of the seabed and subsoil in 200 metres of water had seemed the maximum achievable, but scientists were already talking in terms of a much higher order of magnitude.[108]

This unmistakably testifies that the United States delegate was thinking primarily in terms of over-water drilling into the subsoil[109] since other methods of over-water exploitation of mineral resources had already been actively tested at much greater depths, and the exploitation of organic resources beyond the 200-meter limit was practiced, even though but exceptionally.[110]

[105] 2 *Official Records* 13.

[106] 6 *Official Records* 30.

[107] During the 10th meeting of Committee IV, Marjorie Whiteman (United States) "accepted the depth of 200 metres, with a precise equivalent indicated in fathoms, as an appropriate definition of the limit of the continental shelf, but intimated doubts about the wisdom of adopting the additional criterion of possible exploitation . . ." *Ibid.* 19.

[108] *Ibid.* 40.

[109] This conclusion is particularly strengthened by the comments of Arthur H. Dean, the Chairman of the United States delegation at Geneva, on the Convention on the Continental Shelf and the criterion of exploitability: "The effect of the present language is that exploitability, and therefore the necessary control, will be presumed to a depth of 200 meters, but must be shown beyond that point. Although the [International Law] Commission and the Conference showed themselves aware that technical advances may increase the depth to which control is possible, the 200-meter figure (655 feet) serves to represent the greatest depth at which control is now thought to be possible." Arthur H. Dean, "The Geneva Conference on the Law of the Sea: What Was Accomplished," 52 *American Journal of International Law* 620 (1958).

[110] Regarding the over-water exploitation of minerals lying on the seabed in nodules, it has already been authoritatively stated as not only technically possible but also economical in depths up to 4,000 feet. John L. Mero, "Minerals on the Ocean Floor," 203 (No. 6) *Scientific American* 70 (2 December 1960). As to organic resources, substances such as coral were many years ago exploited under water depths of 900 feet. Donald K. Tressler and James McW. Lemon, *Marine Products of Commerce*, 2d ed. (New York: Reinhold Book Division, 1951), p. 143.

M. W. Mouton, speaking on behalf of the Netherlands against the criterion of exploitability, proposed the depth of 500 meters as a limit and sought to defend it by arguing that the establishment of installations was unlikely beyond that depth,[111] and later stated that "that depth line would give coastal States unlimited rights of exploitation for fifty or more years."[112]

The above references to Canada, United States and the Netherlands should not suggest that only countries most advanced industrially, with more interest in oil than in coral or sponge, were naturally inclined to think in terms of petroleum when considering the criterion of exploitability and other methods of defining the territorial extent of the exclusive coastal rights on the shelf. The delegate of India, accepting the elastic limit of exploitability, was also clearly thinking in terms of oil exploitation when he noted that "at the present stage of economic development the possiblity of exploiting the natural resources of the seabed and subsoil . . . was limited to the confines of the continental shelf as defined in geology, that need not always remain the case."[113] The representative of the United Arab Republic, again with reference to the technological advances in over-water drilling for oil which "woud soon make it possible to do so at 200 or 300 metres," suggested that the criterion of exploitability be abandoned and a firm distance from the shores used instead as a limit.[114] The technological advances in over-water drilling into the subsoil likewise affected the thinking about the territorial limits of coastal shelf rights of the delegations of Lebanon,[115] Bulgaria,[116] Republic of Viet-Nam,[117] Republic of Korea,[118] United Kingdom,[119] Greece,[120] Soviet Union,[121] and even El Salvador.[122]

Yet all these delegations simultaneously accepted the sedentary species as one of the natural resources of the continental shelf – a fact which in itself made any mention of the depth barrier standing in the way of over-

[111] *Ibid.* 37.
[112] *Ibid.* 46.
[113] *Ibid.* 12.
[114] *Ibid.* 27.
[115] "The present limiting depth for exploitation of the resources of the seabed and subsoil was between 60 and 70 metres; in his view, the margin between that depth and 200 metres was more than adequate." *Ibid.* 38.
[116] *Ibid.* 23.
[117] *Ibid.* 24.
[118] *Ibid.* 32.
[119] The British delegate considered that the 550-meter depth "was likely to remain the limit of exploitation of the seabed and subsoil in the foreseeable future." *Ibid.* 36.
[120] *Ibid.* 6.
[121] *Ibid.* 20.
[122] The delegate of El Salvador, defending the criterion of exploitability against the 200-meter depth, interpreted the consideration of the International Law Commission as meaning "that the 200-metre line itself was based on the criterion of possible exploitation, since that depth was considered the maximum present limit thereof, and might conceivably remain the limit for some time." *Ibid.* 24, 33.

water drilling completely unnecessary since other extraction methods, such as coral fishing and mineral dredging, had already been pushing beyond those barriers. Not once during the discussions in Committee IV of the territorial limits was the criterion of exploitability defended by an unequivocal and explicit reference to the existing exploitability limits of organic resources.[123]

The extensive debates in Committee IV on the definition of the "natural resources" of the continental shelf, opened after the criterion of exploitability had been voted into draft article 67, were distinguished by an almost ostentatious unconcern on the part of most delegations with the problem of the depth limit. Yet – or perhaps because of that unconcern – it would be difficult to maintain that the criterion of exploitability was intended by the delegates to mean "exploitability of subsoil mineral resources by methods of over-water drilling," [124] although many of them had thought and spoken in those terms. In any disputes arising under the Convention, anyone arguing on the basis of the narrow meaning of the criterion of exploitability would encounter the unsurmountable objection that a mere misapprehension or misinformation on the part of some delegations cannot stand up against the clear meaning of an accepted and ratified document.

2. Exploitability: Achieved or Implied? Similar difficulty in interpreting the Convention on the Continental Shelf exists with respect to the following questions: if the shelf resources, in a single area and a single instance, are successfully exploited under, for instance, 5,000 feet of water, does that depth determine the seaward limit of exclusive rights of all coast-

[123] According to 6 *Official Records* 25, Garcia-Amador referred in Committee IV to the exploitation off Chile of coral reefs in depths up to 1,000 meters, adding that therefore the reefs could not be considered a part of the shelf in the accepted geological sense, but that such cases should be taken into account when the criterion of exploitability was considered. Since there is no evidence of any exploitation of coral reefs at that depth, the statement can be explained either as a misunderstanding of a previous reference by the Chilean delegate to coal mines reaching a depth of 1,000 meters below sea level and several kilometers from the shore (6 *Official Records* 16) but tunneled from land, an instance irrelevant for a definition of the shelf; or else, as a well informed observer suggested to the present author, the error might have had linguistic origins: an oral reference to "coal seams" could have been inadvertently changed into "coral reefs" during the process of note-taking or while the summary records were being prepared. In any case, no evidence is available to show that the recorded statement did influence any of the delegations at the Conference.

[124] McDougal and Burke, interpreting the problems of the continental shelf by reference to community perspectives and interests, recommended that "the limit established for oil resources should also be established for living resources, particularly since in the case of these latter resources any limit seems arbitrary. If the limit of exploitability of coral were used, for example, to define the area of exclusive access to all resources, including oil, there would be little restriction upon the extensiveness of the area so delimited." Myres S. McDougal and William T. Burke, *The Public Order of the Oceans; A Contemporary International Law of the Sea* (New Haven: Yale University Press, 1962), p. 664 and, in the same sense, p. 619.

al states? Young, interpreting the words of article 1 ". . . to where the depth of the superjacent waters admits of the exploitation of the natural resources . . .," answers the question in the affirmative and, in our opinion, correctly so; considering the language of the Convention, he critically concludes that ". . . every coastal state would seem entitled to assert rights off its shores out to the maximum depth of exploitation reached anywhere in the world, regardless of its own capabilities or of local conditions, other than depth, which might prevent exploitation." [125] Mouton, with reference to the same provision in the first draft prepared by the International Law Commission, arrived at the same conclusion when he stated that the words "where the depth admits of the exploitation" should be interpreted in an objective way meaning that if the coastal state had not available the technical devices to drill at a certain depth, but other states had, that depth did admit of the exploitation; *i.e.*, to the words in question one could add – "if this was performed with the world's best devices." [126]

This interpretation of the treaty provision concerned does not, however, rest on any clear and general consensus during the Conference debates. When the substantive discussion of the problem was drawing to a close in Committee IV, the delegate of the Netherlands was still able to express doubts regarding that consensus; they were reflected in the following paragraph of the summary records:

> With regard to the contention that, if any State should exploit as a certain depth, all States should be entitled to claim sovereign rights over submarine areas at an equal depth beneath the surface, he said that recognition of such a principle might raise important issues of evidence.[127]

And the delegate of Argentina, seeking at the same meeting to clarify the problem, directly acknowledged the reality of the doubts and the lack of a clear Conference consensus when he stated:

> . . . many of the views heard in the course of the debate had been prompted by the apprehension of the poorer States that other more powerful or richer States might come to exploit the resources off their coasts. A clause might therefore be included to the effect that no State could exploit the seabed and subsoil off the coast of another State where the latter was precluded from so doing solely by a lack of technical means already at the disposal of others. Such a provision would at least dispel all doubts.[128]

[125] Richard Young, "The Geneva Convention on the Continental Shelf; A First Impression," 52 *American Journal of International Law* 735 (1958).

[126] M. W. Mouton, *The Continental Shelf* (The Hague: Martinus Nijhoff, 1952), p. 42.

[127] 6 *Official Records* 44.

[128] *Ibid.* 43.

Similar doubts and apprehensions were implied or clearly expressed by several delegations of less as well as more advanced countries,[129] and most clearly by the delegate of the Philippines who stated that

> his delegation did not favour the criterion possible of exploitation, because sovereignty was indivisible and absolute, and did not depend upon the State's ability to develop the natural resources of the area in question,

adding that

> if the criterion of possible exploitation were admitted, less-developed countries would be in danger of forfeiting their untapped natural wealth to those with great industrial and technical facilities.[130]

In the final analysis it was only the separate vote taken by roll call in the plenary meetings on the very words of Convention article 1 embodying the criterion of exploitability that permits the argument that probably a great majority of delegations came to understand those words in their wider, non-restrictive sense; all the delegations of the less-developed countries, previously apprehensive and doubtful, voted for the retention of those words with the exception of Pakistan voting against and Lebanon abstaining.[131] The wider interpretation of the provision in question is also further strengthened, though not fully supported, by paragraphs 2 and 3 of Convention article 2, providing for the existence of a coastal state's right irrespective of any actual activity or occupation.[132] And finally there is the practical consideration that any state, poor or well-advanced, could avail itself of the best technical means of submarine exploitation by the issuance of advantageous exploitation leases or rights to a private concern or even to another state as long as its adjacent submarine areas contain anything worth exploiting within technical reach.

129 Page numbers following names of countries refer to 6 *Official Records*: Ghana 11; Venezuela 21; Tunisia 21; Guatemala 31; France 21, 31; Canada 37; and Lebanon 38.

130 *Ibid.* 41.

131 2 *Official Records* 13. After an earlier vote in Committee IV on the draft article 67 (Convention article 1), the delegate of Guatemala, previously doubtful and apprehensive – he had described the criterion of exploitability as "dangerously vague" and "particularly unfair to under-developed countries" – explained his affirmative vote by the consideration, "in accordance with the principle of the equality of states, that if it became possible for any nation to exploit the resources of the seabed beyond a depth of 200 metres, the rights of all other states over the seabed off their coasts would automatically be extended to the new limit permitted by technological advances." 6 *Official Records* 48.

132 Young, *op. cit.* (note 125), finds full support for the wider meaning of the criterion of exploitability in article 2/2 and article 2/3. However, without reference to the records of negotiation, *i.e.*, the Conference debates, such interpretation is not very easy since the provisions of article 2/2 and article 2/3 assumed that the territorial limit of exclusive shelf rights had already been determined, and were not included to provide for that determination.

Yet here the problems arising from the treaty criterion of exploitability do not end; at this point they actually become more difficult.

3. PROOF OF EXPLOITABILITY. The records of the Geneva Conference provide no specific guide-lines for the interpretation of the criterion of exploitability in terms of what should be recognized as the practically achieved exploitation limit expressed in terms of water depth. Speaking as the Netherlands representative, Mouton touched upon the problem while arguing that the criterion of exploitability was "legally unsound and difficult to apply" and illustrated his point by the following example:

> ... if a technician invented an installation whereby resources could allegedly be exploited at a depth of 300 meters, but the apparatus failed to function after it had been installed, the State concerned would have committed an illegal act.[133]

The main problem implied here is not, of course, any illegality of the attempt; the erection of an inoperative structure could probably be comfortably housed under the *res communis* concept of the high seas and their seabed and subsoil. The problem is rather one of deciding on criteria that determine what really constituted exploitation. If exploitation of coral reefs were undertaken at the maximum depth of 1,200 meters and then abandoned, after some meager results, for any reason: would then the depth of 1,200 meters be still considered the limit of exploitability until surpassed? Or if some oil were obtained by drilling into the subsoil under a maximum of 1,500 feet of water, but the operator abandoned the operation after several months for not getting sufficient returns on his investment, would the limit achieved still hold under the Convention?

McDougal and Burke suggested, without reference to the Convention, that the criterion of exploitability may perhaps be determined 'in terms of the commercial feasibility of extraction" or by "the economics of the enterprise." [134] Earlier Mouton, writing as a private author, also noted that

> exploitation is only proved possible when it actually takes place, and this does not depend only on the technical possibility but also . . . on a consideration of whether the exploitation will be a paying proposition [because] . . . the cost of developing a field is, ultimately, the governing factor.[135]

[133] 6 *Official Records* 37. As a private author, Mouton raised the same argument in one of his writings. See M. W. Mouton, *op. cit.* (note 126), p. 44.

[134] McDougal and Burke, *op. cit.* (note 124), pp. 668, 690.

[135] M. W. Mouton, *Recent Developments in the Technology of Exploiting the Mineral Resources of the Continental Shelf* (U.N. Conference on the Law of the Sea, Prep. Doc. No. 20), U.N. Doc. A/CONF.13/25 (3 January 1958), p. 5.

But not only do the Convention and the Conference records nowhere indicate that the "economics of the enterprise" should be taken into account when defining the maximum achieved exploitation; the criterion of commercial feasbility, while undoubtedly effective in practice, by its very nature defies any attempt to translate it into a principle of legal interpretation. What to a United States oil company may be a completely uneconomical and commercially non-feasible enterprise, may elsewhere be still regarded as economically sound. An oil-starved country, perhaps politically isolated, may operate submarine oil wells or exploit other shelf resources at a sizeable deficit. Without the Convention providing an authoritative answer to these problems, any state party to the treaty and in relation to other treaty members could, at least in theory, determine the outer limits of the "shelf" by extracting from the outlying sea bottom even a small amount of substances falling within the treaty definition of natural resources. The only possible limitations on the coastal state's liberty to do so may lie in the difference between exploratory and exploitative[136] extraction of natural resources, and in the treaty term "adjacent" describing the submarine areas in question.

4. EXPLOITABILITY AND EXPLORATION. Another problem created by the text of the Convention on the Continental Shelf and unsolved by the Conference debates arises from the following treaty provisions: (a) Article 1, embodying the criterion of exploitability in the phrase "to where the depth of the superjacent waters *admits of the exploitation* of the natural resources . . ." and (b) Article 2/1, according to which "The coastal state exercises over the continental shelf sovereign rights for the purpose of *exploring it and exploiting* its natural resources." [137]

The problem is this: If a treaty member establishes the maximum limit of the shelf by proven exploitation at the depth of 1,500 feet, it obviously has no exclusive rights of exploration beyond that limit at a greater depth, but only inclusive rights together with any other user of the high seas. A foreign state or company may explore the deeper neighboring areas at will – but no more than that. It cannot exploit them because, under the wider meaning of the criterion of exploitability, it would automatically lose its

[136] In the course of submarine exploration designed to establish the presence and richness of mineral nodules lying on the seabed at a depth of, for instance, 10,000 feet, hundreds of buckets of natural substances may have to be removed from the bottom of the sea by a drag-dredging method. It may thus be maintained that even a sizeable extraction of samples, but still in quantities too small to be used industrially and commercially, falls within the meaning of exploration and, under the Convention, exploratory activity at any depth does not effect an extension of exclusive coastal rights.

[137] Emphases added.

inclusive rights of exploration and the coastal state's exclusive rights of exploration and exploitation would come into force.

Thus stated, this is seemingly a purely legalistic problem of no practical significance since, quite obviously, no one would invest into submarine exploration without a real chance of ever recovering the investment.[138] In fact, if not in law, all foreign industrial exploration beyond the established coastal limit is thus *a priori* excluded since in practice it would serve no useful purpose unless, remotely, it had the function of an intentional political irritant directed at the coastal state.

But without an undue strain on one's sense of reality the following legal problem may be seen arising in practice between states bound by the Convention:

(Activity.) An industrial operator carries on, for an extended period of time, intensive and costly submarine exploration to determine the richness of mineral nodules on the seabed, with a view to their extraction. While exploring at sea, he engages engineering firms to design and build suitable dredges.

(Position) The explored submarine area has an average depth of 10,000 feet and is over five hundred miles distant from the nearest shores. They are shores foreign to the operator. At the time the operator began exploring in the area, the limit of exclusive coastal rights, established by effective and proved exploitation, was at the depth of 1,500 feet; the exploration area was therefore far removed from the then recognized shelf boundary.

(Conflict.) But as the foreign operator's exploratory work was progressing, the boundary of exclusive coastal rights was continually being pushed closer to the exploration area by proved technological improvements of exploitation methods, until the depth of 10,000 feet was recognized as admitting of exploitation. The foreign coastal state, lawfully under the Convention, claimed exclusive rights of exploration and exploitation over the submarine area in question, and maintained that the foreign operator was obliged either to abandon his project or to pay such fees, bonuses and royalties as prescribed by the coastal authorities.

[138] McDougal and Burke considered this a factor supporting the exploitability criterion in case of oil exploitation: "The test of effective exploitation from a coast also serves to prevent potential foreign initiative from locating just beyond the boundary of present exclusive control, perhaps to the detriment of the shoreward exploiters. Unless all effective exploitation comes within a single exclusive coastal control, it would be possible for other states to sponsor activities that frustrate or greatly diminish the effectiveness of those already exploiting an area." *Op. cit.* (note 124), p. 665.

(Problem.) Could the operator's national state, when asked to intervene on the operator's behalf, do so legally and without violating its obligations under the Convention?

It appears that it could not legally undertake such action. But it then also means that the Convention with its exploitability criterion has much wider effects than its articles suggest, and that it virtually prevents the emergence of a right to the fruits of an exploratory activity lawfully undertaken on submarine areas under the control of no single state but open to the use by all. However, could not the operator's national state still take legal action based on the term "adjacent" used in the Convention to characterize the submarine areas on which a coastal state may acquire exclusive rights of exploration and exploitation?

5. EXPLOITABILITY AND THE TREATY TERM "ADJACENT". Should the term "adjacent" fail to provide the legal means by which the seaward push generated by the criterion of exploitability can be curbed or stopped, then a question asked in Committee IV of the Geneva Conference by the delegate of Ceylon, and an answer given by the delegate of France, are truly relevant and realistic.

The delegate of Ceylon, describing as "regrettably vague" an amendment by India which would replace by the expression "in the vicinity of" the term "adjacent to," [139] asked in the debate

> ... what interpretation should be placed on the article [Convention article 1 providing for the exploitability criterion] in dealing with exploitable areas far removed from any single coastal State. Would all the [sub]marine areas of the globe be parcelled out among the different nations, or would the seabed beneath isolated parts of the high seas be open to exploration and exploitation by all comers?[140]

The French delegate stated, after sharply criticizing the contention of some delegations "that the State had a right to all that was situated off its coasts" and that "the only test to determine the limits of its competence was that of possible exploitation":

> That would ultimately mean that each State had a right to proceed as far as it could, not just at any one moment but for ever, and that there was a "sector" of water opposite its coasts over which it would have exclusive rights as soon as it could assert them.[141]

[139] The Indian amendment appears as Doc. A/CONF.13/C.4/L.29 in 6 *Official Records* 135. The Indian delegate explained that the reason for the amendment "was that, since by definition the continental shelf was separated from the coast by the subsoil and seabed of the territorial sea, the expression "in the vicinity of" would be more appropriate than "adjacent to." *Ibid.* 42. The amendment was later withdrawn. *Id.* 46.

[140] *Ibid.* 43.

[141] *Id.*

Earlier in Committee IV discussions – and the delegations' comments on the term "adjacent" were rather rare and general – the delegate of the Dominican Republic stated that the thought underlying article 1 was that

the continental shelf was a prolongation of the land and, therefore, subject to considerations of contiguity or proximity. Exploitation beyond the point at which the relationship of proximity ended might be based on occupation, but would not be covered by the provisions of articles ... [1 and 2].[142]

On the whole, however, it appears neither from the Conference debates nor from the Convention that the term "adjacent to" ought to be interpreted as "in the vicinity of" or "in the proximity of" the national coasts. And such state practice as there has been after 1958 indicates no tendency of states to ascribe any restrictive meaning to the term "adjacent".

The case in point is provided by a memorandum of 5 May 1961 sent by Thomas J. Cavanaugh, Associate Solicitor, Division of Public Lands of the United States Department of the Interior, to the Director of the Bureau of Land Management within the same Department.[143] The memorandum was to answer a question of the addressee whether phosphate deposits in a submarine area off the coast of California may be leased under the 1953 Outer Continental Shelf Lands Act. The area was described as follows:

The designated area lies some forty miles off the coast of southern California. While it lies closer to the mainland than San Clemente Island, the designated area does not lie between that island and the mainland but rather in the open sea. The soundings in the designated area range between 43 and 670 fathoms, the greater part of the area being at a depth of far more than 100 fathoms. Between the designated area and the mainland lies a deep channel in which the soundings are of 600 fathoms and more.

The memorandum stated further:

The question of the propriety of leasing phosphate deposits in this area under the Outer Continental Shelf Lands Act has been presented to us because it has been frequently said in the past that the continental shelf extends seaward to a point where the water deepens rapidly and that this outer limit is set at the 100-fathom line. Under such a definition the designated area would lie beyond the outer Continental Shelf, and, consequently, the crux of this problem is whether there is in fact a seaward limit to the applicability of the Outer Continental Shelf Lands Act set at the 100-fathom line.

[142] *Ibid.* 9. In the same sense, McDougal and Burke emphasized and recommended the term "adjacent" as effectively limiting the seaward extent of exclusive coastal rights. *Op. cit.* (note 124), pp. 685–686.

[143] The mimeographed document, distributed within the Department by its Duplicating Section under No. 94127–61 and No. M-36615, and entitled "Application of Outer Continental Shelf Lands Act to Designated Area off the Coast of California," was kindly forwarded to the present writer by the United States Department of the Interior. As the document is of only six pages and is not generally available, references to it in the present text are not further and individually defined.

Answering the question, the document concluded that there was no such limit; and that without it "it is possible to hold that with technological progress the act may be applied to areas at greater and greater depth."

The Assistant Solicitor stated that from 1945 on and through the legislative history of the Act the setting of a firm shelf limit had never been contemplated by the United States;[144] his opinion rested primarily on the text of article 1 of the Geneva Convention on the Continental Shelf and its criterion of exploitability. The memorandum noted that the Convention had been ratified by the United States Senate; that it was not in force, but "may be regarded as expressing the present views of the United States"; and that Convention article 1, quoted in full in the memorandum, is "the first definition of 'continental shelf' officially adopted by the United States which sets any seaward limit," and "is an indication of the extent of the area of seabed and subsoil over which the United States asserts jurisdiction, control, and power of disposition." The Assistant Solicitor's memorandum then concluded:

> There is no question that the area designated on the map which you have sent us falls within the scope of the definition in the Convention and is, therefore, subject to leasing under the Act.

The memorandum did not indicate whether any restrictive meaning was found in the term "adjacent." The entire problem of proximity was dismissed with ease in one statement: "The distance of 40 miles from the mainland is of little importance since in the Gulf of Mexico activities under the Act are conducted at a greater distance . . ." It is, of course, doubtful, considering the arguments and the spirit of the memorandum,[145] whether this last quoted sentence was meant to express a real concern about some restrictive effects of the criterion of proximity implied by the term "adjacent." [146]

144 This rather difficult task was accomplished through several means: first, by the assertion that "any description in the legislative history of the continental shelf as a geographic concept may be regarded as an effort to give the Congress a general idea of the area over which the United States was asserting jurisdiction rather than a precise definition applicable to the statute;" further, by stressing that the 1945 Truman Proclamation had not mentioned the seaward shelf limits; third, by pointing out that both the Proclamation and the accompanying press release "emphasized the importance of technology in determining the seaward limits of exploitation"; and finally the fact was ignored that the press release as well as a statement of the Secretary of the Interior, whose description of the physical properties of the shelf was actually quoted in the memorandum, had described the United States continental shelf, by giving its extent as 750,000 or 760,000 square miles, as a definite, measurable area. For earlier references to the press release and to the Secretary of the Interior statements see pp. 76, 84 – 85.

145 It should be noticed, for instance, that the author of the memorandum, while relying on the text of the Convention, did not consider the question whether exploitation at the depths of the designated area had been shown to be possible and recognized as such.

146 Some such concern, however, may be noted in a remark by the United States delegate (Marjorie Whiteman) in Committee IV of the 1958 Geneva Conference when she attempted,

A seaward distance of 40 miles is admittedly relatively small; even if the term "adjacent" were to be interpreted restrictively, submarine areas so close to the shores would easily fall within the meaning of such a qualification. But it is not apparent from the Convention at which point, in terms of miles from the shore, a submarine area may be described as not adjacent to any coast. McDougal and Burke noted that some members of the International Law Commission had emphasized the notion of contiguity or proximity as qualifying the range of exclusive coastal rights acquired by proven exploitability, the qualification having been defined by the term "reasonable proximity." [147] While this is almost impossible to interpret, McDougal's and Burke's own definition of what does not constitute proximity is only slightly more helpful: they speak of exploitation reaching "a point at which it is not possible even to identify a coastal state – **i.e.,** with no one state bordering on the common ocean or being especially related to a particular area or more immediately affected by activities there." [148] But even if it could be shown beyond doubt that states represented at the Geneva Conference did ascribe some such meaning to the term "adjacent," interpretation would be still extremely difficult for two reasons: first, exact measurements can always reliably determine which state is the closest to a definite point on the high seas, while no measurements are likely to show what might be meant by "especially related" or "more immediately affected"; second, the term "adjacent" acquires special significance when it is remembered that 50 per cent of the world's shelf area, and a great majority of shelf exploitation, is in the mediterranean areas of the world with many states grouped together – our next problem to consider.

6. Exploitability and Interstate Shelf Boundaries. The determination of shelf boundaries between neighboring states or states whose coasts are opposite each other is provided for by article 6 of the Convention on the Continental Shelf:

Article 6

1. Where the same continental shelf is adjacent to the territories of two or more states whose coasts are opposite each other, the boundary of the continental shelf appertaining to such states shall be determined by agreement between them. In the absence of agreement, and unless another boundary line is justified by special

by reliance on technological limits, to alleviate fears that the criterion of exploitability could lead to parcelling out the entire sea floor: "Exploitation could not ... continue indefinitely towards the middle of the ocean; the continental slope fell away steeply and rapidly, so that exploitation beyond a certain limit would not be an economic proposition." 6 *Official Records* 40.

147 McDougal and Burke, *op. cit.* (note 124), pp. 658, 686.

148 *Ibid.*, p. 665.

circumstances, the boundary is the median line, every point of which is equidistant from the nearest points of the baselines from which the breadth of the territorial sea of each state is measured.

2. Where the same continental shelf is adjacent to the territories of two adjacent states, the boundary of the continental shelf shall be determined by agreement between them. In the absence of agreement, and unless another boundary line is justified by special circumstances, the boundary shall be determined by application of the principle of equidistance from the nearest points of the baselines from which the breadth of the territorial sea of each state is measured.

3. In delimiting the boundaries of the continental shelf, any lines which are drawn in accordance with the principles set out in paragraphs 1 and 2 of this article should be defined with reference to charts and geographical features as they exist at a particular date, and reference should be made to fixed permanent identifiable points on the land.

This text was developed in Committee IV from International Law Commission's article 72 and there adopted, after some five hours of debate, by 36 votes to none with 19 abstentions,[149] while the plenary meeting accepted the article practically without debate by 63 votes to none with 2 abstentions.[150] In Committee IV the debates as well as amendments proposed by several delegations dealt primarily with the reference to special circumstances in paragraphs 1 and 2 of article 6, with the question of baselines, and with the problem of islands. The reference to "special circumstances", eventually adopted, was meant to refer to geographical and geological variations, irregularities and exceptional configurations of sea bottom as well as the coasts. Thus it was said during the Conference debates in defense of the "special circumstances" clause that the "situations . . . in different parts of the world were too varied" [151] to justify the adoption of a median line as the general rule, and that account would have to be taken "of the great variety of complex geographical situations." [152]

The Conference debates, however, provided no evidence that the delegates were aware of the potentially dangerous problems arising from the conjunction of the criterion of exploitability and the adopted method of determining the self boundaries of neighboring states. Indeed, the prevailing opinion at the Conference seems to have been that expressed later by McDougal and Burke:

With respect to the boundary between states sharing a common ocean bottom, the use of the exploitability limit merely means that at some point in time it will

149 6 *Official Records* 98.
150 2 *Official Records* 15.
151 Venezuelan delegate, 6 *Official Records* 94.
152 United States delegate, *ibid.* 95.

be necessary to agree upon a common boundary, but this problem is not unique to this particular limit.[153]

The seriousness of the problem can be best illustrated by reference to submarine areas of the North Sea between southern Norway and the eastern Scottish coast. There the continental shelf stretches due east from the shores of Scotland for some three hundred miles,[154] with the depth of the superjacent waters generally fluctuating around 50 fathoms (91.5 meters). Only when the shelf reaches within approximately 40 miles off the Norwegian coast does the seabed fall off into the greater depths around 200 fathoms (about 366 meters), and does not rise again until approximately 5 miles off the Norwegian shores. These simple geographical facts may lead to complex problems.

Assuming that both Great Britain and Norway have ratified[155] the Convention on the Continental Shelf without any reservations to article 6, and that depths beyond 200 meters were not recognized as admitting of the exploitation of the shelf resources, Great Britain could lawfully control shelf exploration and exploitation[156] up to some 40 miles off Norway where depths over 200 meters occur, while the corresponding Norwegian rights would be confined to an extremely narrow coastal strip of the shelf mostly under the Norwegian territorial waters. But, as soon as technology would permit industrially and commercially meaningful exploitation in depths up to or over 366 meters, the entire submarine area between British and Norwegian coasts would become one uninterrupted continental shelf expanse as defined by the treaty criterion of exploitability. Areas previously falling under British control would suddenly shrink some 100 or more miles in surface distance back toward British coasts.

While capable of creating this problem, the Convention fails to provide for its solution. The "special circumstances" clause, as we have noted, was

[153] McDougal and Burke, *op. cit.* (note 124), pp. 666–667.

[154] Basic features of the submarine area concerned, lying between 57° and 59° N parallels and between the British and Norwegian coasts, are clearly shown by United States Hydrographic Office, Map No. 4842 (The North Sea – Middle Sheet), natural scale 1 : 186,557 (Washington D.C., 1922). All data referring to the area in the present text have been derived from the map cited herein.

[155] The United Kingdom ratified the Convention on the Continental Shelf, by the summer of 1964. At this time, Norway is unlikely to become a party to the Convention; it failed to sign it, and its delegation at Geneva had abstained from voting on it.

[156] In 1962–64, this was not a purely imaginary possibility. Exploratory work in search for oil was done off the east coasts of Great Britain in 1962, while in the spring of 1963 reports were published about a forthcoming seismic survey sponsored by a consortium of petroleum companies (Shell, British Petroleum, and Standard Oil Company of New Jersey) and designed to cover larger areas of the North Sea shelf. Among the factors leading to the submarine search were also the limited oil deposits discovered in Scotland and the prevailing suspicion that bigger fields may lie eastward under the sea. See Alexander MacLeod, "North Sea Oil: Object of Search," *The Christian Science Monitor*, 15 March 1963, p. 4. – Currently, formal agreement governs Anglo–Norwegian shelf relations.

not intended to allow for similar situations; and even if it were, it would be of little assistance unless the two states concerned have agreed to a mutually acceptable solution or to international adjudication. Further, the situation as described above need not be "special" if this Convention term in the phrase "special circumstances" is understood to mean "exceptional"; a close inspection of sufficiently detailed hydrographic maps and charts discloses that the problems arising from the conflict between the exploitability criterion of Convention article 1 and the method of delimitation of state shelf boundaries of article 6 might be fairly common in several mediterranean areas of the world, though involving different depths and distances.[157]

It may thus be said that Convention article 6, stressing the median line in the determination of interstate shelf boundaries, partially aims to restore what has been destroyed by article 1 which defines the shelf by the 200-meter depth and by the exploitability criterion – namely, the term "adjacent" now receives the meaning of "closer to one coast than to another." For instance, article 1 would permit installations to be constructed, under exclusive British control, some 15 to 20 miles off Cuban coast and thus immediately outside the territorial sea claimed by Cuba, in some 4 fathoms of water covering the southwestern edge of the Great Bahama Bank, and about 80 miles from the nearest British land. But article 6, as soon as shelf exploitation is recognized as practicable under about 500 fathoms of water, would tend to push the interstate shelf boundary back towards the Bahamas.[158]

The legal problem clearly stems from the failure of the Convention to provide any indication how the conflicts created by the incompatibility of the two articles can be settled if bilateral negotiations break down and international adjudication is not accepted.

At the same time, moreover, the combination of the two articles undermines the validity of the concept of geographical and geological land-and-shelf contiguity, a concept on which several delegations at Geneva based their claimes to *ipso jure* coastal sovereignty over the contiguous submarine areas. In the above case of the Bahamas-Cuba shelf situation, or in the North

157 Similar problems, for instance, might arise; between the United States and Cuba in an area north off the Cuban Pinar del Rio province and south-west of Florida, with about 1,000 fathoms as the crucial depth admitting of the exploitation of shelf resources; or, more clearly and with greater shelf areas involved, between the Bahamas and Cuba, in an area north-east off the Cuban Camaguey province, where depths of perhaps no more than about 500 fathoms in the Old Bahama Channel, few miles off the Cuban coast, prevent under the Convention Cuban access to the submarine riches of the Great Bahama Bank; still another, even more complicated situation exists south-west off Jamaica between that country and both Nicaragua and Honduras. All these situations are clearly visible on, for instance, a West Indies map prepared as Atlas Plate 23 by the Cartographic Division of the National Geographic Society for *The National Geographic Magazine*.

158 For geographical reference see preceding note.

Sea position of Great Britain and Norway discussed earlier, the median line principle, applied to submarine areas definable under the treaty criterion of exploitability as "continental shelf," would bring under the exclusive control of Cuba and Norway parts of the continental shelf geographically and geologically contiguous to foreign coasts and separated from Cuba and Norway by deep-sea channels.

Aspects of the Functional Limits

The most important aspects of the functional limits set by the Convention to the exclusive coastal rights on the shelf grow from article 2/1 according to which "The coastal state exercises over the continental shelf sovereign rights for the purpose of exploring it and exploiting its natural resources." This provision seems clearly to imply that for other purposes the coastal state has no exclusive rights on the adjacent shelf; and even the restricted rights provided by the Convention are still further limited by the duty of the coastal state not to impede the laying and maintenance of submarine cables or pipelines (article 4), not to interfere unjustifiably with navigation, fishing or the conservation of the living resources (article 5/1), and to make possible oceanographic and other scientific research on the shelf (article 5/1 and 5/8). The right of the coastal state to construct and operate on the shelf installations necessary for shelf exploration and exploitation and to establish protective safety zones around them (article 5/2 and 5/3) is limited by the duty to report the construction of such installations, to equip them with warning devices, and to remove them when not used (article 5/4), and by the further obligation of the coastal state to protect the living resources of the sea, within the safety zones, from harmful agents (article 5/7). Also, installations are not allowed where their presence would interfere with international navigation in recognized sea lanes (article 5/6). While in its provisions regarding the territorial limits of exclusive coastal rights the Convention appears excessively liberal, it seems more restrictive in the area of exclusive functional rights.

1. Exploration and Exploitation, and Other Uses of the Shelf. The Conference debates did indicate a considerable consensus of states that the exclusive coastal rights should be limited to rights of exploration and exploitation of the natural shelf resources. But they did not indicate any conviction on the part of the state delegations that this limitation had already been established by a binding customary rule; not did they suggest that the intended effect of that limitation was to safeguard on the continental shelf

inclusive rights other than those specifically provided for, such as the laying and maintenance of cables and pipelines and scientific research. The discussions in Committee IV show the "exploration and exploitation" limitation to have been the product chiefly of one underlying assumption and an apprehension: the assumption that the continental shelf offers little more than its natural resources; and the apprehension that a failure to express that limitation in the treaty might be used as a basis for claims to exclusive rights in the superjacent waters rather than to other uses of the shelf itself.

During the Committee IV debates some delegates did demand that the coastal rights on the shelf be described by the all-embracing terms "sovereignty." [159] But even these delegates were thinking and speaking primarily in terms of the exploration and exploitation of shelf resources with but two clear exceptions. During the general debate, the delegate of Chile attempted to defend the recognition of full coastal sovereignty on the adjacent shelf by reference to such other uses of the shelf as the construction and maintenance of radar installations,[160] and the delegate of Ceylon argued that

> If the coastal State's rights were confined to exploring and exploiting the natural resources of the continental shelf, a situation might arise in which another State would wish to erect installations on the continental shelf for some entirely different purpose – say, that of interstellar communications – and the coastal State would be unable to protest.[161]

However, this type of argument was not only rare; it was also generally disregarded. Judging by the contents and the spirit of the Conference debates, the view most widely adopted was that expressed by the Greek delegate; as he stated it, the words "exploring and exploiting' seemed to cover all the uses which could possibly be made of the continental shelf." [162] The Convention on the Continental Shelf thus fails to provide unequivocal answers to problems that may arise through such uses of the shelf as modern technology may discover and develop, and several of them are currently being developed. One such instance appears to be the use of the shelf for building military installations of some such type as the so-called radar "Texas Towers" erected by the United States in the Atlantic.[163]

159 See statements in Committee IV by the following delegations (all references are, at pages indicated, to 6 *Official Records*): Argentina 2–3; Philippines 8, 41–42; Colombia 10; Peru 11; Mexico 15; Chile 16, 57–58; Republic of Korea 23; El Salvador 24; and Ceylon 67.

160 *Ibid.* 16.

161 *Ibid.* 67.

162 *Ibid.* 6. Earlier, Mouton privately expressed a similar view: "Whether this limitation means anything is questionable. It is difficult to imagine that in practice control and jurisdiction over the continental shelf could be exercised for any other purpose than exploration and exploitation of the natural resources of the seabed and subsoil. Mouton, *op. cit.* (note 126), p. 281.

163 The only three "Texas Tower" type radar stations operated by the United States Air Force (and in 1963 reported abandoned and in the process of being dismantled) were constructed in the

In Committee IV, the Bulgarian delegation emphasized that "the continental shelf should not be used for military purposes, such as the erection of military bases or installations aimed at the safety of other States." [164] In a still broader version, the same view was expressed by India in a proposed additional article providing that "The continental shelf . . . shall not be used by the coastal State or any other State for the purpose of building military bases or installations." [165] The proposal was rejected by 31 votes to 18 with 6 abstentions.[166] McDougal and Burke suggest that the negative votes might have been inspired by

> a combination of circumstances, including an unwillingness to single out for prohibition this single instance of use while leaving other uses unmentioned, the notion that the coastal interest in security in the modern world might outweigh the slight impediment to freedom of the seas caused by a few radar towers, and conviction that the erection of military installations was a permissible use of the area.[167]

. . . a use permissible, presumably, to the coastal state alone.

But it appears that the complex needs of society may find other uses for the continental shelf. Some of them have already been found. We have noted earlier that the United States policy and practice permit the use of the shelf as a ground on which to build or place submerged storage facilities for petroleum whether it was or was not produced from the continental shelf.[168] Next, apart from the radar towers, the United States operates through its Office of Naval Research and in cooperation with thirty academic, industrial and governmental scientific groups a research tower known as Argus Island standing atop an extinct volcano in 200 feet of water 30 miles southwest of Bermuda; the steel tower, as a part of the so-called Project Artemis, serves as a relay point for faint sound signals picked up by hydrophones placed on the deep ocean floor. The purpose of the project is to develop, by using complex sonar devices, a detection system aimed at enemy submarines.[169]

Still another use for the continental shelf is found in current proposals

late 1950's as modifications of the oil-drilling Gulf of Mexico platforms. Two of them were placed on the shelf in water 87 feet deep, one 50 miles east of Nantucket Island, another 110 miles east of Chatham, Cape Cod. The third, TT-4 (TT-1 was never built), stood in 185 feet of water about 117 miles south-east of New York at a point where the Hudson Gorge of the continental shelf goes into great oceanic depths. It was this last station that collapsed in January 1961. *The New York Times*, 17 January 1961, p. 30. Also, *Time*, 27 January 1961, pp. 15–16.

[164] 6 *Official Records* 23.

[165] United Nations Doc. A/CONF.13/C.4/L.57, in 6 *Official Records* 141.

[166] *Ibid.* 91.

[167] McDougal and Burke, *op. cit.* (note 124), p. 717.

[168] See note 38 above. Also the possibility of placing on the shelf mooring stations and storage platforms was already seriously discussed by McDougal and Burke, *op cit.* (note 124), pp. 719–. 720.

[169] *The New York Times*, 1 June 1961, pp. 1 and 16.

outlining the conversion of 28 United States floating drydocks – surplus from World War II – to missile-age uses. An engineering firm already submitted proposals to the United States Air Research and Development Command, to the National Aeronautics and Space Administration, and to the United States Air Force Ballistic Missile Division, on adapting the drydocks for use as satellite tracking stations, mobile missile launchers, and as pads for firing nuclear ramjet engines. The converted drydocks, standing on their hydraulically extended legs, could be positioned in waters up to 150 feet deep. According to a published report, specific plans were submitted by Lockheed Aircraft Corporation to the Ballistic Missile Division to use the converted drydocks as a tracking site for the Midas and Samos satelite network off African coast because "efforts to acquire land sites in Africa have been thwarted by the unstable political situation." [170]

All these uses of the continental shelf, and perhaps many other, admittedly are in the developmental stage and because of their rarity may be considered as highly exceptional. Yet they open the way to future methods of utilizing the shelf, methods on which the Convention is completely silent. One might observe, of course, that the silence itself need not be meaningless; since the Convention does provide for the protection of established inclusive rights on the shelf such as the right to lay and maintain cables and pipelines, and for a limitation of other inclusive rights such as scientific oceanographic research, it may be deduced that the use of the shelf as a ground on which to place storage equipment, tracking and detection sites and other installations was not considered at Geneva to belong to established inclusive rights requiring special protection or modification.

2. Exploitable resources. We need not dwell excessively on the problem of what resources did the Convention include among those falling under the exclusive control of the coastal state. We have already noted above that the exploitation of sedentary species living on the shelf has not been brought about or materially affected by the continental shelf doctrine;[171] and that the treaty definition of the natural resources of the shelf, with its inclusion of the sedentary species, was arrived at by the Geneva Conference through a process of a political compromise exacted by a considerable number of countries primarily interested in immediate revenues from a controlled exploitation of the living organisms rather than in the costly and time consuming process of searching and drilling for minerals. Eventually, the major dif-

[170] William S. Reed, "Docks Proposed as Offshore Launch Sites," *Aviation Week*, 12 September 1960, pp. 122–127.
[171] Pp. 46–47.

ferences at the Conference did not center upon whether or not to include living resources within the exclusive coastal control of the shelf but upon the range of species to be put within the coastal rights of exclusive exploitation;[172] because of its character of a political compromise, however, such consensus as did exist at the Conference on the inclusion of the sedentary species may indeed be called but a *seeming* consensus[173] – a consensus, that is, on what was politically prudent rather than legally desirable or even previously established and unavoidable.

What was significant at the Conference was, however, its primary concern with the type of shelf resources rather than with the methods of their exploitation. Although the concept that the security of the coastal state would be jeopardized by the erection on the adjacent shelf of installations controlled by foreign interests was among the impulses leading to the development of the continental shelf doctrine, it has not been clearly embodied in the Convention. The Government of the Netherlands referred to the problem in 1957 in its comments to draft article 67 of the International Law Commission defining the continental shelf by the 200-meter depth and the exploitability criterion; this definition, the Netherlands Government said,

> may create a dangerous situation in the future, because if in the future an exploitation of minerals at ocean depth might be possible by means of a dredging installation on a ship, the coastal State must be prevented from claiming a monopoly by basing itself on the present text. This kind of exploitation must remain free in principle, just as at present fishing is free for any State.[174]

During the Conference this problem was completely pushed aside by the governing concern of the delegates with the type of resources to be controlled by the coastal state.

3. FUNCTIONAL RIGHTS AND STATE RESPONSIBILITY. By controlling under the Convention the exploration and exploitation of the adjacent shelf, the coastal state assumes varying degrees of responsibility for not permitting any undue disturbance of other inclusive uses of the shelf and the superjacent waters. The term "undue" is being used advisedly; it is vague to about the same degree as the corresponding terms used in the Convention and emphasized in the following quotations of the appropriate paragraphs:

[172] This conclusion was also expressed by McDougal and Burke, *op. cit.* (note 124), p. 660.
[173] *Ibid.*, p. 661.
[174] 1 *Official Records* 110. (Comments by Governments on the Draft Articles concerning the Law of the Sea adopted by the International Law Commission at its Eighth Session, Doc. A/CONF.13/5/Add. 1.)

Article 4

Subject to its right to take resonable measures for the exploration of the continental shelf and the exploitation of its natural resources, the coastal state may not impede the laying or maintenance of submarine cables or pipelines on the continental shelf.

Article 5

1. The exploration of the continental shelf and the exploitation of its natural resources must not result in any unjustifiable interference with navigation, fishing or the conservation of the living resources of the sea, nor result in any interference with fundamental oceanographic or other scientific research carried out with the intention of open publication.

. . . .

6. Neither the installations or devices, nor the safety zones around them, may be established where interference may be caused to the use of recognized sea lanes essential to international navigation.

7. The coastal state is obliged to undertake, in the safety zones, all appropriate measures for the protection of the living resources of the sea from harmful agents.

8. The consent of the coastal state shall be obtained in respect of any research concerning the continental shelf and undertaken there. Nevertheless, the coastal state shall not normally withhold its consent if the request is submitted by a qualified institution with a view to purely scientific research into the physical or biological characteristics of the continental shelf, subject to the proviso that the coastal state shall have the right, if it so desires, to participate or to be represented in the research, and that in any event the results shall be published.

The size of the problem that arises from the obvious need of finding a balanced measure of coexistence between the various inclusive and exclusive uses of the shelf may be illustrated by reference to the drastic measures adopted by the Humble Oil and Refining Company to isolate an oil well burning at sea. The area involved was in the Galveston Bay in Texas and not under the high seas. The well was burning out of control from October 1961 until March 1962. The company, to insure that the surrounding waters are not polluted, ordered the erection – at a cost of a quarter of a million dollars – of a fence of interlocking sheets of steel extending six feet above the water and driven thirty feet into the floor of the bay.[175] The obvious question is whether a state would be held internationally responsible under the Convention to take similar drastic measures should the accident occur on the continental shelf beneath the high seas.

Understandably, the Conference debates completely fail to alleviate the vagueness of the treaty provisions in this respect; it is almost impossible to define in general terms and without reference to specific circumstances what

[175] News report, 16 (No. 5) *Offshore* 17 (March 1962).

type of interference with navigation would be justifiable or what protective measures might be reasonable.[176]

A still greater problem however, is hidden behind the question whether the coastal state's responsibility as provided for by the Convention may not eventually result in a partial extension of national jurisdiction over the users of the high seas themselves. The coastal state, to provide for the safety of navigation, may have to issue shipping regulations and designate specific sea lanes in areas of the high seas under which the mineral resources are intensively exploited – but it may also need to enforce such regulations if it is to discharge its responsibility effectively. The Government of Denmark is undoubtedly among the first who would fully understand the scope of the problem. That government, legally obligated to preserve and maintain a safety system protecting all ships navigating the high seas off Denmark[177] – shallow seas full of shoals and reefs – invited the International Law Commission to formulate a rule enlarging the jurisdiction of Denmark over foreign ships navigating the Danish Sound, and stated: "In order to accomplish [the] task efficiently and safely, it must be possible to enforce the regulations issued by the Danish authorities . . . with binding effect on everyone navigating the said waters." [178] The situation developing on the high seas covering rich continental shelves may become closely comparable to that off the Danish coast and, not provided for by the Convention on the Continental Shelf, may continue as a point of considerable legal uncertainty until, perhaps, a customary rule might grow up and fill the gap.

Looking back at both the descriptive and the analytical section of this study, the contours of a legal regime of the continental shelf are far from clear. Among the many component rules of that regime only the very core – the rule giving the coastal state exclusive rights on the adjacent continental

[176] The draft article 73 providing for compulsory adjudication of disputes was intended by many delegations to induce some self-control of states capable to blunt the dangers created by the unavoidable vagueness of some of the provisions. 6 *Official Records* 89–106. The article was adopted in Committee IV by 33 votes to 15 with 14 abstentions (*ibid.* 106), but in the plenary meeting received 38 votes in favor and 20 against with 7 abstentions and, having thus failed to obtain the required two-thirds majority, was rejected. 2 *Official Records* 55.

[177] The responsibility of the Danish Government for making the freeways among the shoals and reefs of the Danish Sound rests partly on an old practice and partly on the express provision in Article 2 of the Treaty on Abolition of the Sound Dues of 14 March 1857. By agreement between the Danish Lighthouse Authority and the corresponding authorities of the neighboring countries, the area of responsibility of each country in the waters outside the territorial sea has been delimited. On the origins and the exercise of Danish responsibility for the safety of all shipping off Danish territorial waters, Charles E. Hill, *The Danish Sound Dues and the Command of the Baltic* (Chapel Hill: Duke University, 1926).

[178] United Nations International Law Commission. Comments by Governments on the Provisional Articles concerning the Regime of the High Seas and the Draft Articles on the Regime of the Territorial Sea adopted by the International Law Commission at its 7th Session. Doc. A/CN.4/99/Add.9, pp. 7–8.

shelf beneath the high seas – appears relatively firm; yet it lacks the company of other equally firm rules that would define it in space and substance, that is, the company of rules setting up the territorial and functional limits of the exclusive coastal rights.

Throughout the thirteen years from 1945 to 1958 the practice of states with regard to the continental shelf was generous indeed. It was a practice consisting, first, of issuing unilateral statements of policy motivated by the national interest of each national community; second, of accepting policy modifications induced by the need of political compromises, clearly demonstrated mainly during the 1958 Geneva Conference; and third, of actual acts of state control over shelf activity encouraged by declared national policies. However, the sum of all these manifestations of different national interests differently expressed makes a heterogeneous whole. There are often wide gaps, if not inconsistencies, between the optimum goals sought by each state with regard to the continental shelf, the political minima acceptable to each state when confronted by the policies of other countries, and the realistic extent to which the national policies can be materially implemented.

Yet it is somewhere within this amorphous mass of state acts and their consequences that the political discretion of governments is being narrowed down and forced into specific patterns of legally ordered behavior – patterns, that is, also definable as customary rules of international law. And our aim now is to examine whether any such rules have emerged to comprise a meaningful legal regime of the continental shelf, and how their contents, force and scope could be determined.

CHAPTER IV

BILATERAL PERSPECTIVES OF THE LEGAL REGIME OF THE CONTINENTAL SHELF

With the methods and implications of shelf utilization and control already surveyed and their political and legal problems outlined in some detail, we proceed with the examination of the legal regime of the continental shelf through a study of various bilateral situations, existing or assumed. Our main aim now is to study the various relevant factors effecting the emergence of bilateral and multilateral relationships developing on the continental shelf.

AMERICAN AND BRITISH SHELF PRACTICE IN THE 1940'S

The bilateral approach both enables us and demands that we begin at the very roots of the international shelf practice, in the American mediterranean and at the time of the 1945 Truman Proclamation concerning the continental shelf. However, to consider the Truman Proclamation as a unilateral governmental act of general legal significance but unrelated to a specific situation on the continental shelf might lead to generalities.

By analysis and deduction, one may indeed reach certain conclusions as to the political and legal significance of the act; yet the abstract nature of such conclusions seriously weakens their persuasive potential.

The Truman Proclamation, by the wide scope and the reciprocal character of the policy it initiated, represents an attempt – decidedly novel in nature – of changing the extent of national territorial jurisdiction; but even in 1945 it did not face a world wholly unaware of its interest in the continental shelf resources and totally inactive in the field. One of the leading journals of the United States petroleum industry, the weekly *Oil and Gas Journal* published in Tulsa, Oklahoma, since 1902, did describe the action taken by President Truman as a "surprise Proclamation." [1] It might have been surprising indeed in the method adopted; it was not surprising in its material implications. In fact, the following inquiry into the specific relation between the United States

[1] 44 (No. 22) *Oil and Gas Journal* 72 (6 October 1945).

and Great Britain, created in 1945 by the Truman Proclamation, shows, as already discussed above, that the act of the United States Government was actually prompted by specific interests of the oil industry and its need for a climate of stability and certainty so necessary to encourage and make possible heavy investment required by exploration and exploitation of continental shelf areas under the high seas.

One may first consider the relation between the Truman Proclamation and the British Submarine Areas of the Gulf of Paria (Annexation) Order in Council of 6 August 1942. As we have seen above,[2] the Order in Council was intended primarily to implement the Treaty of the Gulf of Paria between the United Kingdom and Venezuela, and to provide for an orderly exploitation of petroleum resources of the submarine areas of the Gulf. But in fact the Order went beyond the legal scope of the bilateral Treaty and claimed for Great Britain an exclusive right to control the use of the defined shelf territory, its soil and subsoil. No country protested against the aspirations of the Order; none, until 1945, recognized and accepted its aspirations directly or indirectly.[3]

The Truman Proclamation of 1945 did constitute such a recognition by the United States. After 1945, it is difficult to imagine the United States claiming any kind of right to the resources of the Gulf of Paria shelf. Legally, the British Administration of Trinidad and Tobago might be able successfully to defend its position against any such claim by pointing out:

a) That the Truman Proclamation, publicly made and not revoked by word or deed, was sufficient for the British Government reasonably to expect and assume the United States acceptance of the British claims in the Gulf of Paria, especially since both the Proclamation and the Order in Council sought the same goal (orderly exploitation of petroleum resources) under the same conditions (undisturbed freedom of navigation on the high seas, no claim in either case to exclusive control of high sea fisheries).

b) the United States itself permitted, in accordance with its proclaimed policy, the administration and leasing of continental shelf areas under the high seas adjacent to the United States territorial waters.[4]

c) Aware of this situation, the British Administration of Trinidad and Tobago continued to administer, and permitted and encouraged investment in,[5] the Gulf of Paria continental shelf; it thus accepted responsibilities and incurred expenses it may not have so freely undertaken if the United States

[2] Pp. 73–74.

[3] The absence of protest, of course, need not be significant; as we have seen (p. 74), no overwater drilling operations were undertaken in the high seas of the Gulf until 1955, and the Order in Council itself may not have been considered an occasion for protest.

[4] Louisiana offshore lease sale in 1945, Table II, p. 52.

with its industrial and technological potential had not clearly indicated its disinterest in the Gulf of Paria submarine areas.

d) Consequently, from the British viewpoint, the Truman Proclamation would represent an estoppel potentially capable of invalidating a subsequent United States claim to the Gulf of Paria shelf resources.

But even this situation contains a strong admixture of unreality since the Gulf of Paria is but a small area of sea almost completely enclosed by Venezuelan and British land and accessible only through narrow channels. An effective exploitation of its continental shelf resources would depend on cooperation from the shore, either British or Venezuelan. The possibility of an active United States interest in asserting any right in the Gulf was in 1945 extremely remote. Furthermore, the mutual positions of the United States and Great Britain are not wholly comparable in the limited Gulf of Paria perspective; whatever might have been the effects of the Truman Proclamation seen as an estoppel to a United States claim to Gulf of Paria shelf rights, Great Britain could probably still find enough legal room if it chose to argue that in the Gulf of Paria it had acted under special geographical circumstances and on a strictly limited scale, and without any intention to affect the British position concerning the legal status of the continental shelves in general.

However, in 1945 the Gulf of Paria Order in Council and the Truman Proclamation were not the only two signs of an active American and British governmental interest in the continental shelf resources and their control. On 3 April 1945 the Bahamas Petroleum Act was passed,[6] followed by Regulations of 20 June 1945[7] made under the Act by the Governor in Council. The two documents stipulate conditions under which exploration and prospecting licenses and oil mining leases could be issued for crown and alienated lands and submarine areas, the latter being defined by article 2 of the Act as "land underlying the sea waters below high water mark." In itself, none of the two documents represents a claim, or even refers, to submarine areas under the high seas.[8] It should be noted that the Bahamas (Alteration of Boundaries) Order in Council,[9] extending the boundaries of the

[5] For early Gulf of Paria shelf activity, *cf.* p. 73, especially footnote 8.

[6] Full text in "Bahamas, Acts passed in the year 1945," No. 1, p. 1 (Nassau, 1945). Excerpts from the Act in 1 *U.N. Legislative Series* 30–31 (1951).

[7] Text with several annexed forms of exploration, prospecting and oil mining licenses and leases in Bahamas, Appendix to the Statutes of 9 George VI, Orders in Council and Rules and Regulations Made During the Year 1945.

[8] The only such reference, in a negative sense, is to be found in Article 6 of the Act, providing that no exploration and prospecting license or an oil mining lease "shall be granted in respect of New Providence *or the land underlying the sea within four miles thereof* except with the consent of the Legislature." Emphasis added.

[9] *U.N. Legislative Series* 31–32 (1951). For the chronological position of the Order in Council in relation to unilateral declarations and enactments of other countries, p. 44.

colony so as to include the adjacent continental shelf, was issued only some three years later, on 26 November 1948.

Yet still in 1945, under the authority of the Petroleum Act, the colony proceeded to regulate exploration, prospecting and oil mining activities on the adjacent shelf under the high seas. On 24 October 1945, less than a month after the Truman Proclamation, the Bahamas Petroleum Board, established under the Petroleum Act, issued two oil exploration licenses to Bahamas Oil Company, Ltd.[10] in respect of 7,801 square miles of the continental shelf area adjacent to the Colony islands. A close inspection of the area plans annexed to the licenses shows that a great majority of the submarine acreage licensed for exploration lies beneath the high seas. The larger[11] of the two areas, between Florida and Andros Island, is at some points, particularly in the vicinity of the Biminis, about 50 miles off Miami, Florida. The smaller area[12] lies southwest of the larger and is separated from it by the approximate 50-mile width of Santaren Channel.

In their form,[13] the two 1945 licenses issued to Bahamas Oil Company are identical except for area definitions and fees payable to the Petroleum Board of the Bahamas. The Board itself, a statutory corporation, is an administrative body of the Bahamas Governments. Not only does the Bahamas Petroleum Act 1945 vest the oil rights in the Government;[14] the license itself provides (clause 15) under what conditions "the Licensee shall immediately

[10] The Bahamas Oil Company, Ltd., incorporated under the laws of the Bahama Islands, was formed in 1944 as a subsidiary of the Superior Oil Company, a California corporation. It was through the courtesy of the Superior Oil Company and its attorney, F. P. Jones, Jr., that the writer was able to procure copies of four licenses granted by the Petroleum Board of the Bahamas Government to the Superior's subsidiary, and by this note he also wishes to express his gratitude for the excellent cooperation he received. The following text, unless otherwise indicated, refers to documents and correspondence supplied by the Superior Oil Company.

[11] The first of the two licenses includes a submarine area of 6,958 square miles, covering the northern part of the Great Bahama Bank east of the Straits of Florida. From its northernmost tip in the vicinity of the Isaacs Lighthouse, some twenty-five miles north of the North Bimini Island, the area is on the west side bounded by a slightly curved line running south for some 140 miles – the line marked on the license plan as the "10 fathom line" – to 24°16′ N. lat. From this line the area extends generally to the east toward Andros Island whose northern part is also included in the license. However, the land area licensed for exploration – part of Andros Island, the Biminis and certain adjoining cays – is measured separately and accounts for additional 1,195 square miles. Making a liberal allowance for submarine areas under territorial waters, one still finds more than 6,000 square miles of the continental shelf licensed for oil exploration to be under the high seas.

[12] The second oil exploration license, of the same type and issued on the same date as the first, includes what is known as the Cay Sal Bank; the major part of the 843 square miles of the submarine area covered by the license lies between 79°30′ and 80°30′ W. long., and 23°30′ and 24°10′ N. lat. Two additional square miles represent land area of the included cays. The plan annexed to the license again shows the boundary line as the "10 fathom line" – and a major portion of the licensed submarine area is again a part of the continental shelf covered by the high seas.

[13] "Form A. Oil Exploration License. Crown Lands, Alienated Lands and Submarine Areas'. *Cf.*, note 7.

[14] Article 3 of the Act. *Cf.*, note 6.

release to the Government any . . . lands or areas when required to do so by the Board." Thus, in law as well as in fact, the grant of the licenses was a governmental act.

By undertaking it, the British Government asserted its exclusive oil rights in continental shelf areas under the high seas and proceeded to assign them to private parties on an exclusive basis: in clause 1 the Petroleum Board grants to the Licensee in consideration of a certain fee "the sole right and license . . . for the term of two years . . . to explore and search the surface of the said lands and the said areas for petroleum." The same clause then reserves "to the Governor [of the Colony] full power and liberty at all times to enter into and upon and to grant or demise to any persons whomsoever liberty to enter into and upon such Crown lands and areas . . . for all and every purpose other than that for which this License is granted . . ."

The Government thus asserted for itself, and exercised, full rights of exclusive control over oil exploration on the continental shelf under the high seas. But the Petroleum Act 1945 and the license we are here discussing do not limit themselves to oil exploration. The Act provides for control over higher levels of activity as well – oil prospecting (article 12/2) and oil mining (article 12/3). By its license (clause 19), the Bahamas Oil Company was entitled to an oil prospecting license or licenses "in respect of so much of the said lands and areas as the Licensee may select." The oil prospecting license[15] in turn establishes the right of the Licensee to an oil mining lease (clause 41).

The oil exploration license issued to the Bahamas Oil Company provides still further interesting evidence as to the scope and character of the rights the British Government of the Bahamas asserted and exercised in 1945 over the continental shelf under the high seas. The license (clause 12) reserves to the Petroleum Board the right to revoke the license should the Licensee cease to be a company incorporated in the Colony. A special clause (13) provides that if the Licensee "shall be or become controlled directly or indirectly by an alien or a company incorporated outside His Majesty's dominions . . . two of the Directors and the Resident Manager shall be British subjects"; by the same clause, the Board may further require a majority of the Licensee's employees active in the licensed area to be British subjects. However, the so-called "reciprocity clause" [16] (clause 14) is in our context of a still wider importance and deserves a full quotation:

[15] "Form B. Oil Prospecting License. Crown Lands and Sub-marine Areas." A copy of a Form B license issued to Bahamas Oil Company in 1946 by the Bahamas Petroleum Board was also supplied to the writer by the Superior Oil Company.

[16] Included in the license in accordance with article 9 of the Bahamas Petroleum Act 1945, note 6.

14. This License shall be determined if the Licensee shall be or become controlled directly or indirectly by a national of or by a company incorporated in any country the laws and customs of which do not permit British subjects or companies incorporated in His Majesty's dominions or companies incorporated in that country controlled directly or indirectly by British subjects or by companies incorporated in His Majesty's dominions to acquire hold and operate petroleum concessions on conditions which in the opinion of His Majesty's Principal Secretary of State for the Colonies are reasonably comparable with the conditions upon which such rights are granted to nationals of that country with the addition of conditions corresponding to those imposed by this Clause and the immediately preceding Clause hereof.

At the time the license was issued, the Bahamas Oil Company, Ltd., was a subsidiary of the Superior Oil Company, a California corporation. In the opinion of the British Government, the applicable laws and customs of the United States obviously were comparable with those on which the license was based. The reciprocity clause was included to provide for nondiscrimination against British subjects and companies operating abroad. But the comparability of treatment depended to some degree on the continental shelf practice adopted by the United States. Should the United States view the continental shelf beyond the territorial limits as *res communis,* it could still permit, regulate and protect the activity of its nationals and of United States companies venturing onto the shelf, in the same manner as it regulates the activity of United States registered ships on the high seas – but it could not permit, regulate and protect in the same area a similar activity of foreign nationals and companies. Thus the issuance of the license – with its reciprocity clause – to the Bahamas Oil Company also represented a recognition by the British Government that the United States had established over the adjacent continental shelf a regime that would permit it to accord to British subjects and companies the same treatment as that given to the United States industry.

However, even without the reciprocity clause in the Bahamas Petroleum Act 1945 and its application in the oil exploration license issued to the Bahamas Oil Company, it is impossible to view each of the two acts, the Truman Proclamation and the British unproclaimed practice[17] in the Bahamas continental shelf, as two unrelated unilateral acts of policy and without

[17] While the Bahamas Oil Company seems to have been the first one to receive a continental shelf exploration license issued under the authority of the Bahamas Petroleum Act 1945, it was closely followed by others. In 1946, Standard Oil Company (New Jersey) launched a search for oil on 2,000 square miles of licensed submarine area off Grand Bahama Island, east of West Palm Beach, Florida, and separated from the United States mainland by the relatively deep water of the Florida Straits. News report, 122 (No. 10) *The Oil Weekly* 36 (international section, 5 August 1946); and 123 (No. 6) *The Oil Weekly* 22–23 (international section, 7 October 1946).

any legal consequences. Indeed, one could read much into clause 15 of the 1945 oil exploration license providing that:

> 15. In the event of the inclusion by inadvertence in the [attached area plans] . . . of land or areas *over which it may subsequently be proved that the Government are not entitled to the oil rights,* or of lands or areas in respect of which the oil rights have already been granted to other companies, the Licensee shall immediately release to the Government any such lands or areas when required to do so by the Board.[18]

Among other things, this clause may even be taken as an evidence of British uncertainty as to its international legal position regarding the continental shelf. However, and whatever might have been the future *erga omnes* legal effects of the British actions and of the Truman Proclamation, it seems beyond any doubt that a special normative relationship arose between the United States acting within its own sphere, and Great Britain acting on behalf of the Bahamas. In the case of a dispute, the British Government could argue that the Truman Proclamation made it believe that the United States would accept such British actions in the Bahamas shelf as were undertaken, that, acting on this justified belief or expectation, Great Britain established a special legal regime over continental shelf areas under the high seas in no essential way different from that provided for by the Truman Proclamation; and further, that by establishing that regime the British Government created in the area concerned conditions of stability giving an impetus to the oil industry to undertake there heavy investment in oil exploration and, as a result, the British Government assumed certain contractual and other obligations not to be lightly disregarded.

One can hardly insist that the normative relationship of the United States and Great Britain thus produced in 1945 was of a permanent nature. The two governments could undoubtedly change it again by acting unilaterally, but their actions would have to be parallel. One can no longer presume that the discretion of either of the two governments to practice or proclaim its own continental shelf policy remained as wide as before. The British Government, by its action on the Bahama shelf and the concurrent failure to protest against the Truman Proclamation and its application, seems to have deprived itself of the possibility to consider the continental shelf under the high seas as *res communis.*

Projected into practice, this conclusion would for instance mean the following: the British Government, allowing the United States to believe that the British shelf practice closely parallels that outlined in the Truman Proclamation, created a certain set of expectations in the United States on both

[18] Emphasis added.

the governmental and industrial level, namely, that Great Britain would claim no rights on the continental shelf under the high seas adjacent to United States territorial waters, and that it was without any visible risk for the United States Government and American oil industry to begin deliberate and unhurried preparations for exploring and exploiting its continental shelf without as yet actually venturing upon it everywhere. After permitting such expectations to exist and be acted upon, could the British Government seek legally to protect a British oil company based for instance on the Biminis and operating without a United States permit on the continental shelf under the high seas immediately outside the United States territorial waters off Miami, Florida?[19] In this case, neither *res nullius* nor *res communis* concept of the continental shelf would seem to provide sufficient defense against a possible United States contention that had Great Britain clearly indicated its disagreement with the Truman Proclamation policy, the United States would not have acted to its detriment and would have actually begun operations on the disputed shelf area so as to materially establish its rights there.

We thus submit that, in a specific case and under specific circumstances, a policy proclamation such as President Truman made, or unproclaimed practice as the British adopted, could have almost immediate though perhaps temporary effects in limiting the earlier legal discretion of the government concerned. It only remains to ask what were, in 1945, the operative legal and material elements that produced the specific United States – United Kingdom relationship with respect to the continental shelf.

The dominant legal factor in both instances – one, the United States policy *vis a vis* the British Gulf of Paria practice and, two, the United States policy *vis a vis* the British Bahamas practice – is an estoppel arising out of the reasonable expectations engendered in one government by the actions of the other. Comparing the two instances, however, it seems obvious that the estoppel may be of varied intensity under different conditions.

First, if there were only the two initial, verbal acts – the British Submarine Areas of the Gulf of Paria (Annexation) Order in Council and the Truman Proclamation – but no actual implementation of the proclaimed policies, the intensity of the estoppel would be rather weak. For instance, unless the United Kingdom could show in case of a dispute that it had actually acted in accordance with the expectations created by the Truman Proclamation

[19] The Biminis and Florida do not have a common shelf. While the distances between the Biminis and the areas immediately outside Florida's maritime limits would easily permit operations by a company based on the Biminis, the waters of the Florida Straits separating the two land areas reach maximum depths of 800 meters. Harald U. Sverdrup, Martin W. Johnson, and Richard H. Fleming, *The Oceans, Their Physics, Chemistry and General Biology* (New York: Prentice Hall, 1942), p. 37.

engaging the good faith of the United States, and that a reversal of the United States shelf practice would harm British interests which had been involved on the shelf as a result of such expectations, the estoppel could probably be overcome by a new declaration of policy. By implication, the effectiveness of the initial estoppel produced by the formal and verbal acts would increase when the policy enactments are acted upon; and they would increase in proportion to the volume of the material involvement in the newly created international situation.

Second, it is likewise obvious that the actual length of time elapsed since the inception of the policy is an element of dubious importance; if the United States and the United Kingdom each only proclaimed a shelf policy and never actually acted in accordance with it although they could have had, it is likely that the effectiveness of the policy statements would gradually decrease while the unrealized intentions would become buried deeper and deeper in some not very significant recesses of history. In the bilateral situation of the United States and the United Kingdom, the duration of time necessary to elapse would seem to be only that necessary for communicating the policy of the one to the other – a rather swift process considering the political closeness of the two states, the immediate geographical neighborhood of the seabed areas involved, and the common and lively interest of both countries in the public order of the seas and their properties.

Third, one may ask if anything definable as *opinio juris* could have possibly attended the initial actions of the two states. There is certainly no indication in the original acts of the United States and the United Kingdom that either government acted with the conviction that it was obligated to act in that particular way. At the most, one can only assume that each of the two governments merely hoped to have its own continental shelf policy accepted by other states as one consistent with the existing international law. But, while it would be difficult to read more into the Truman Proclamation and into the British acts, one can say without much strain that both governments probably acted with the knowledge that their shelf practice entails certain modifications in the then existing law of the sea, or at the least that their practice might eventually lead to an addendum to the body of legal rules. After the two countries adopted the new shelf policies and an estoppel between them arose, then, of course, one might search for *opinio juris sive necessitatis* as a motive behind *further* governmental acts and omissions. For instance, the fact that an American oil company obtained from the British authorities in Bahamas a lease entitling it to exclusive rights of oil exploration in the seabed under the high seas adjacent to Bahamas territorial waters, and that the United States made no diplomatic or other moves to deter the

British from exercising exclusive control over the areas involved, may be attributed to the conviction of the United States Government that it was legally bound not to interfere due to the estoppel created by the Truman Proclamation and by further acts implementing it. However, it is unnecessary to search for this type of *opinio juris*; in the situation described, it does not represent one of the prerequisites for the emergence of a legal relationship but a consequence of it. Here it can be simply defined as an admission by the United States that, as far as its relationship with the British administration in the Bahamas was concerned, it had an obligation not to act otherwise. The essential point here is, of course, that there is no need to expect and look for any *opinio juris* as a precondition of the emergence of a local custom between the United States and the United Kingdom. Even if the newly adopted practice represented a radical departure from the then existing international law, the legal force of the estoppel between the two countries would be thereby undiminished.

Summed up, the legal fabric of the newly created relation between the United States and the British Government, having the character of a mutually operative estoppel, consists of certain expectations created by the acts of one state in the other – expectations, that is, which need to be fulfilled in the interests of public order.

But what are the limits of that relation? What could the United States and the United Kingdom reasonably expect, and demand, from one another? Answers can be best sought through artificially constructed situations that could conceivably develop between the two countries during the 1945-1948 period.

1. Seaward limits of shelf rights

Throughout the first three years in question, the actual administrative practice of both the United States and the United Kingdom was limited to relatively narrow strips of seabed under the high seas adjacent to the territorial waters. The practice was thus confined to the continental shelf in its strict geographical sense and nowhere even approached its geographical seaward edges. The United States policy, outlined in the Truman Proclamation and interpreted in other official statements, likewise contains nothing to indicate that the policy framers intended to claim exclusive rights on the seabed beyond the geographical boundaries of the continental shelf.[20] The

[20] On geographical limits of shelf rights claimed in 1945 by the United States Government, see pp. 81–82. For an official view, in our opinion erroneous, advanced in 1960 and suggesting that the Truman Proclamation should have been understood as claiming submarine areas even beyond the geographical limits of th continental shelf, see pp. 108 ff. and accompanying note 144.

British policy was not embodied in proclamations and its geographical reach can therefore be measured only with reference to administrative practice such as, for instance, the leasing of shelf areas for exploration and exploitation. Only in November 1948 the Bahamas (Alteration of Boundaries) Order in Council was passed to extend the boundaries of the Bahamas so as to include "the area of the continental shelf" "beneath the sea contiguous" to their coasts[21] – but even here nothing disturbs the accumulated evidence that both countries did not define the continental shelf by anything except geographical and geological criteria. Under these conditions, the United States seems to have had the right to expect that the United Kingdom would not seek for its ships and firms uncontrolled access to the shelf resources in the Gulf of Mexico; but the United Kingdom would have been still legally free to demand from the United States non-interference should British-flag ships engage, for instance, in the dredging for phosphate some fifty or sixty miles off California coast under waters over 500 fathoms deep as long as that area could be reliably defined as not forming a geographical part of the continental shelf – an area, that is, which was later described with reference to the exploitability limit as a part of the United States legally defined continental shelf.[22]

2. *Functional limits of shelf rights*

As to the mutual American and British expectations concerning the functional limits of coastal shelf rights, the actual practice of shelf administration was in both cases identical; it was confined to oil exploration and exploitation. As we have seen earlier, the Truman Proclamation directly asserted no exclusive rights for the United States other than those of jurisdiction and control over the exploration and exploitation of the natural resources of the shelf, with a heavy emphasis on subterranean mineral resources.[23] But the Bahamas (Alteration of Boundaries) Order in Council of November 1948 sought to do exactly what its title suggests: to incorporate fully the area of the adjacent continental shelf so that it would make an integral part of the sovereign domain of the Bahamas. But, before the Order in Council was issued, the British authorities had been exercising on the Bahamas shelf exclusive rights only of control over the use of petroleum resources. It may thus be said that in this narrow area – the control over petroleum shelf resources –

21 1 *U.N. Legislative Series* (1951) 31.
22 Pp. 108 ff.
23 Pp. 81 ff.

the practices of both states were sufficiently parallel to form a mutually operative estoppel. But what would be their mutual legal position should the United States decide to erect, without first securing British consent, some type of a non-military observation tower on the Bahamas shelf not far beyond the outer limit of the territorial waters of Bahamas? Politically speaking, this hypothetical situation is, of course, highly improbable. But its legal complexion, though not very clear-cut, can be defined: the British government, should it object against the United States course of action, could rely on both the text and the spirit of the Truman Proclamation. It could argue, perhaps with success, that the expectations aroused by earlier American acts and relied upon by the United Kingdom in its Bahamas shelf policy were not entirely confined to the exploitation of mineral resources. In fact, the argument could continue, one of the reasons why the British authorities accepted the American practice and followed it on the Bahamas shelf was the argument set out in the Truman Proclamation that "... self-protection compels the coastal nation to keep close watch over activities off its shores which are of the nature necessary for utilization of these resources" – that is, as the entire text of the document suggested, activities connected with over-water exploitation of mineral resources such as oil and involving the erection of relatively permanent platforms, towers and other similar installations. The United States thus estopped itself from asserting that the erection on the Bahamas shelf of a similar installation, though used for purposes other than mineral exploitation, lies within the scope of legal discretion the United States might have possessed before 1945.

3. Problem of state responsibility

One needs to consider if any expectations could have been created by the shelf policy of the United States and Great Britain in the area of state responsibility. Again, an artificially constructed case illustrates the problem: A fishing boat under the British flag, operating on the high seas in the northern Gulf of Mexico outside the usual lines of navigation, suffers damage by hitting at night an unlighted oil-drilling platform. The operator of the platform was licensed by the United States Government. The obvious question is whether the United States responsibility could have been engaged by the then existing practice of the two countries – and the answer appears to be that it could have been so engaged. Since the very inception of their continental shelf practice both the United States and the British authorities on the Bahamas ordered and regulated the use of safety and warning devices on the shelf installations. Even if the primary and perhaps the only motivation here were in each case the national concern for maintaining an easy access to the ports and thus their prosperity, the shipping of the other party had a right to expect that every installation would employ some system of reasonably clear signals to warn passing ships. Should the British vessel fail to obtain redress through local remedies within the United States, the British authorities would have a strong case when demanding satisfaction on the intergovernmental level.[24]

As in all situations artificially constructed and, therefore, without the often decisive details of an actual case, one cannot reach conclusions as exact as might be those of a court dealing with a specific issue. However, it would appear that all a policy-maker himself usually has when defining the international legal position of his state as a guide to the state's future conduct are, in fact, mainly artificially constructed, hypothetical situations. His question would necessarily be how much legal room would he have for a contemplated political move in the light of the earlier acts of his own state and in the light of the relevant practices of other countries, and whether and how he could defend his acts should one or another foreign state protest. In a quest for a meaningful assessment, an analysis of the legal position of the state *vis a vis* other individual countries would seem to be the most accessible road. Should the United States face in 1947 a question concerning its rights and duties with respect to the outer continental shelf, it could hardly resolve it by reference to some general rules of law comprising a definite legal regime of the shelf: What rules could it then have discovered that would apply equally to its position *vis a vis* Great Britain as well as *vis a vis* the Soviet Union, then without any known shelf policy and practice, and also *vis a vis* a disinterested and landlocked country such as Afghanistan? But it could assess the scope of its newly formed legal relationships in bilateral terms by adopting some such method of inquiry as we have employed above.

To sum up the section concerning the effects of the shelf practice adopted by the United States and the United Kingdom during the 1945-1948 period, one might say that due to reasonable expectations aroused in each of the two countries by the acts of the other, each was entitled to assert certain rights and was obligated to fulfill specific duties towards the other; namely, each was estopped, at the least, from demanding for its subjects or itself free

[24] At this point, we are concerned only with the legal situation as it existed bilaterally, between the United States and the United Kingdom. on the continental shelves controlled by the two governments. Of course, the question of coastal state's responsibility for the safety of foreign users of the high seas above the utilized areas of the continental shelf invites an inquiry into multilateral legal relations produced by the continental shelf practice, a problem dealt with further below.

access to the mineral resources in the geographically defined continental shelf massif adjacent to the coasts of the other, and each was obligated, at least as against the other, to maintain reasonable safety standards on the high seas above the utilized portions of its own shelf. As to the factors which had produced this bilateral legal relationship, there appears to be no need to force them into any specific category such as (a) the repetition of governmental acts (b) spread over a long period of time and (c) accompanied by *opinio juris*. The bilateral relationship itself might be described as a tacit agreement effected by actions giving rise to the mutually parallel estoppels limiting the legal discretion of each of the two states. And what was necessary for the unilateral acts of each to have that legal effect was the clarity of the political intent behind the acts, and the time needed for reliably communicating that intent from one party to the other. It is somewhat difficult to find an *opinio juris* in the motives of the two states at the inception of their shelf practices.

COASTAL RIGHT OF EXCLUSIVE CONTROL IN BILATERAL PERSPECTIVES

To arrive at a relatively reliable picture of the varied legal relationships of individual countries ordering their shelf policies, the resort to imaginary situations must be tempered by an effort to base the artificial contructions on ascertained facts. Since 1945, there have been between the various states no actual bilateral situations, publicly dealt with, in which the existence of rules comprising the legal regime of the continental shelf was discussed in any detail. However, for the want of a better case, one might take the 1951 Abu Ahabi arbitration and project specific artificially constructed issues against its situational background.

The Abu Dhabi arbitration[25] was to settle a dispute concerning the interpretation of a written contract of 1939 between Sheikh Shakhbut, the ruler of Abu Dhabi, and Petroleum Development (Trucial Coast) Ltd., a British oil firm. Set up under an arbitration clause of the contract, the adjudication was not an international one; possibly not even quasi-international in the sense in which the term is implied regarding the so-called quasi-treaties between independent states and foreign companies, since Abu Dhabi was a British-protected entity whose foreign relations were controlled by Great Britain. The arbitration has received wide attention in international legal writ-

[25] The text of the Abu Dhabi Award of Lord Asquith of Bishopstone appears in the United States Naval War College, *International Law Situation and Documents* 1956 (Washington, D.C.: Government Printing Office, 1957), pp. 137–155. References to the Award in the present section – *e.g.* Award 154 – are to the text and page of the United States Naval War College volume.

ings for two reasons: because Lord Asquith of Bishopstone, the umpire, delivered with his award a reasoned opinion on the legal status of the continental shelf doctrine, and due to the prominence of counsel – among the legal representatives of the oil company was Professor H. Lauterpacht and, on behalf of the Sheikh, Professor C. H. M. Waldock, in addition to others.

Yet the arbitration, limited as it was in legal international significance, does furnish a realistic background for our problem.

The issue arose primarily from article 2(a) of the agreement between the Sheikh and Petroleum Development (Trucial Coast) Ltd. reading –

> Article 2. (a) The area included in this Agreement is the whole of the lands which belong to the rule of the Ruler of Abu Dhabi and its dependencies and all the islands and the sea waters which belong to that area. And if in the future the lands which belong to Abu Dhabi are defined by agreement with other States, then the limits of the area shall coincide with the limits specified in this definition.[26]

– and from the Sheik's decision in 1949 to award oil mining rights in the subsoil of submarine areas under the high seas adjacent to Abu Dhabi's territorial waters to a foreign oil firm, a wholly-owned subsidiary of The Superior Oil Company of California, a decision disputed by Petroleum Development (Trucial Coast) Ltd. who claimed to own such rights by the terms of the agreement.[27]

The first finding of the umpire was that the 1939 agreement did assign to the British company oil rights in the seabed and subsoil of Abu Dhabi's territorial waters – rights disputed by the Sheikh.[28]

Secondly, the umpire refused to "read back into the contract the implications of . . . [the shelf] doctrine not mooted till seven years later, and . . . not even today admitted to the cannon of international law." [29] This view was based on a brief but broadly based inquiry as to the existence of an unwritten rule of international law governing the shelf – an inquiry touching upon such problems as the divergent shelf and high sea claims of individual states, the uncertainties of the seaward shelf limits, the technical difficulties of shelf apportionment in shallow seas with irregular configuration such as the North Sea, as well as the question whether occupation of the subsoil is possible, and whether it can be effected by a unilateral proclamation. Lord Asquith opined that all these were questions mostly unresolved either by the practice of nations or by the pronouncements of learned jurists, and that "in no form can the doctrine claim as yet to have assumed . . . the definitive status of

[26] Award 139–140, translation by the Sheikh relied upon by Lord Asquith. See Award 142.
[27] Award 138–139.
[28] Award 144.
[29] Award 145.

an established rule of international law." [30] The umpire thus rejected the company's premise "that the doctrine of the Shelf has become and, indeed, was already in 1939, part of the *corpus* of international law." [31]

Thirdly, and on the basis of the foregoing, the umpire also denied[32] the company's claim resting on the second provision of article 2(a) of the agreement – and it may be repeated:

And if in the future the lands which belong to Abu Dhabi are defined by agreement with other States, then the limits of the area shall coincide with the limits specified in this definition.

The company argued that by this provision the leased area was expressly extended to any after-acquired area of Abu Dhabi; and that the effect of the Abu Dhabi proclamation of 10 June 1949, by which the Sheikh declared the contiguous submarine areas under the high seas to "appertain to the land of Abu Dhabi . . . subject to its exclusive jurisdiction and control," [33] if not retrospective, cannot be less than to add the shelf to the area originally covered as from the date when the proclamation was promulgated. The umpire rejected this argument; by implication he thus held that the Sheikh's proclamation had no legal effect if it did not have the broadest one possible – to make an *erga omnes* rule of law operate for Abu Dhabi as well.

Fourthly, according to the Award, the argument based on the future-oriented provision of contract article 2 (a) would have failed independently of the question of a legal rule governing the shelf, since there had been no definition of anything "by agreement with other States." [34] This in itself invites some questions. Did Lord Asquith interpret the phrase "by agreement with other States" to mean "with all other states?" Obviously not, since he also stated, albeit passingly, that in his opinion the entire future-oriented provision affected only dry land[35] – in other words, that it involved only the determination of Abu Dhabi's vague boundaries with Qatar, Dubai, and Saudi Arabia.[36] Yet the umpire's earlier assertion that there had been no

[30] Award 149.
[31] Award 150.
[32] Award 152.
[33] Award 148.
[34] Award 152.
[35] *Id.*
[36] Abu Dhabi's boundaries with the two Sheikhdoms – Qatar to the west and Dubai to the east – are said to be vague only to some extent. In the interior, however, Abu Dhabi's territory virtually blends into the sands of Rub' al Khali desert of Saudi Arabia. The Award mentions (at 137) that the interior boundary is so indeterminate that Abu Dhabi's area has been estimated at anything from 10,000 to 26, 000 square miles.Yet a look into the standard world gazeteer, usually reliable, suggests that the uncertainty may be still graeter: the total area of all seven Sheikhdoms comprising the Trucial Oman, Abu Dhabi included, is said to be about 6,000 square miles. See Rand McNally (publ.). *World Guide* (New York: 1953), p. 328.

definition of anything "by agreement with other States" comes back: while there was no formal treaty signed between Abu Dhabi and the surrounding states concerning their respective adjacent submarine areas, they all acted on them in unison. Not only did Dubai and Qatar, the two coastal neighbors of Abu Dhabi, as well as the other six Arab Sheikhdoms under British protection, issue the same proclamation as Sheikh Shakhbut, uniformly claiming that "the right of any littoral State to exercise its control over the natural resources of the seabed and subsoil adjacent to its coasts has been established in international practice by the action of other States";[37] Saudi Arabia, their closest neighbor on the Persian Gulf, preceded them by days with its Royal Pronouncement[38] essentially the same as their proclamations. One need not go any further; the question whether all these actions did not actually constitute an agreement – though a tacit one, of regional scope and without any general effect – offers itself quite forcefully.

Against this background of the Abu Dhabi case we may now project specific, artificially constructed situations to study the elements involved in ascertaining the existence of customary legal rules.

Situation 1: Abu Dhabi v. Petroleum Development (Trucial Coast) Ltd.

In essence, Lord Asquith adjudged as correct the Sheikh's contention that the contract in question did not give Petroleum Development (Trucial Coast) Ltd. any rights over submarine areas under the high seas contiguous with Abu Dhabi's territorial waters. Such would be the meaning of the umpire's statement that "the Sheikh succeeds as to the subsoil of the Shelf" [39] since, while delivering his opinion, the umpire in no way suggested, and in fact denied, that the submarine areas in question legally fell under the Sheikh's rule.

Upon this ground one may erect the following construction: If Petroleum Development Company had no persuasive political reasons to act otherwise, or if it felt free and were willing to risk substantial investments, it conceivably could proceed to explore and exploit the submarine areas under the high seas contiguous with Abu Dhabi's territorial waters. Doing so, the company could shield itself against the Sheikh's protests by the legal umbrella of Lord Asquith's award which nowhere showed the disputed submarine areas as falling under the Sheikh's rule. What would be Sheikh Shakhbut's position?

[37] 1 *U.N. Legislative Series* 23–30.
[38] *Ibid.* 22.
[39] Award 154.

A. He could not rely on a general customary rule specifically denied by Lord Asquith. Nor on his own proclamation by which he declared the adjacent submarine areas under the high seas to appertain to Abu Dhabi, since the umpire clearly considered that proclamation to have had no legal effect other than that of one of the many elements from which, sometime in the future, a binding rule may emerge. And he could not even rely on his own assertion of 1939 at the time the company's contract was negotiated that the adjacent seas to a distance as much as 100 miles from Abu Dhabi's coast belonged under his rule, for Lord Asquith found that assertion to have been "a rhetorical flourish" of the same class as "Britannia rules the waves" rather than "a sober contractual stipulation." [40]

B. The Sheikh could not easily acquiesce in the company's view of the submarine areas beyond the three-mile line as *res nullius* or *res communis*. To do so, he would be choosing a dangerous policy of inconsistency; by submitting to the company's claim and action he might seriously threaten or even void his own proclamation of 10 June 1949. For if he should fail to assert his control over the adjacent submarine areas regarding Petroleum Development Ltd., why should not, for instance, the Arabian-American Oil Company operating in Saudi Arabia also freely indulge in exploring and exploiting the outer submarine areas adjacent to Abu Dhabi,[41] declared by Lord Asquith and shown by the Sheikh as areas controlled by no one?

C. The third course the Sheikh could take to prevent Petroleum Development Ltd. from freely developing the submarine areas adjacent to Abu Dhabi may seem somewhat unusual but not impossible. His dispute being with a private company and not a state, he could possibly base his case on the following points: (1) In line with Lord Asquith award, the Sheikh could admit that no new and generally binding principle of international customary law gives him exclusive rights over the adjacent submarine areas. (2) Again in line with the Award, he could consider his own proclamation of 10 June 1949 and his further acts of control over the disputed areas as mere stepping stones toward the eventual establishment of those rights. (3) Thus the submarine areas in question, not yet fully under Abu Dhabi's control and jurisdiction, could not automatically fall under the company's contract with the Sheikh even if the terms of the contract would otherwise apply to them. (4) But the Sheikh could also maintain that, as a ruler of Abu Dhabi, he was

[40] Award 153.

[41] Aramco had the technical means as well as the experience necessary for such a venture. There is, of course, no indication whatsoever that the company ever contemplated any similar move. Whatever may have been the legal status of Abu Dhabi's outer submarine areas after the Award and its possible consequences in our artificially constructed situations, it was in the interest of the oil companies active in and around the Persian Gulf not to disturb the orderly regime of coastal jurisdiction being established there, even if it was a system costly to the companies.

entitled, *vis a vis* a private company, to an opportunity to test internationally his policy regarding the adjacent submarine areas – to test, in fact, the acceptance of, or acquiescence in, his policy by other states. And this could perhaps be taken as one form of a practical definition and application of what has been called an imperfect or inchoate right.

Situation 2: United States v. Abu Dhabi (Great Britain)

But the problem, again stripped of political realities down to its legal bones, has much wider implications. One can visualize the following sequence of events: (1) Petroleum Development Ltd., in line with Lord Asquith's 1951 award, proceeds in 1952 to explore and exploit outer submarine areas adjacent to Abu Dhabi, on the theory that if they do not fall under the Sheikh's control anyone may exploit them freely. (2) The subsidiary of American-owned The Superior Oil Company of California, to whom the Sheikh had leased the submarine areas in question for fees and royalties, refuses to pay but continues its own exploration and exploitation activities and, faced with serious objections by the Sheikh, turns in 1953 through its parent company to the United States Government for assistance.

Our problem now is the problem the United States Government would face if it were willing and able to take diplomatic action along legal lines on behalf of The Superior Oil Company. However, the United States would be dealing not with Abu Dhabi but with Great Britain as the power protecting the Trucial Sheikhdoms and representing them internationally. How could the United States construct its case?

A. It could hardly maintain that submarine areas under the high seas are a *res communis* to be freely exploited by the first comer. In fact, by bringing up such an argument the United States would expressly revoke the policy initiated by the Truman Proclamation and, thereby, seriously endanger the accomplished implementation of that policy on the entire continental shelf adjacent to its territorial areas. Even then, however, it might find it extremely difficult to maintain the *res communis* argument in the specific case of Abu Dhabi. It could still be confronted with the formidable objection by Great Britain as well as by other countries that, by having maintained its previous continental shelf policy for eight years and by implementing it administratively[42] and legislatively,[43] the United States created a definite

[42] See the estimate at p. 64 that, in 1948, some sixty governmental agencies of the United States were directly involved in the implementation of the continental shelf policy.

[43] The Committee on Interior and Insular Affairs of the United States Senate hald a number of public hearings between 1949 and 1953 with a view to legislating in conformity with the

expectation on the part of other countries that it would not claim any rights on the continental shelf adjacent to their respective coasts; and that it was therefore estopped from claiming such rights wherever the expectation has been acted upon, as in the Sheikhdoms of the Trucial Coast, and wherever the reversal of United States policy would work to the detriment of such countries.

B. Next – and with a slightly lesser strain on imagination – the United States could rely on the *res nullius* concept of the shelf, and thus on the law governing the acquisition of territorial rights by occupation. In the present situation the United States could argue that the Sheikh of Abu Dhabi, by suffering on outer submarine areas adjacent to Abu Dhabi the uncontrolled activities of Petroleum Development Ltd., had abdicated the right to perfect his claim to control over such areas, and without a valid title had no right to interfere with the interests of the American-owned company. Whatever form the United States' representation would take, by espousing the *res nullius* concept the United States would encounter a number of problems.

First, it would again jeopardize its entire continental shelf policy by officially renouncing the terms and spirit of reciprocity[44] embodied in the 1945 Truman Proclamation, since reciprocity is clearly foreign to the law of territorial acquisition by occupation.

Second, by insisting on material acts of occupation beyond the initial manifestation of a mere *animus occupandi* expressed by governmental decrees and proclamations of the kind Sheikh Shakhbut and President Truman had made, the United States would throw serious doubt on the legal status of most of its continental shelf. Most probably the United States would be able to defend its rights on the continental shelf in the Gulf of Mexico where it had encouraged considerable investment accompanied by multiple and continuous acts of state control.[45] It is also likely that it could defend for itself its rights over the entire Gulf of Mexico continental shelf adjacent to the United States by showing that it represents a geopolitical and economic

continental shelf doctrine as promulgated by President Truman. See U.S. Congress, Senate, Committee on Interior and Insular Affairs, under the title *Submerged Lands*, Hearings on: S.155, S.923, S. 1545, S.1700, S.2153, held 4–10 October 1949 (81st Congress, 1st Sess.); on S.J. Res. 195, held 14–19 August 1950 (81st Congress., 2nd Sess,); on S.J. Res. 13, S.294, S.107, S.107, Amendm., S.J. Res. 18, held 10, 17–20 and 23–27 February and 2–4 March 1953 (83rd Congress, 1st Sess.); on S.1901, S. 1901Amendm., held 16, 18–23, 25 and 28 May and 1 June 1953 (83rd Congress, 1st Sess.). And, also, U.S. Congress, House of Representatives, Committee on Interior and Insular Affairs, *Investigation and Study of the Seaward Boundaries of the United States*, Report, 1953 (82nd Congress, 2nd Sess., H. Rept. 2515). The Outer Continental Shelf Lands Act (67 Stat. 462) was approved on 7 August 1953.

44 On the terms and spirit of reciprocity of the 1945 Truman Proclamation see pp. 75–79.

45 See sections on the industrial and state involvement on the United States continental shelf in the Gulf of Mexico, pp. 52–53 and 59–63.

unit – a well-defined geographical whole[46] within which a uniform system could best serve the requirements of order and security as well as those of economical exploitation and exploration. It is doubtful, though, whether the full effects of the acts of occupation in the Gulf of Mexico could be said to radiate to areas east of Florida and, perhaps, to those off the entire Atlantic coast. And it is impossible to imagine that such effects could be reasonably seen as crossing the Isthmus to apply off California, Washington, Oregon, Alaska and Hawaii.

Third, the British position would be affected but little. The British Government would have an opportunity to attempt expanding westward, and as far as the three-mile distance from the shores of Florida, its well-established control over the continental shelf of the Bahamas.[47] It might or might not be able to defend such actions by reference to occupation leading to territorial acquisition. However, the reliance by the United States on the *res nullius* concept of the shelf would obviously erase the estoppel – created through the reciprocal meaning of the Truman Proclamation and the British acquiescense in it – on British freedom of action.[48]

Fourth, even the adoption of the *res nullius* concept of the shelf and the demand for effective occupation and control may be insufficient to defend the United States claim that the submarine areas adjacent to Abu Dhabi are a *res nullius* without a ruler. The British Government could again argue with force that the United States was estopped from pressing such contention by the eight years during which it maintained a reciprocal policy of the continental shelf and thus created a justified expectation on the part of Great Britain and of Sheikh Shakhbut that the United States Government would claim no rights on outer submarine areas adjacent to foreign coasts. Had the United States originally adopted the *res nullius* concept coupled with the demand for effective occupation, the British argument could continue, all necessary steps would have been taken long ago by the British and Abu Dhabi authorities to establish and perfect Abu Dhabi's territorial title in the adjacent submarine areas. As always in estoppel cases, the general principle of good faith was engaged and could not be disregarded.

C. Thus there would seem to be but one accessible road open to the United States if the rights of the American-owned company on Abu Dhabi's outer submarine areas were to be reasonably protected. After advising the company to pay to the Sheik the agreed fees and royalties, the United States

[46] On the question of geographical limits within which acts of occupation may be recognized as effectively creating a title see Norman L. Hill, *Claims to Territory in International Law and Relations* (New York: Oxford University Press, 1945), pp. 146–154.

[47] See pp. 124 ff. above on British practice in the Bahamas.

[48] See discussion of estoppel on British freedom of action in the Caribbean at pp. 128 ff.

Government could proceed to defend the company's right to work undisturbed on its leased area and under conditions stipulated by its contract with the Sheikh. This, in effect, would be a demand on the Sheikh to reassert his exclusive control over the submarine areas in question in the exercise of which he had signed the contract, and to exclude from the licensed acreage those operating there unlawfully.

Situation 3: Japan v. Abu Dhabi (Great Britain)

It remains to be seen what legal relationships could be detected if we inject into our picture a new element: the right freely to explore and exploit the outer submarine areas adjacent to Abu Dhabi now asserted by a state without any heretofore proclaimed or practiced continental shelf rights. Choosing between France and Japan as two countries with a well developed and internationally active oil industry to which the Persian Gulf has not been without interest,[49] one is inclined to select Japan because of its more pronounced views concerning the exclusive coastal control over the adjacent continental shelf. The French delegate at the 1958 Geneva Conference simply held that Committee IV of the Conference "had the opportunity of legislating in a field not previously regulated by international law." [50] The Japanese delegate, on the other hand, stated in the early stages of the Conference that Japan found it difficult

> to admit that it was necessary to vest a monopoly of rights in the coastal State. The Conference was dealing with a new concept, and it was accordingly important that the interests of the whole international community should be considered rather than those of any nation or group of nations.[51]

[49] In 1955, Compagnie Française des Petroles actually started exploratory work on a large Abu Dhabi offshore concession obtained from Sheikh Shakhbut. In 1957, the Japanese Petroleum Development (Export) Company acquired large offshore concessions from Saudi Arabia and Kuwait.

[50] U.N. Conference on the Law of the Sea, 6 *Official Records* 22, para. 36. During the forty-two meetings of Committee IV and in the three plenary meetings devoted to the continental shelf, the French delegation actively participated in the shaping of the draft convention by discussion and proposals.

[51] *Ibid.* 14, para 1. The second and last contribution by the Japanese delegation to Committee IV discussions came thirteen days and eleven meetings later, after the general debate had been closed, views of the majority of states presented, a recommendation by the Federal Republic of Germany for an internationalization of continental shelves (U.N. Doc. A/CONF.13/C.4/L.1 in *ibid.* 125) virtually ignored and pushed aside, and the first article defining the continental shelf adopted by 51 votes to 9 with 10 abstentions (*ibid.* 47); only then, obviously accepting the demonstrated political realities, did the Japanese delegate admit that "unfortunately the solution of international exploitation [of submarine resources as a source of prosperity for mankind] ... was not yet feasible." *Ibid.* 56, para. 11. In the plenary meetings, Japanese voice was heard but twice on problems of the continental shelf: when the Japanese delegate stressed that in Committee IV his delegation did not vote for any of the substantive draft articles on the regime of the

Under these circumstances, the following legal construction may be erected on the background of the Abu Dhabi problem as it existed in 1953.

A Japanese oil company, considering Lord Asquith's award and Sheikh Shakhbut's submission to the uncontrolled activity by Petroleum Development Ltd. on the outer submarine areas adjacent to Abu Dhabi as opening the door to free exploitation of such areas by anyone, proceeded to explore and exploit them. Faced by the Sheikh's interference, the Japanese firm turned for protection to Tokyo. Japan then approached the British Government through diplomatic channels and with a legal argument based on the view that submarine areas under the high seas are a *res communis* and therefore, while not appropriable by anyone, open to use by all. Obviously, Japan was not estopped from choosing that course by any positive action on its own part. Could it be found estopped by its failure to act at an earlier time?

A. The British Government could remind Japan that in June 1949 Sheikh Shakhbut proclaimed the submarine areas under the high seas adjacent to Abu Dhabi to be subject to his exclusive jurisdiction and control, and proceeded to control their uses. In a sense, the arbitration with Lord Asquith as umpire was one of the instances showing that the Sheikh did intend to control those areas, for otherwise there would be no cause for the arbitration. During the arbitration itself the Sheikh had contended not any lack of title to control the outer submarine areas but an absence of duty on his part to consider them as falling under the terms of his 1939 contract with Petroleum Development Ltd. And in any case Japan could not rely on the Award as it was applicable only to the essentially domestic relations between Abu Dhabi and a private company and not to those of the generality of nations. Finally, the British Foreign Office could point out that the Government of Japan had failed to protest effectively against the Sheikh's assumption of exclusive control and jurisdiction over the disputed areas; that it had permitted Abu Dhabi reasonably to expect for four years that the latter's claim to control the submarine areas was sound and well-established; and therefore the Government of Japan was now estopped from claiming on those areas rights whose existence it had not asserted in time.

Provided the British response was as simple as indicated, Japan could hope to succeed only by showing that the alleged estoppel had insufficient time, and roots too weak, to come to existence. First, only four years elapsed from the Sheikh's proclamation, not long enough to enable a state that might have considered itself as possessing rights in the disputed areas, or having

continental shelf except draft article 74 providing for compulsory settlement of disputes (*ibid.* 106, para. 44, and 2 *Official Records* 19, para. 49), and when he explained that he had voted against the Convention because no reservations were admitted to the first three articles and because article 74 had been rejected. *Ibid.* 57, para. 36.

a claim to such rights, to have – taking into account the complicated relation of the Sheikhdom of Abu Dhabi to Great Britain, Abu Dhabi's unsettled and purely discretionary system of justice,[52] and the fact that the disputed areas of several thousand square miles are beneath the sea – a reasonable possibility for ascertaining the existence of a state of things contrary to its rights. Second, the existing state of things was the more difficult to ascertain as there were but very few manifestations of Sheikh Shakhbut's control over the outer submarine areas; beyond his initial proclamation, he did no more than to decide to lease the disputed areas to a foreign oil company, and submitted to an arbitration initiated by the action of another private company – an arbitration resulting in an award giving no support to the Sheikh's stand. Third, the Japanese Government cannot be estopped from defending its rights in the outer submarine areas adjacent to Abu Dhabi by an allegation that Japan, by its four-year silence, permitted the economic life of Abu Dhabi to become materially attuned to revenues obtained through its control of the areas in question, and the Abu Dhabi Government to undertake investments and establish any special administrative apparatus in prosecution of its disputed policies. The economic involvement of Abu Dhabi in the outer submarine areas adjacent to it was even lesser than the political involvement.

At this point, some reorientation of our inquiry is necessary. Admittedly, in the narrow confines of a Japan *v*. Abu Dhabi (Great Britain) dispute, the Japanese Government could succeed in demonstrating persuasively that it was not estopped by its four-year silence from claiming, in 1953, its own rights in the disputed submarine areas adjacent to Abu Dhabi. However, a right to claim is not a right to get. Could, then, the Japanese Government defend its substantive rights off Abu Dhabi?

Any such defense would inevitably lead from the relatively simple relations between Japan and Abu Dhabi (Great Britain) into those of the generality of states. The Japanese Government would have to defend its rights in the disputed areas as arising from the *res communis* concept of the continental shelf. But Japan would not be taking the *res communis* stand entirely because it was so inclined and by its free choice; in fact, the *res nullius* view would be a largely impractical alternative since Japan could hardly aspire to establish on the submarine areas off Abu Dhabi an exclusive title superior to that of Sheikh Shakhbut. Here our situation necessarily expands.

B. Defending its inclusive rights, Japan would run into two related and difficult questions. (1) Could the Japanese Government, acting alone, defend on the disputed submarine areas off Abu Dhabi specific rights for the entire international community without first showing that the members of that

[52] So described by Lord Asquith, *Award* 142.

community were aware of, and anxious to retain, such rights? (2) The Sheikh's proclamation of Abu Dhabi's exclusive control over the disputed submarine areas, though a unilateral act, was but a response to, and in recognition of,[53] similar acts by other countries regarding similar areas off their respective coasts; was not the Japanese Government now estopped from claiming inclusive rights off Abu Dhabi's coasts by its failure from 1945[54] and on until the present to take appropriate action with a view to stopping a chain of developments it now considers unlawful?

One may be inclined to believe that the two above questions in fact, and under all circumstances, represent but one: a question whether or not, at the time, there existed a general rule of international customary law giving to the coastal state exclusive rights on the adjacent outer continental shelf, a rule resting primarily on the practice of several nations and acquiescence by many, *i.e.*, on a general international consensus. We have seen, however, how inconclusive were the debates concerning the existence of such a rule, and it is unlikely that Japan could answer the problem convincingly.

If obliged to answer the two questions, could the Japanese Government reasonably avoid addressing itself to the problem of a general customary rule of international law? It seems that it could so avoid it by an exact and painfully detailed examination of its actual legal relations with individual

[53] According to the Sheikh's proclamation, "the right of any littoral State to exercise its control over the natural resources of the seabed and subsoil adjacent to its coasts has been established in international practice by the action of other States." 1 *U.N. Legislative Series* 23 (1951).

[54] Not to complicate the situation unnecessarily, the postwar status of Japan as an occupied country is here generally disregarded. However, one might be able to defend the contention that Japan, when it regained the status of a sovereign state, was still obligated to honor such commitments as it may have had undertaken through its actions or inaction while under "hostile occupation." (For a definition of "hostile occupation" distinguishing it from "belligerent," "pacific" and "peaceful" occupation, see William G. Downey, Jr., "Revision of the Rules of Warfare," 1949 *Proceedings of the American Society of International Law* 103). The defense, in general, would probably have to rest on the principle that a "military occupant, especially one who has conquered and subjugated a country, has supreme power over the territory occupied, and, to all intents and purposes, is the sovereign during the period of occupation" (6 Hackworth, *International Law* 385–414), and on the consequent view that Japan, once more sovereign, was bound by the actions of its previous military government. Of course, an argument could possibly be also raised that the relation between Japan and the United States as one of the governing military powers was of a special character and that Japan could not be forever bound by the acts and omissions of a temporary military govermnent, especially if such acts and omissions would directly benefit the occupant even after the occupation was ended. This argument would probably be further strengthened by evidence showing that, during the period of occupation, such Japanese authorities as might have been then recognized notified the military occupant of their disagreement with the latter's continental shelf policy considered potentially harmful to the future interest of Japan. However, no such evidence is known to exist, and it is not our task here to resolve this particular problem of the continuity of the state of Japan; for our purposes, we might as well consider Japan as a state responsible for the acts or omissions of its postwar governments, whatever their character.

states who have hitherto applied or positively accepted the doctrine of the continental shelf.

Thus the Japanese Government could recognize that in 1953 it was, perhaps, estopped from asserting any inclusive rights to the mineral resources of the outer continental shelf adjacent to the United States. Not only did it fail to object against the Truman Proclamation; Japan also acquiesced in a long chain of further acts taken by the United States in implementing the proclamation, and thus assisted in encouraging the United States to become deeply involved on the adjacent outer continental shelf politically as well as materially. Further, Japan also assisted, by its prolonged silence, in encouraging on the outer continental shelf adjacent to the United States an industrial activity carried on from the high seas and so dense after a time that it has come to require effective regulation in order not to interfere with the freedom and safety of high sea navigation and fishing, a regulation which the United States provided and Japan was not in a position to undertake. Thus the Japanese acquiescence may be said to have led on the part of the United States and *vis a vis* Japan to a prescriptive reight.[55] A right, that is, the admission of which by Japan in no way militates against the Japanese *res communis* concept of the shelf.

In fact, even in 1964 the Japanese Government refused to admit formally that the United States had acquired exclusive rights on the continental shelf. During a series of discussions with U.S. representatives on the effect of the

[55] The term "prescriptive right" is used here advisedly to signify a specific right within an area rather than a full territorial title acquired by prescription. As to the usual requirement of a long operation of time for the existence of prescriptive rights no agreement appears to exist among writers as to any specific duration. "No general rule can be laid down." L. Oppenheim, *International Law :A Treatise*, 6th ed., ed. by H. Lauterpacht, v. 1 (London: Longmans, Green fh Co., 1947), p. 527. And – "... le Droit International ne comporte pas de delais determines des prescriptions, et il est un peu naif de la part de certains auteurs d'avoir essayé de les chiffrer (quarante ou cinquante ans) ..." Georges Scelle, *Manuel de Droit International* Public (Paris: Domat-Montchrestien, 1948), p. 160. – Also, compare the view of Josef L. Kunz regarding the claims of some Latin American states to a two-hundred-mile breadth of their territorial sea: "... it is very important for the United States to take correct action in order not to make possible the argument of acquiescence. That a new rule of customary international law may come into being by acquiescence is not to be feared, as the overwhelming majority od states are strongly opposed to a two-hundred-mile limit of territorial waters. But acquiescence may lead to a prescriptive right. True, the United States has protested. As long as foreign states only enact municipal legislation, contrary to international law, or even conclude treaties of this type without doing anything to apply them, a strong protest is sufficient to preserve the rights of the protesting state. But when such states, as it is here the case, insist constantly and everywhere upon their unlawful claims and enforce them by forceful action and in their own courts, things are different. First, protests must be repeated. But even repeated protests may be insufficient in law, may become mere 'paper' protests, unable to bar title by prescription. In such case ,more than mere protests is required by international law, international tribunals and courts. Protests in such cases must be supported by further action." Josef L. Kunz, "Continental Shelf and International Law: Confusion and Abuse," 50 *American Journal of International Law* 852 (1956).

United States legislation S. 1988[56] the Japanese Government maintained its position that it was not bound by the law of the Convention on the Continental Shelf. The United States then assured Japan that prior to implementing the legislation with respect to fishery resources of the continental shelf, the United States will consult with the Japanese Government and that in such consultations full consideration will be given to the views of the Japanese Government and to Japan's long-established king crab fishery.[57] Subsequently the United States did consult with the Japanese Government and in December 1964 the two countries concluded an agreement on an interim regime of their king crab fishery in the Bering Sea. Their joint announcement stated that

> faced with the opposing legal positions of the two governments regarding rights under international law to the king crab resource, the two delegations agreed on practical arrangements without prejudice to the legal position of either side.[58]

In subsequent diplomatic communications exchanged between the United States and Japan the disagreement of the two countries regarding the regime of the fishery resources of the continental shelf was again noted.[59] The point is, of course, that in practice the main Japanese opposition to the Convention on the Continental Shelf was motivated by the intense Japanese interest in the freedom of continental shelf fishing, and there was no real or formal indication that the Japanese held equally strong views with regard to the mineral resources of the continental shelf.

Thus our simulated case set in 1953 and describing the Japanese Government as estopped from asserting any inclusive rights to the mineral resources of the outer continental shelf adjacent to the United States need not be so unrealistic as it may have appeared at the outset. And the feeling of unreality can be still further weakened by setting forth the assumption that the same estoppel capable of limiting the Japanese claim against the United States need not have existed between Japan and other countries asserting an exclusive control over the mineral resources of their adjacent continental shelves. We have seen that by 1952 only twenty-one states publicly demonstrated their interest in acquiring exclusive national jurisdiction over their adjacent continental shelves; and that in the early 1950's all of these states except the United States, Saudi Arabia and, possibly, the United Kingdom (insofar as the Bahamas, Gulf of Paria and some of the Arab sheikhdoms

[56] Public Law 88–308, "to prohibit fishing in the territorial waters of the United States and in certain other areas" by foreign vessels, 78 Stat. 194–196, 1964.

[57] 50 *Department of State Bulletin* 936 (June 15, 1964).

[58] 51 *ibid.* 829–830 (7 Dec. 1964).

[59] *Ibid.* 892–893 (21 Dec. 1964).

are concerned), were but nominally engaged on their respective shelves through acts of political control and economic involvement. It is, therefore, quite possible that, as in our simulated case of Japan *v.* Abu Dhabi (Great Britain), the Japanese Government could point to several other instances in relation to which its own process of deepening acquiescence has not reached a degree sufficient to create an estoppel on the part of Japan and a prescriptive right – *vis a vis* Japan – on the part of the state concerned.

Finally, even if in 1953 Japan could legally claim inclusive rights on the disputed submarine areas off several countries, would it be able to maintain its eventual protests and to defend its claims without a parallel action taken by other states? And what legal relations regarding the continental shelf rights might have developed between Japan and countries which have not claimed or exercised exclusive continental shelf rights themselves?

SHELF UTILIZATION AND RESPONSIBILITY OF STATES: FROM BILATERAL TO MULTILATERAL PERSPECTIVES

Rather than to answer such questions *in abstracto,* it might be useful first to examine the other important question raised by the international application of the doctrine of the continental shelf: whether, at any particular time, it has become the duty rather than an asserted right of a coastal state to supervise industrial and other activity on the adjacent continental shelf. We have already seen in the case of the American-British shelf relations that as between the two countries the obligation of coastal authorities to provide for the safety of the users of the high seas above the utilized portions of the continental shelf did exist. But it might be said that such an obligation extended even beyond the bilateral scope within which we have examined it: there is a standing expectation among all the users of the high seas that each of them would observe and enforce certain safety standards so as not to injure the interests of others. One need not recite in detail, for instance, the rules of high sea navigation with regard to the system of colored lights assigned to different classes of ships and the attendant rules governing the right of way, such as those that the United States Supreme Court had an occasion to examine in the case of *The Scotia*; suffice it to say that even before the British orders in council of 1863 provided for the system of colored navigation lights – a system adopted by the United States in 1863-64 and subscribed to by an overwhelming majority of maritime states – every user of the high seas expected, and because of a well-established usage had a right to expect, that every other user would employ some signal indicating his presence on the waters in dark or in fog.

This rather rudimentary yet fundamental expectation of all seafarers does, in a special way, relate to the doctrine and practice of the continental shelf. If the existence of the expectation is admitted, any coastal nation encouraging or causing the utilization of its adjacent continental shelf by way of the high sea, and claiming a right exclusively to control such utilization, appears to assume automatically a duty to fulfill the expectation that the safety of others will be protected.

However, it is more difficult to determine if, at any particular time after 1945, it has become the duty of all coastal states, whether or not they had claimed and exercised the right to an exclusive control of the adjacent continental shelf, to extend their jurisdiction to, and assume some responsibility for, such activity as may take place on that shelf.

To examine this problem we will again employ the bilateral approach and simulated cases based on such facts as may have existed during the period under discussion. However, before we begin our hypothetical cases, it is necessary to re-emphasize the dynamics of the growth of customary rules; the impact of national acts on the scope and content of the rules creates a need to evaluate each legal relationship with reference to a definite and defined point in time. The necessity for this time-consciousness arises from the relative rapidity of the development (i.e., change) of the shelf policies of some states, particularly those used in our simulated situations further below. For instance, in 1958 Norway refused to recognize the existence of an effective legal rule giving the coastal state exclusive rights over the adjacent shelf, and was still considering, as an alternative, the possibility of international acceptance of the outer continental shelf as *res communis*.[60] The Norwegian delegation participated in the discussions leading to the adoption of the draft Convention on the Continental Shelf, but by July 1966 Norway did not ratify the Convention. It appears, however, that the Norwegian shelf policy did undergo considerable change as the need for an orderly exploitation of shelf resources increased. By 1963, Norway enacted a Law on the Exploration and Exploitation of the Natural Resources of the Seabed establishing, in municipal law, Norwegian jurisdiction over shelf activities and declaring the right to natural resources "in the seabed or in its subsoil, as far as the depth of the superjacent waters admits of exploitation" to be vested in the state.[61]

The development of the shelf policies of the German Federal Republic after 1958 was even more rapid. In 1958 representatives of that state at the

[60] U.N. Conference on the Law of the Sea, 6 *Official Records* 4, Dec. A/CONF.13/42.

[61] Richard Young, "Offshore Claims and Problems of the North Sea," 59 *American Journal of International Law* 511–512 (1965).

Geneva Conference maintained an internationalist policy; they denied the existence of an international legal rule giving the coastal states any exclusive rights on the continental shelf beyond the outer limits of the territorial sea, and proposed the adoption of a body of new rules internationalizing the continental shelf and providing for the regulation of activities on the submerged *res communis*.[62] By 1963, the Federal Republic of Germany still did not ratify the Convention or otherwise accept its law. The following year, however, the Federal Government published a proclamation accepting the Convention on the Continental Shelf as general international law, and it was suggested that Bonn's hesitation with the actual ratification of the Convention was no longer motivated by some internationalist sentiments or policies but, rather, by a hope of negotiating bilateral agreements giving Germany larger shelf areas than it would have under the general international law as represented, in the German view, by the Convention.[63]

These relatively dramatic developments emphasize still more the need not only to see the emergence of certain legal rules of international custom in their bilateral context (e.g., what was the German-Norwegian shelf relationship in 1958, and how did it change by 1964?) but to see them in the context of time. It may be difficult to speak in general terms of French-German or French-Norwegian legal relationship concerning the continental shelf; but it is possible to speak about such relationships as they may have existed in 1948, or 1960, or at any other definite point in time.

Situation 1: Norway and France, 1948

The selection of the two countries and the date are not entirely arbitrary. Neither Norway nor France have formally accepted the existence of an international rule giving the coastal state a right exclusively to control the use of the continental shelf under the high seas adjacent to the belt of territorial waters. As late as 1958, the representatives of the two states declared that no such rule existed at the time. As to the date, we have already submitted that in 1948, if not much earlier, there existed between the United States and the United Kingdom a specific legal relationship: it consisted not only of a mutual acceptance by the two countries of each other's right to control exclusively particular forms of continental shelf activity, but also of the mutual obligation to maintain certain standards of safety with respect to the users

[62] Memorandum of the Federal Republic of Germany, Doc. A/CONF.13/C.4/L.1, in U.N. Conference on the Law of the Sea, 6 *Official Records* 126–127.

[63] See Richard Young, *op. cit.* (note 61) 513.

of both the shelf and the high sea above. Could any such relationship be found to have existed in 1948 between Norway and France?

There certainly was no question of their mutual recognition of the coastal state's right to exercise exclusive control over the adjacent shelf. There was between them no treaty regulating the problem, and if they both denied the existence of a general customary rule on the subject in 1958, they certainly did not feel bound by it in 1948; even if there were such a rule then, they were free to disregard it as between themselves.

Our artificially constructed situation consists of the following points: (a) A foreign oil company constructs a platform on the continental shelf adjacent to the coast of France but clearly outside the French territorial waters as well as the contiguous zone. The French Government is aware of the undertaking but, in line with its continental shelf policy, takes no official notice of it and does not interfere with its operation. (b) A Norwegian fishing vessel, while pursuing its lawful trade on the high seas, is damaged while it navigates in fog and hits the platform insufficiently equipped with warning devices. The Norwegian fisherman, seeking reparation, finds that the platform is operated by a group of private companies of different nationalities, none of them with a majority interest in the venture. Unable to obtain redress privately, the Norwegian fisherman turns to its own government for assistance.

What courses of action would be open to Norway? The Norwegian Government could hardly choose to view the stationary platform as a vessel and, finding it has not been registered in any one country and has flown no flag, to exercise its assumed right and seize the platform as if it were a vessel without nationality.[64] Nor could the Norwegian Government turn to France in an attempt to obtain redress in French courts or through diplomatic channels; by its own continental shelf policy, Norway was estopped *vis a vis* France – a country maintaining a similar stand – to claim French negligence in not enforcing reasonable safety standards on the outer continental shelf beyond the limits of the asserted and recognized French jurisdiction.

Unless the artificially constructed situation were enriched by further details opening new alternatives, the Norwegian Government would appear incapable to intervene on behalf of its national whose right to navigate safely the high seas was impaired by the negligence of another user of the high

[64] See, concerning the right of a state to seize a vessel without an identifiable national character the case of Molvan *v.* Attorney General for Palestine, 1948 Appeal Cases (Great Britain) 351. According to Rienow, "the entire legal system which States have evolved for the regulation of the use of the high seas is predicated on the possession by each vessel of a connection with a State having a recognized maritime flag." R. Rienow, *The Test of the Nationality of a Merchant Vessel* (New York: Columbia University Press, 1937), p. 13.

seas. Possibly the only promising course of action open to Norway would be to ascertain the nationality of the ships which had brought in the platform and assisted in its construction, and thus left behind an obstacle to high seas navigation; should they fly the flags of a state or states bound by the 1929 International Convention for the Safety of Life at Sea[65] and should the provisions of that treaty be found applicable,[66] Norway could perhaps seek reparation on legal grounds through either diplomatic or legal action. But should the ships have flown, for instance, the flag of Honduras, not a party to the 1929 Convention, the Norwegian Government would encounter greater difficulties.

Situation 2: France, Norway, and Gabon, 1960

Now we assume that the Norwegian fishing vessel was damaged by running into an unlighted oil-drilling platform off the coast of Gabon; the structure was erected on the Gabon continental shelf beyond the seaward limit of the territorial waters of Gabon. The Norwegian ship, having failed to obtain redress through local remedies, turns to its government for assistance. An investigation shows that the platform, owned jointly by the Royal Dutch Shell Group and the Societé des Petroles d'Afrique Equatoriale[67] was erected on the site by ships flying the French flag, and that it was managed and operated by a French crew under a license properly issued by the Gabon Government.

The first set of questions arising from the situation concerns Gabon. Could the Government of Gabon disclaim its responsibility for occurrences on the

[65] The text of the Convention can be found in: U.S. Congress. Senate. *Treaties, Conventions, International Acts, Protocols, and Agreements between the United States of America and Other Powers* 1923–1937, vol. 4 (Washington, D.C.: Government Printing Office, 1938), pp. 5134–5209. (75th Congress, 2d Sess., Doc. No. 134).

[66] Possibly, the following provisions of the 1929 Convention might indirectly apply:

Article 34 [Chapter V, Safety of Navigation]: The master of every ship which meets with dangerous ice, a dangerous derelict, a dangerous tropical storm or any other direct danger to navigation is bound to communicate the information ....

Each Administration [note: the term Administration designates a signatory state] will take all steps which it thinks necessary to ensure that when intelligence of any of the dangers specified in the previous paragraph is received, it will be promptly brought to the knowledge of those concerned and communicated to other Administrations interested. *Ibid.*, p. 5144.

As between the contracting governments, the 1929 Convention was replaced and abrogated by its 1948 version which entered into force on 19 November 1952 .The text of the 1948 Convention is in 3 *U.S. Treaties and Other International Agreements* (No. 2495) 3450 ff. The two cited paragraphs of article 34 of the 1929 Convention have become, in the 1948 version, paragraphs (a) and (b) of Regulation 2, Chapter V on Safety of Navigation. *Ibid.* 3644.

[67] These companies did in fact jointly search for oil off Gabon in 1960. 13 (No. 2)*Offshore* 18 (August 1960).

high seas arising from activities licensed by Gabon? If – as Norway would maintain – the Government of Gabon had no right under international law either to permit or prohibit the utilization of the resources of the outer continental shelf beneath the adjacent high seas, did it have either the right or the duty to supervise the methods of such utilization?

The answer to these questions would appear to be that Gabon did have the right in 1960 to control and supervise the utilization of its outer continental shelf as long as that right had not been subjected to a successful challenge. But once Gabon assumed that right, it also accepted the duty to ensure an effective measure of safety and order on the high seas above the utilized portions of the shelf; in fact, ships of all nations, acquainted with the safety measures employed off the United States coasts, in the Bahamas, in the Persian Gulf, off Libya and the United Arab Republic as well as off Nigeria, in the waters off Borneo and in other segments of the high seas above utilized segments of the continental shelf, had a right to expect a safety system established and enforced off Gabon too.

Yet there is no certainty that Norway, not accepting the right of the coastal nation to control the adjacent outer continental shelf, would address its representations to Gabon. Choosing not to recognize any Gabonian rights and duties in the area involved, the Norwegian Government could turn to France whose flag endowed the operation of the oil-drilling platform with French nationality.

We do not intend to run through all the possible variations of a French response. The combined France-Norway-Gabon situation appears sufficiently clear to suggest that, while in theory there might develop a conflict of responsibility and jurisdiction, in 1960 the Government of Gabon would carry the primary burden of supervising such activities on its outer continental shelf over which it had assumed control.

Situation 3: Federal Republic of Germany, Norway, and Japan, 1958

The Government of the Federal Republic of Germany suffers an extensive network of oil-drilling platforms to be built off its shores and beyond its territorial waters in the North Sea. The platforms are operated and owned by the Japanese Petroleum Export Company, a firm with considerable experience in submarine drilling.[68] Norwegian fishing interests consider the platforms a danger to their ships and an obstacle to navigation in a segment of the sea with a relatively heavy traffic. The Norwegian Government ap-

[68] P. 143, footnote 49.

proaches the Government of Japan. The Japanese, however, while maintaining their position that the continental shelf beyond the seaward limit of territorial waters represents a *res communis,* nevertheless refer the Norwegian authorities to the Federal Republic of Germany; they are rejecting the Norwegian representations on the grounds that the German Government itself publicly stated that it was improper to subordinate the control over such comparatively immovable fixtures as oil-drilling platforms to the law of the nationality of the operator and that the control, and thus the responsibility, should be vested in the coastal state closest to the installation.[69] But should Norway, thereupon, approach the Federal Republic of Germany, the latter could state that it never assumed such rights and responsibilities of control; although it did feel that the law of nationality of the operator was inapplicable, Germany merely proposed in 1958 the vesting of the rights of control in the coastal state by and on behalf of the international community. But the international community never accepted the proposal.

It thus appears that in the Japan-Norway-Germany triangle the primary responsibility for maintaining a reasonable measure of safety and order on the high seas would ultimately rest with the state whose flag provided the continental shelf operator with its nationality. This, admittedly, would be a somewhat impractical solution; Japan would be actually under a duty to issue to its nationals a set of regulations befitting the special circumstances of a high seas area thousands of miles from Japan and, not to be charged with negligence, would have to supervise the shelf operations to ensure compliance with the regulations.

But it is also obvious that the states involved, should they be determined to preserve their policy of not admitting the exclusive coastal rights on the outer continental shelf, could choose a more tractable path: the Federal Republic of Germany could exercise jurisdiction and control over the foreign operator off its coasts as a right and responsibility delegated to Germany by a treaty with the operator's national government; thereby, and as between the two states, the *res communis* concept of the continental shelf would have been preserved and the practical requirement of order on the high seas effectively served.

The situation, of course, could be different if, instead of Norway, the complaining state would be one of those with a long-standing policy of claiming and exercising exclusive coastal rights on the outer continental shelf and, consequently, maintaining the view that every coastal state is re-

[69] Memorandum by the Federal Republic of Germany, U.N. Doc. A/CONF.13/C.4/L.1, is included as an annex in UN Conference on the Law of the Sea, 6 *Official Records* 126 (Doc. A/CONF.13/42).

sponsible for securing an orderly conduct of the continental shelf operators utilizing the seabed and subsoil under the adjacent high seas. The Federal Republic of Germany itself admitted during the 1958 Geneva Conference on the Law of the Sea the general need for controlling the activities of continental shelf operators,[70] its government was aware that in all cases where over-water utilization of the continental shelf had been undertaken, the necessary system of controls was established and maintained; in the various high sea segments above the utilized shelves ships flying the German flag complied with, and benefited from, such systems of control; the Federal Republic of Germany thus assisted in the forming of an expectation on the part of international shipping that every coastal state provides for the safety of navigation on the adjacent high seas above the exploited areas of the continental shelf.

PROVISIONAL CONCLUSIONS

The inquiry into the specific United States-United Kingdom legal relationship arising from their continental shelf policies and practice in the early postwar years, as well as the artificially constructed situations involving other states and different aspects of the shelf doctrine, indicate both the multiplicity of possible legal threads from which the continental shelf regime might actually consist, and the importance of pinpointing to a specific time period every inquiry seeking to determine the legal status of individual rules comprising the regime.

To obtain a reasonably balanced picture of the political scope and legal intensity of the continental shelf regime at any given time would in fact presuppose an examination of bilateral relations as they may have developed, or failed to materialize, with regard to the following groups of suggested norms governing the continental shelf:

[70] The German memorandum of 1958 admitted there was no "world organization capable of supervising the enforcement" of the necessary continental shelf rules "on behalf of the international community" and, after proposing that the coastal state be empowered to undertake such controls, stated the functions of the coastal state as follows:

"(a) To satisfy itself that the operator fulfills the necessary conditions qualifying him to carry out the proposed work;

(b) To supervise the concerns engaged in prospecting and exploitation;

(c) To delimit the prospecting and exploitation areas of each operator."

Among the necessary rules the Federal Republic of Germany listed provisions such as: "the operations of prospecting and exploitation shall not prejudice unnecessarily navigation or fishing, telegraphic communications, sea bathing, etc. – *e.g.*:

(i) They must not unduly obstruct the movements of shipping;

(ii) They must not cause excessive pollution of the sea;

(iii) They must not cause undue harm to marine fauna and flora ..."

Ibid.

(1) Exclusive coastal rights to (a) explore and exploit the mineral resources of the shelf; (b) explore and exploit both mineral and other defined natural resources of the shelf; (c) utilize the physical properties of the shelf, as for submarine storage, the erection of various structures, or the grounding of undersea apparatuses (*e.g.*, sonic devices).

(2) Inclusive or common rights of states to (a) lay and maintain submarine cables and pipelines: (b) utilize the continental shelf for the grounding of various types of fishing gear; (c) dredge the seabed for various materials by means of freely moving vessels; (d) carry out scientific research.

(3) The determination of the seaward extent of coastal rights defined by (a) geographical and geological criteria; (b) political and legal criteria; (c) a combination of the two.

(4) The definition of coastal responsibility for (a) maintaining general order in shelf utilization; (b) providing for safety of navigation above the utilized portions of the shelf; (c) protecting the rights of other users of the shelf and of high-sea fishermen; (d) preventing the pollution of sea waters harmful to the rights of others.

A bilaterally oriented inquiry into the existence and clarity of each of these and other rules of the shelf complex may, of course, yield different answers for different sets of countries. This alone, perhaps, may be a disturbing thought; yet there appears to be no sound reason why varied systems of international legal rules operating at the same time in different parts of the world and for different groupings of states should be considered as incapable of fulfilling their basic role, *i.e.*, the maintenance of public order. The diversity of continental shelf rules need not produce conflicts as long as the relationships between the diverse systems are definable and defined – and here again the bilateral approach is of some assistance. Hypothetically, it may show that several states of western and northern Europe as well as other countries not accepting and practicing the exclusive coastal right of shelf exploitation have been developing among themselves a different system which includes the recognition of the *res communis* character of the outer shelf; yet, in the absence of effective protests directed by these states against different practices elsewhere, they may be estopped – through their own acquiescence and through prescription on the part of others – from carrying their own system to other shelves where exclusive coastal control and jurisdiction have been sufficiently established. At the same time, the countries claiming and exercising the exclusive right of the coastal state to control the adjacent shelf may be found estopped, through their own acts, from demanding on the shelves off foreign coasts such rights as, off their own shores, they deny to others.

A bilaterally oriented inquiry into the legal regime of the continental shelf may show this diversity to be multiple and affecting most of the component rules. This, however, is not unusual in the international legal system with its considerable treaty component; here, uniformity and universality would be much more surprising.

CHAPTER V

THE CONTINENTAL SHELF AND INTERNATIONAL CUSTOM: ASSESSMENT AND CONCLUSIONS

We have set out to inquire, through a study of the legal regime of the continental shelf, into some of the processes through which states, by acting or failing to act in respect of a specific international issue or situation, narrow their choice of policies in that particular sphere up to the point of being bound by legal rules. We have found some of the traditional methods of inquiry into the validity of customary rules not to be very helpful as a guide, especially where they strive directly to assert or to deny the existence of a general rule of international customary law and, consequently, lose the sight of the gradual, dynamic process of the growth of custom, of its complexity and flexibility. In an attempt to overcome this difficulty, we have utilized, in the specific case of the continental shelf regime, a method of inquiry characterized as the bilateral approach: a method whereby one examines a customary rule as a composite and dynamic pattern of varied bilateral state relationships, and follows its growth from its historical beginnings toward a broader application; and a method, too, which neither denies nor asserts in advance that a rule of custom must or cannot acquire universal validity.

While advocating this method of inquiry into the existence of rules comprising the legal regime of the continental shelf, we do not suggest its use for every other customary rule. The norms of international customary law regulate an extremely wide range of subjects in the diplomatic, political, economic and social relations of states. To insist that a bilateral approach be employed in the examination of each of them would mean only to replace one rigid generalization by another.

However, the use of the bilateral approach, with the necessary acceptance of the possibility that a bilaterally oriented inquiry might not yield evidence of a general rule where such a rule would otherwise seem feasible and desirable, may in more than one instance well serve in a world of some hundred and thirty states and harboring different legal, political and social systems with cultural and economic diversities and a variety of geographical and geopolitical situations. In such a world a diversification in the methodology of international legal inquires may not only be functional, but unavoidable as well.

In the closing sections below, the conclusions of this study are presented in two separate yet closely related parts: first, we offer an approximate assessment of the rise of a customary legal regime of the continental shelf at two different stages, in 1950 and in 1958; it is followed by an evaluation of the legal role of the various factors affecting – and sometimes effecting – the emergence of that legal system of the continental shelf.

The scope of both concluding parts needs some qualification. The assessment of the rise of the continental shelf regime is qualified as approximate since it is based only on data presented in the previous chapters of this study; while their volume might be thought considerable, they fall far short of representing a full-fledged inquiry into the minute details essential for a bilaterally oriented study of the status of the continental shelf regime. However, for our purpose of demonstrating the feasibility and the problems of the bilateral approach to the study of the growth of a system of international customary rules, approximate assessment appears sufficient.

The qualification of the second concluding part – the evaluation of the legal role of various factors affecting the growth of customary rules – is less restrictive: it consists merely of a recognition that such conclusions as we reach regarding the significance and role of the various legal factors, while applicable to the growth of the continental shelf rules, need not be equally valid in other areas of international custom. To determine their more general validity would, of course, require a different, comparative type of a study.

THE CONTINENTAL SHELF REGIME

The bilateral approach does not deny the need for an inquiry into the general validity of the rules comprising the legal regime of the continental shelf; it merely reverses the process of inquiry. Instead of first assuming the eventual emergence of a general rule and then proceeding to prove or disprove it, one begins with the bilateral manifestations of the rule and, at the end, may or may not arrive at the contours of a general norm.

The Shelf in 1950

It is technically possible to subject to a bilaterally oriented inquiry every rule of the legal complex of the shelf to cover, eventually, the entire community of states. The results could even be tabulated to indicate the intensity and territorial validity of each rule. The following is a segment of a possible table indicating for 1950 the geographical spread of the exclusive coastal right to exploit the mineral resources of the adjacent continental shelf:

	As against						
State and its right	United Kingdom	United States	France	Norway	U.S.S.R.	Mexico	Saudi Arabia
United Kingdom		A	Ad	Ad	Ad	A	A
United States	A		A	A	A	A	A
France	Ad	A		N	N	A	A
Norway	Ad	A	N		N	A	A
U.S.S.R.	Ad	A	Nd	Nd		A	A
Mexico	A	A	Nd	Nd	Nd		A
Saudi Arabia	A	A	Nd	Nd	Nd	A	

A Affirmative; right established
Ad Right established, yet some doubt remains
N Negative; right not established
Nd Right not yet established, but its roots have begun to appear

The symbols indicate mere approximations of the bilateral legal relationships between the various states, and have been arrived at on the basis of the relevant facts outlined above in this study.

As to the data shown in the table, the first horizontal row indicates that, in 1950, there might have been some doubt concerning the British right, as against France, Norway, and the Soviet Union, to exploit exclusively the mineral resources of the adjacent shelf. The second horizontal row admits no such doubt in the case of the United States' right. A detailed examination would show the difference to lie in the different methods adopted by the British and the United States Governments when asserting their shelf rights. The Truman Proclamation applied to the resources of the entire shelf "contiguous to the coasts of the United States"; the British Government, on the other hand, proceeded by individual acts for each of its possessions and protectorates and by 1950 did not explicitly act with reference to the continental shelf off the coasts of Great Britain and Northern Ireland. It is thus possible to admit that, at the time, countries such as Norway and France, both generally opposing the establishment of exclusive coastal shelf rights, could have been estopped from claiming inclusive rights off, for instance, the Bahamas, whose continental shelf had not only been declared as falling under the control of the Bahamas Government, but had also been actively administered by that Government, while at the same time no such estoppel or other legal hindrance would have prevented Norway or France from viewing the outer continental shelf off Great Britain and Northern Ireland as a *res communis*.

In the case of the Mexican shelf rights as against Norway and France, the table above again indicates doubt, although the Mexican declaration asserting national control over the adjacent shelf dates as far back as October 1945, only one month after the Truman Proclamation, and its scope is not specifically restricted. The difference, a detailed examination might reveal, could arise from the simple fact that the policy statement of the Mexican Government was not implemented in practice before 1950. Unlike the United States shelf, the seabed and subsoil claimed by Mexico saw no industrial and administrative activity except well within the limits of the Mexican territorial waters, and in the absence of an actual Mexican economic and administrative involvement on the outer continental shelf, Norway and France could possibly still successfully protest the Mexican assertion of exclusive shelf rights.

Of course, we do not suggest that a mere tabulation of the bilateral relations of states regarding each rule would automatically show the general or particular character of the various norms. In more than one instance something more may be needed for a realistic assessment of the obligatory force of laws applicable at different points of the globe than a mechanical calculation of numerical majorities and minorities of states observing, ignoring or rejecting a specific practice or doctrine. However, an examination of bilateral relationships along the lines suggested in this study, with the results tabulated or not, is capable of providing the inquirer with a relatively solid foundation for a further study.

How much could a bilaterally oriented examination of specific continental shelf relations actually reveal? Using again broad approximations based on the data assembled in the chapters above, one may actually arrive at a composite picture – a fabric woven from multiple legal threads – of the following relationships pertaining to the rule of exclusive coastal control over the exploitation of the mineral resources of the shelf in 1950.

The Shelf as a Res Nullius

By 1950, no state claimed or established for itself exclusive rights to exploit the resources of an outer continental shelf adjacent to another state. Thus the practice of states did not admit of the possibility to view the outer continental shelf as a *res nullius* open to a discretionary find-grab-and-hold contest.

Impact of Active Shelf Policies

By 1950, nineteen states claimed for themselves the right of exclusive control over the resources of the outer continental shelf adjacent to their territories. The national claims and acts appear to have had the following legal consequences:

(a) Each of the national assertions of coastal control over the shelf had the potential of depriving, almost automatically, the submarine areas involved of the character of a *res nullius* should another state seek to view them as such. The coastal claim, reinforced by the facts of geographical proximity and geological unity and by the relative ease of control from the coast, was bound to prevail over an attempt by any other state to claim the distant submarine areas for itself by virtue of its own, necessarily isolated acts of occupation. To illustrate, the 1945 Mexican shelf declaration itself, unless revoked or abandoned, eliminated for any other country the theoretical legal possibility of occupying and appropriating a part or the whole of the Mexican shelf merely because no other individual country could show, in relation to that shelf, a title superior to that of Mexico.

(b) Within the group of states with active continental shelf policies, relatively stable relationships were formed. The national claims were sufficiently similar to each other in their purpose and in the spirit of reciprocity to estop each of the claiming states from denying the corresponding assertion of exclusive rights to another within the group. The legal regime thus established by and within a group of states involved approximately 25 percent of the total expanse of the geographically defined continental shelves of the world.

(c) It does not follow, however, that these active continental shelf policies effectively, generally, and permanently removed the submarine areas involved from the *res communis* category. It is a fact that none of the states which failed to assert any claims of their own deemed it appropriate to protest the national claims to exclusive coastal control. However, we have seen that by 1950 the actual economic and administrative involvement of the claiming states on the adjacent submarine areas was minimal. It is submitted that sustained protests by the non-practicing states could have been still effective in preventing the full rise of the claimed coastal rights, even if such protest would be without any legal effect on the inner relationships of the practicing states. The protests could possibly fail only in those instances where they would encounter the barrier of prescription established through a deeper involvement of the coastal nations in their shelf ventures; the area thus removed, at least for a time, from the *res communis* category, would represent, at the most, some 10 percent of the entire shelf expanse in the world.

Impact of Passive Shelf Policies

While by 1950 the passive stand of a majority of states could have resulted for some of them, and as against some of the practicing states, in a prescriptive estoppel reducing or destroying the effectiveness of a later protest, the non-practising states do appear to have had at the time sufficient legal room for the establishment, by unilateral though parallel actions, of one or more diverse systems of control over some 75 to 90 percent of the total expanse of geographically defined continental shelves of the world. They could thus still successfully defend a *res communis* concept of the outer continental shelf against the general spread of the doctrine of exclusive coastal control.

Summary

Thus, by 1950, a number of states established between themselves different legal relationships ordering their continental shelf policies – relationships different in their legal character, intensity and stability but, seen bilaterally, sufficiently clear to function. However, it is difficult to assert the existence in 1950 of an *erga omnes* customary rule giving the coastal state generally exclusive rights on the adjacent continental shelf. Such an assertion would have to rest not on the actual facts of the general development and application of the shelf doctrine but on an estimate as to what course that development may take in the future. It was indeed highly reasonable to expect in 1950 that the doctrine of exclusive coastal shelf rights would eventually mature into a general legal system. The political complexion of the world preconditioned the tendency of states to view the adjacent outer continental shelf as an area within which the state's security would be threatened by prolonged and intensive foreign activities. Economic nationalism, like a gravitational force, pulled the outer shelf – a potential source of wealth – within the available coastal control. Industrial utilization of the shelf could directly affect the accessibility of the nearby ports. Mineral resources in the shelf subsoil often formed a geological extension of deposits under the adjacent land. Coastal cooperation was essential for some, useful for most methods of the utilization of the shelf resources. Objectively, of course, all these interests and advantages of the coastal state could have been effectively protected by, and utilized under an international system of shelf control giving the coastal state extensive powers progressively diminishing with the shelf distance from the coast. Further, in 1950, tendencies were already visible among some states, in Western Europe in particular, to move toward closer cooperation especially in the economic field and, consequently, toward some measure of limitation on their sovereign attributes. Thus the argument based on the alleged reasonableness of exclusive coastal control over the outer continental shelf, asserted to be generally valid, represented a prediction – even if not an incorrect one – that the states will be politically incapable to develop a cooperative system of outer shelf control preserving both the *res communis* character of the shelf and the legitimate coastal interests. A prediction of this type can indeed serve as a useful political guide. In 1950, however, while a preponderant percentage of the world shelves was still untouched by acts of states and while many governments did not as yet limit their legal discretion by deciding for or submitting to any particular form of shelf control, that political prediction would have to serve as the almost sole basis of a world-wide international legal system – a suggestion difficult to accept.

The Shelf in 1958

As in the previous chapters of this study, the selection of the years 1950 and 1958 for the assessment of the status and scope of the legal regime of the continental shelf has its specific reasons. In 1950, the doctrine of the continental shelf was for the first time defined by a prominent writer as expressing an established, general international customary law. In 1958, the United Nations Conference of the Law of the Sea was held in Geneva and one of its results was the Convention on the Continental Shelf, a treaty now in force; the comments of tens of governmental delegates at that Conference on the draft articles of the Convention, a product of several years of expert efforts of the United Nations International Law Commission, demonstrated significant areas of agreement and disagreement of states regarding the legal status of the continental shelf.

A bilaterally oriented examination of the various component rules of the continental shelf regime established by 1958 through international custom would yield the following approximate results:

Exclusive Coastal Control

With the work of the United Nations International Law Commission on the law of the sea and the reflections of that work in the Sixth (Legal) Committee of the General Assembly, international communication regarding the various national shelf policies was intensified; thus, in many bilateral situations, the more profound governmental awareness of the legal significance and scope of the continental shelf practice would appear as a factor speeding up the process of acquiescence through a failure to protest. A tabulation of bilateral relationships regarding the rule of exclusive coastal control would still show areas of doubt, but they would be more regional in character, the largest of them involving the countries of Western Europe with the exception of Portugal. The position of several states would have been found changed significantly through the performance of their representatives in the Sixth Committee. There the Soviet representative, for instance, discussed the problems of the continental shelf so as not to commit his government to any specific and definitive policy prior to a conventional agreement on the shelf; however, his comments would tend to increase the expectation of a state with an active continental shelf policy that the Soviet Government would not protest against the exercise of an exclusive coastal control over the adjacent outer shelf. Further, even in the bilateral relations the fact that state X failed to protest against the practice of coastal control exercised by states A to M would make a protest by X against the same practice on the part of state N extremely difficult if that protest sought to preserve the *res communis* character of the continental shelf and unless it rested on exceptional circumstances. On the whole, and as far as one can estimate without careful measurements on the global scale, a bilaterally oriented inquiry into the 1958 legal status and scope of the coastal right exclusively to control the utilization of the adjacent shelf would probably show the practice asserting or accepting that right widely spread in the international community and possessing the character of relative generality; *i.e.*, a majority of states, by their commissions or omissions, were obligated to accept the existence of such a right on the part of those who had claimed or exercised that right, and a majority of coastal nations were obligated to accept the existence of that right on the part of those coastal states who had not proclaimed any particular shelf policy. A bilaterally oriented inquiry would not enable us to go beyond this broad definition of a rule which is general, or prevailing, but not universal.

Geographical Extent of Coastal Control

An examination of bilateral relations of states regarding the geographical extent of coastal shelf control as established by custom by 1958 would show the continental shelf to be primarily and overwhelmingly a geographical concept. It is true that several states in Latin America, in the Mediterranean regions of Europe and the Middle East, and in Asia, did claim their control to extend beyond the geographical boundary of the shelf and up to the limits of exploitability of the shelf resources. But we have also seen that by 1958 no administrative or industrial activity ever reached anywhere close to the geographical limits of the shelf. Thus between the countries asserting their right of control beyond the geographical boundaries of the shelf a form of estoppel may have been created by their various proclamations preventing them, for the duration of their policies, from denying the parallel claims of others. Yet there was, without actual national involvement of an economic or administrative character, nothing to form the basis of a more permanent right on their part and *vis a vis* the states not claiming or practicing a shelf control beyond the geographical boundary; and, therefore, no definable measure of acquiescence on the part of the states not claiming the more extensive area of national control could have resulted to endow the principle of the limit of exploitability with the character of any significant generality. On the contrary, divergent systems of shelf measurement appear to have existed side by side in 1958 and to have formed the essence of various bilateral relationships: the geographical one, taking the shelf as a defined formation of the sea-bottom; another, limited to some Latin American states, defining the shelf by a 200-mile distance from the shores; and the dynamic limits determined by the depth of the superjacent sea in which industrial exploitation of the shelf resources was possible.

Functional Limits of Coastal Control

A bilaterally oriented examination of the functional limits of coastal shelf rights would result in a complex of diverse systems of national control. While parallel policies of some states claiming full sovereign control over the adjacent outer shelf may have led to their mutual recognition of exclusive rights encompassing all methods of shelf utilization and exploitation, the actual practice of states, in terms of concrete acts and industrial involvement, went but rarely and in extremely insolated instances into areas other than the exploitation of petroleum and gas resources by drilling from relatively stationary structures. At one point, for instance, it appeared entirely possible – judging by the relative initial reluctance of some West European states to accept the new idea of exclusive, and extensive, coastal rights on the adjacent shelves – that in the West European area and as between some states certain uses of the shelf will be recognized as outside coastal control, such as, for instance, dredging for mineral nodules from moving ships, an activity akin to fishing; in other instances, different species of marine life in constant contact with the seabed may have been included in or excluded from the control of the adjacent state; finally, while the shelf was used, in isolated instances again (primarily by the United States and the United Kingdom), for such purposes as submarine storage for oil and as the ground for the construction of observation towers, no other practice was developed and no specific policies were proclaimed in this area of shelf utilization to provide a basis for a conclusion, except on the uncertain grounds of reasonableness, that a legal rule of any appreciable scope was formed by 1958.

State Responsibility in Shelf Areas under National Control

Since 1945, there was never any doubt expressed by any state that the right of exclusive coastal control over the adjacent outer continental shelf carried with it the duty to maintain reasonable standards of order and safety on the high seas above the utilized portions on the shelf. But it appears that this obligation of the coastal state did not emerge as a product of the new continental shelf practice; in fact, it represents an application of the old and generally valid principle that the users of the high seas are bound to conduct their business so as not to threaten the safety of, or to deprive of their rights, other lawful users of the international waters. The application of this principle on the high seas above nationally controlled continental shelf does, of course, raise certain problems of jurisdiction over ships. There is a question what enforcement and punitive measures, short of revoking the exploitation license, the coastal authorities could take against foreign-flag ships engaged in continental shelf operations licensed by the coastal state, if the operating ships do not comply with the orders and regulations issued by the coastal state. And it is even less clear how the coastal state can ensure compliance with its rules by foreign ships navigating the high seas above the utilized portions of the adjacent outer continental shelf. An examination of the continental shelf practice from 1945 to 1958 would show that states controlling the adjacent outer continental shelf also automatically assumed responsibility for the maintenance of order and safety on the high seas above the shelf; thus, while protecting primarily the interests of their ports and of coastal navigation, they were also discharging their international duties. But there was by 1958 an insufficient amount of practice to form the basis of legal norms assigning to the coastal state new and extensive rights of jurisdiction over foreign users of the high seas above the utilized continental shelf. One can expect that, with the growth of continental shelf utilization, this segment of the continental shelf regime may see a rapid development and possibly some changes in the law of jurisdiction over ships. By 1958, however, the situation would seem to have paralleled rather closely the practice established in the Danish Sound, where Denmark has an international responsibility for the maintenance of a system of signals and lights guiding high sea shipping through reefs and cays, but the Danish authorities have no jurisdiction over ships violating the rules of passage. An examination of the continental shelf practice, bilaterally oriented or a general one, does not show that by 1958 a different system of jurisdiction over ships was legally established anywhere.

It may be thus said that some parts of the 1958 Convention on the Continental Shelf did, for some countries participating in the Geneva Conference, express a law then existing between them. For most of them, the right of the coastal state to control exclusively the exploitation of the natural resources of the adjacent outer continental shelf, with the accompanying responsibility of the coastal nation for the order and safety on the high seas above the shelf, represented then existing rules of behavior. However, the definition by the criterion of exploitability of the extent of the exclusive shelf rights was then a reciprocally established and recognized policy between but a few of the participants, while the Convention articles determining the functional limits of exclusive coastal rights on the shelf, *i.e.*, the definition of the exclusively controlled resources and the method of their exploitation, represented merely one among several existing international systems, some of them more and others less restrictive. On the whole, the Convention could not be said to have represented a codification of existing rules of international customary law simply because, as may so often be the case in the field of custom, there existed by 1958 no unified, world-wide regime of the continental shelf.

INTERNATIONAL CUSTOM: ASPECTS OF GROWTH

As soon as one adopts for the study of an international customary rule the method of bilaterally oriented inquiry, the notion of a broadly conceived, non-technical estoppel describing the legal customary relationship of two or more states is bound to emerge. The term "estoppel," as used here and in the chapters above, is not intended to signify a simple one-sided legal bar merely hindering state A from obtaining, through its own inconsistency or a policy reversal, an undue advantage at the expense of state B which has relied on the policy representations of A and would suffer damages by A's change of policy. The estoppel, operating as a preclusion capable of limiting a state's alternatives, may be the eventual consequence of a number of legal relationships created by unilateral acts of states – policy statements and actions, protests, acquiescence or, eventually, by such unilateral yet parallel behavior of two or more states as to indicate consensus and an implied agreement.

By this notion of a broadly conceived estoppel or a preclusion we do not seek to displace other well established concepts of international law. A strong argument, of course, can be made that the notion of estoppel is not foreign and superfluous, for instance, to the concept of an implied agreement obligating two or more states to behave in a certain prescribed way. Indeed, an implied agreement between two or more states regarding a specific policy may exist on the basis of parallel and compatible views of the states before such views find their way to the actual practice of the states and before any actual reliance by one state on the policies of the other can be reasonably proved.

However, the essence of the problem lies in the general perspective adopted rather than in the compatibility or incompatibility of abstract concepts. Seen by an outside observer, the behavior of two states may, indeed, be interpreted as both the source and the evidence of a fully binding implied agreement. If the behavior of the two states includes acts deeply involving the governments and the national communities in the specific practice, the bonds of the implied agreement are that much stronger, the evidence thereof that much more persuasive. And it is possible to make still another conceptual step and ask whether in the field of the implied agreement – a relationship closely akin to a treaty but for its less formal origins – one should not consider the possible application of the doctrine of *rebus sic stantibus* and the consequent question in what ways an implied agreement no longer corresponding to international realities could be dissolved. Indeed, the conceptual perspectives of the various ways by which a state may limit its discretion to act in a specific manner are numerous and may lead to interesting legal analyses.

Then there is a different perspective from which to view the operation of the *ius non scriptum* – the perspective, adopted for this study, of the national decision-maker determining whether and how the scope of his political discretion has been legally limited by his own earlier acts and those of other states. His problem is not a problem of basic concepts but of consequences. He *may* ask, but need not determine, whether he is bound to obey the prescriptions or prohibitions of an implied agreement, or of an act-and-acquiescence sequence implying an agreement, or of some other legal relationship. But, inevitably, he *must* ask whether he is legally free to adopt and pursue a certain policy, whether by his own earlier acts or omissions he has not put a legal obstacle in his way, whether, eventually, by pursuing a new course of action, he would not harm both, the other states who may have relied on his earlier stand and, in the long run, his own interests in a certain measure of stability – and thus of the predictability – of the international public order. In other words, the decision-maker, after having determined what the power of his state would enable him to undertake politically, is bound to ask whether he is not legally barred, precluded, estopped from that undertaking.

The above policy-oriented perspective embodies the notion of an estoppel as it has emerged from this study. Clearly, it is not important whether or not a term other than "estoppel" is used to describe the eventual consequences of a legal customary relationship of two or more states; in this sense, the estoppel is an abstract embodiment of the international necessity and obligation of states to fulfill between themselves such expectations as each of them may have created in others by its actions or inactivity. To state this is, of course, to state the obvious: in its broadest sense, an estoppel represents but the duty of a state to behave or not to behave in a certain way which one or more states have a right to consider as an international prescription or prohibition. And our main question is how that estoppel emerges, grows and, sometimes, disintegrates, what factors determine its legal quality and intensity.

The study of bilateral customary relationships leads into a realm different from that governed by the notion of general rules of international custom and by the traditional requirements for the establishment of such rules, namely, the generality and consistency of state practice, its duration, and the attendant *opinio juris sive necessitatis*. These elements do not disappear in a bilaterally oriented study; only their meaning becomes much more specific and particular.

Considering bilateral customary relations of states, one obviously does not start with the study of the generality of state practice but, rather, with the study of the reciprocal character of unilateral acts of the states or the mutuality and compatibility of a specific mode of their behavior. Seen from the perspective of general international law, the 1945 Truman Proclamation on the Continental Shelf was but a statement of policy of uncertain legal significance. In bilateral relations of states, however, the unilateral act of the United States Government clearly played a definite legal role. After first limiting the previous assumed discretion of the United States to view the continental shelf as either a *res communis* or a *res nullius,* it had almost immediate legal consequences in changing the legal relationship between the United States and those countries whose policies and practices created a receptive climate for the continental shelf doctrine embodied in the Proclamation. Such new legal relationship – for instance, between the United States and the United Kingdom – was at first weak and could have been of only brief duration. However, its legal intensity and its relative permanence were increasing through the activity which was a direct implementation of the initiated shelf policy and a consequence of it. Thus the legally relevant state practice encompasses more than a formulation of policy and its formal implementation; it consists of the entire chain of events generated by the policy within the national community and resulting, as we have seen in some detail, in a relatively deep economic and social involvement in the policy by the national body.

The speed and depth of this national involvement, in turn, affects the freedom of action on the part of other countries. It is, first, significant politically in that it testifies to the permanence of the proclaimed policy and thereby induces others to orient themselves toward it, positively or negatively. Second, it is significant legally; the rapidity of the national involvement in a newly proclaimed policy, rather than the mere time elapsed after the proclamation, determines the process of acquiescence in that policy on the part of other states; in terms of state action, a foreign government's possibility of effectively protesting the proclaimed policy decreases in relation to the increasing national involvement, on the part of the proclaiming state, in its new policy.

We have had no opportunity to examine the question of protests directed against national claims to the coastal control over the outer continental shelf since no state has actually protested. However, from the bilaterally oriented examination of the process of acquiescence in the national assertions of exclusive control over the outer continental shelf some conclusions regarding the role of protest may be deduced. It appears that in the specific case of the continental shelf the possibility to protest effectively is determined by – apart from the rapidity of the national involvement in the proclaimed shelf policy – several factors:

Among them is, first, the speed of communication between the state proclaiming a new policy and the foreign government whose acceptance of, acquiescence in, or protest against that policy may shape the relationship of the two countries. The process of communication – the transmission of the text of the policy statement, the evaluation by the foreign government of its political and legal significance, and the foreign government's orientation toward the new policy – obviously differs in speed from one bilateral situation to another. As in the case of the *Norwegian Fisheries* where the International Court of Justice considered the relative position of Great Britain toward Norway and saw the traditional British interest in maritime matters as a factor obligating Great Britain either to react to the Norwegian policy or to accept the legal consequences of inaction, so in the case of continental shelf policies; Great Britain, for instance, itself practicing shelf control in the Caribbean area at the time of the 1945 Truman Proclamation, would have been expected to be in a position to react faster to that Proclamation than a distant state whose government would have to study the entire concept of the continental shelf from the very beginning in order to define its own interests and position.

In the case of the continental shelf studies through bilateral situations, the role of *opinio juris* conceived as a separate element creative of legal relationships is largely invisible. Where a new, previously nonexistent and undefined legal relationship emerges between two states through the operation of parallel practices, implied agreement or through the act-and-acquiescence formula, one does not search for *opinio juris* as a prerequisite of that relationship; *opinio juris,* the consciousness that a specific international practice is pursued with a sense of legal obligation, is but the ultimate outcome of state practice having passed from the realm of discretionary activity into the phase of legally ordered behavior. In some instances, as between the United States and the United Kingdom in their 1945 relationship in the shelf policies, that passage from discretionary practice to legal obligation could be almost instantaneous; in other cases, where acquiescence had to develop on the basis of an increasing shelf activity of one state and the silence of another state, the emergence of a definable *opinio juris* is a slower process. This view of *opinio juris,* of course, automatically eliminates its conception, sometimes advocated, as an experssion of a state's agreement to abide by a specific rule; it rather appears to represent, in the instances of acquiescence, a complete failure of a state to express and defend a different will or, simply, a failure to disagree effectively. However, for a bilaterally oriented inquiry into the emergence of international customary rules of the continental shelf regime the concept of *opinio juris* as a creative element in the rise of legal obligations is wholly unhelpful. It may seem to have a larger meaning if one considers the question whether a network of bilateral relationships is sufficiently dense and of sufficiently compatible threads to amount to a general rule of international customary law. But even then, in the case of the continental shelf rules, it remains to define the varied substantive factors which may have led to a general consciousness of a legal obligation to follow a specific practice, and the concept of *opinio juris* again translates itself into a sum of specific legal relationships.

All these observations eventually lead toward one basic finding regarding both the growth of international customary rules and the method of an inquiry into their legal status – the finding of an all-pervasive principle of relativity.

It does appear that in at least some instances such as that of the continental shelf rules the adoption of a bilaterally oriented approach may be necessary in order to avoid imprecise generalizations and subjective impressions. However, the usefulness of such an approach may be limited to only some customary rules of international law. The appropriate method of a meaningful examination may be relative to the basic characteristics of the rule, *i.e.,* to the geographical, economic, political, social or cultural type of state relations regulated by the rule.

But not only the appropriate method of assessing the status of an international customary rule may differ from case to case; also the role of the various factors effecting the emergence of a customary norm is relative to the conditions in which those factors operate. Thus, the legal impact of international acts of a state lies in their potential to create justified expectations in other states that a specific behavior will be followed consistently. However, the legal potential of state acts may be determined by the economic, social and psychological consequences of those acts: the international expectation that a state would follow a certain mode of behavior is relative to the volume of the national involvement in that activity on the part of the practicing state, and the volume of its involvement, if allowed to increase without protests, also reinforces the expectation of the practicing state that it can follow its policy without being internationally disturbed. Thus the speed of acquiescence or the rapidity of the formation of a prescriptive right are not given by some generally set time limits; they are relative to the underlying dynamics of the implementation of national policies. The potential of the acts of a state to create international expectations may be affected by the relative position of the state in the world community: if a state, politically and economically capable and legally able to adopt alternate methods of behavior decides on one specific, internationally and legally relevant, form of activity, other states have a right to expect that the deliberate choice of the specific policy is of some permanence and not just a passing response to a sudden necessity. The 1945 Truman Proclamation on the continental shelf was issued under such circumstances. Similarly, the legal potential of the international acts of a state may be determined by the intensity of the state's participation in that field of international activity into which its policies fall: a proclamation of a new maritime policy by the United Kingdom, Norway, or the United States, is bound to have a greater impact on the formation of customary rules than a similar act of another country with less pronounced traditions, involvement and interests in orderly maritime affairs.

Thus the principle of relativity permeating the field of custom is the consequence of a great number of variables – of variables which lend dynamism to the customary rules and thereby create problems in ascertaining their legal force and scope. But beyond this principle of relativity lies the constant and endless process in which a state by its acts creates expectations in others and thus provides for certain predictable and therefore orderly paths of international relations.

Bilaterally oriented studies in different areas of international customary law may, as in the case of the continental shelf, show the impact of the many variable factors on the emergence of international expectations and, eventually, on the rise of relationships governed by rules of custom; but, above all, they may lead away from abstract generalizations regarding the growth of customary rules toward a sounder, because a more realistic, assessment of the ceaseless interplay of politics and law in the relations of states.

SELECTED BIBLIOGRAPHY

Except for a few works containing particularly rich material on the subjects of the continental shelf and international customary law, this bibliography includes only monographic treatments of the two areas.

BOOKS

Alexander, Lewis M., *A Comparative Study of Offshore Claims in Northwestern Europe.* Final report under contract Nonr. 1349(03), U.S. Office of Naval Research, 1960. Mimeographed.

Azcárraga y de Bustamante, José Luis de, *La Plataforma Submarina y el Derecho Internacional.* Madrid: Colección de estudies de derecho internacional marítimo, 1952.

Ballareau, Denise, *La Coutume dans la Jurisprudence Internationale.* Paris: Recueil Sirey, 1941.

Elizalde Montes de Oca, Angel, *Las Fuentos del Derecho Internacional: La Costumbre.* Mexico City: Universidad Nacional Autonóma de México, 1946.

García-Amador y Rodríguez, Francisco Victor, *The Exploitation and Conservation of the Resources of the Sea: A Study of Contemporary International Law.* 2d ed. enlarged. Leyden: Sijthoff, 1959.

Gianni, Grégoire, *La Coutume en Droit International.* Paris: Pedone, 1931.

Gonet, Yvon, *La Coutume en Droit Constitutionnel Interne et en Droit Constitutionnel International.* Paris: Pedone, 1932.

Kemler, Emory N., and Rosencrants, Edward W., *Offshore Summary.* Spring Park, Minn.: Summary Reports, 1954 (mimeographed).

López Villamil, Humberto, *La Plataforma Continental y los Problemas Juridicos del Mar.* Madrid: Juan Bravo, 1958.

McDougal, Myres S., and Burke, William T., *The Public Order of the Oceans: A Contemporary International Law of the Sea.* New Haven: Yale University Press, 1962.

Mouton, Martinus W., *The Continental Shelf.* The Hague: Nijhoff, 1952.

Oda, Shigeru, *International Control of Sea Resources.* Leyden: Sijthoff, 1963.

Scelle, Georges, *Plateau Continental et Droit International.* Paris: Pedone, 1955.

Shalowitz, Aaron L., *Shore and Sea Boundaries.* (Vol. I: Boundary Problems Associated with the Submerged Lands Cases and the Submerged Lands Acts.) Washington, D.C.: Government Printing Office, 1962.

Sorensen, Max, *Les Sources du Droit International: Étude sur la Jurisprudence de la Cour Permanente de Justice Internationale.* Copenhagen: Munksgaard, 1946.

Steele, Gabriel, "The Development of Law on the Continental Shelf." Unpublished Master of Law thesis, Columbia University, 1964.

Tellez Benoit, Maria Emilia, *La Plataforma Continental.* Mexico City: Universidad Nacional Autonóma de México, 1946.

Tressler, Donald K., and James McW. Lemon, *Marine Products of Commerce.* 2d ed.New York: Reinhold, 1951.

U.S. Naval War College. *International Law Situation and Documents 1956.* (Vol. LI: Situation, Documents and Commentary on Recent Developments in the International Law of the Sea, by Brunson MacChesney.) Washington, D.C.: Government Printing Office, 1957.

U.S. Naval War College. *International Law Studies 1959–1960.* (Vol. LIII: The Law of the Sea; Some Recent Developments, by Carl M. Franklin.) Washington, D.C.: Government Printing Office, 1961.

Zoričič, Milovan, *Teritorijalno More, s Osvrtom na Otvoreno i Unutarnje More, Vanjski Pojas i Pitanja Kontinentalne Ravnine.* Zagreb: Jugoslavenska Akademija Znanosti i Umjetnosti, 1953.

ARTICLES

(a) Law, especially customary

Ago, Roberto, "Positive Law and International Law," 51 *American Journal of International Law* (1957) 691–733.

Bos, M., "L'Universalité du Droit des Gens: Postulat et Programme," in *Varia Juris Gentium – Liber Amicorum Presented to Jean Pierre François* (Leyden: Sijthoff, 1959) 62–72.

Bowett, D. W., "Estoppel Before International Tribunals and Its Relation to Acquiescence," 33 *British Year Book of International Law* (1957) 176–202.

Brown, Philip M., "The Codification of International Law," 29 *American Journal of International Law* (1935) 25–39.

Friede, Wilhelm, "Das Estoppel-Prinzip im Völkerrecht," 5 *Zeitschrift für Ausländisches Öffentliches Recht und Völkerrecht* (1935) 517–545.

Hagemann, Max, "Die Gewohnheit als Völkerrechtsquelle in der Rechtssprechung des Internationalen Gerichtshofes," 10 *Schweizerisches Jahrbuch für Internationales Recht* (1953) 61–88.

Hurst, Cecil J. B., "A Plea for the Codification of International Law on New Lines," 32 *Transactions of the Grotius Society* (1946) 135–153.

Jennings, R. Y., "The Progressive Development of International Law and Its Codification," 24 *British Year Book of International Law* (1947) 301–329.

Kopelmanas, Lazare, "Custom as a Means of the Creation of International Law," 18 *British Year Book of International Law* (1937) 127–152.

Kunz, Josef L., "The Nature of Customary International Law," 47 *American Journal of International Law* (1953) 662–669.

Lauterpacht, Hersch, "Codification and Development of International Law," 49 *American Journal of International Law* (1955) 16–43.

MacGibbon, I. C., "Customary International Law and Acquiescence," 33 *British Year Book of International Law* (1957) 115–145.

–. "The Scope of Acquiescence in International Law," 31 *British Year Book of International Law* (1954) 143–186.

–. "Some Observations on the Part of Protest in International Law," 30 *British Year Book of International Law* (1953) 293–319.

Séfériades, S., "Aperçus sur la Coutume Juridique Internationale et Notament sur Son Fondement," 43 *Revue Générale de Droit International Public* (1936) 129–196.

Silving, Helen, "Customary Law: Continuity in Municipal and International Law," 31 *Iowa Law Review* (1946) 614–633.

Tunkin, G. I., "Remarks on the Juridical Nature of Customary Norms of International Law," 49 *California Law Review* (1961) 419–430.

Visscher, Charles de, "Contribution à l'Étude des Sources du Droit International," 14 *Revue de Droit International et de Législation Comparée* (1933) 395–420.

(*b*) *The Law of the Continental Shelf*

Azcárraga y de Bustamante, José Luis de, "Los Derechos sobre la Plataforma Submarina," 2 *Revista Española de Derecho Internacional* (Madrid 1949) 47–99.

Bingham, Joseph W., "The Continental Shelf and the Marginal Belt," 40 *American Journal of International Law* (1946) 173–178.

Boggs, S. Whittemore, "Delimitation of Seaward Areas under National Jurisdiction," 45 *American Journal of International Law* (1951) 240–266.

Borchard, Edwin, "Resources of the Continental Shelf," 40 *American Journal of International Law* (1946) 53–70.

Briggs, Herbert W., "Jurisdiction over the Sea Bed and Subsoil beyond Territorial Waters,' 45 *American Journal of International Law* (1951) 338–342.

Brinton, J. Y., "Jurisdiction over Sea-bed Resources and Recent Developments in Persian Gulf Area," 5 *Revue Egyptienne de Droit International* (1949) 131–133.

–. "Problems of the Continental Shelf," 6 *Revue Egyptienne de Droit International* (1950) 165–170.

Daniel, Price, "Sovereignty and Ownership in the Marginal Sea and Their Relation to Problems of the Continental Shelf," 3 *Baylor Law Review* (1951) 241–266.

Goddard, G., "The Land under the Sea," 6 *Indian Year Book of International Affairs* (1957) 81–103.

Goldie, L. F. E., "Australia's Continental Shelf: Legislation and Proclamations," 3 *International and Comparative Law Quarterly* (1954) 535–575.

Gutteridge, J. A. C., "The 1958 Geneva Convention on the Continental Shelf," 35 *British Year Book of International Law* (1959) 102–123.

Hurst, Cecil J. B., "The Continental Shelf," 34 *Transactions of the Grotius Society* (1949) 153–169.

–. "Whose Is the Bed of the Sea?" 4 *British Year Book of International Law* (1923–24) 34–43.

Kunz, Josef L., "Continental Shelf and International Law: Confusion and Abuse," 50 *American Journal of International Law* (1956) 828–853.

Lauterpacht, Hersch, "Sovereignty over Submarine Areas," 27 *British Year Book of International Law* (1950) 376–433.

Mouton, Martinus W., "The Continental Shelf," 85 *Recueil des Cours de l'Académie de Droit International de la Haye* (1954), 347–458.

O'Connell, D. P., "Sedentary Fisheries and the Australian Continental Shelf," 49 *American Journal of International Law* (1955) 185–209.

Oda, Shigeru, "The Continental Shelf," 1 *Japanese Annual of International Law* (1957) 15–37.

Phleger, Herman, "Recent Developments Affecting the Regime of the High Seas," 32 *Department of State Bulletin* (June 1955) 934–940.

Vallat, F. A., "The Continental Shelf," 23 *British Year Book of International Law* (1946) 333–338.

Waldock, C. H. M., "The Legal Basis of Claims to the Continental Shelf," 36 *Transactions of the Grotius Society* (1950) 115–145.

Whiteman, Marjorie M., "Conference on the Law of the Sea: Convention on the Continental Shelf," 52 *American Journal of International Law* (1958) 629–659.

Yepes, J. M., "El Problema del Mar Territorial o Jurisdiccional y de la Plataforma Submarina ante el Nuevo Derecho Internacional," 8 *Revista Universitas* (Bogotá) (1955) 45–69.

Young, Richard, "The Geneva Convention on the Continental Shelf: A First Impression," 52 *American Journal of International Law* (1958) 733–738.

–. "The International Law Commission and the Continental Shelf," 46 *American Journal of International Law* (1952) 123–128.

—. "The Legal Status of Submarine Areas beneath the High Seas," 45 *American Journal of International Law* (1951) 225–249.
—. "Lord Asquith and the Continental Shelf," 46 *American Journal of International Law* (1952) 512–515.
—. "The Over-Extension of the Continental Shelf," 47 *American Journal of International Law* (1953) 454–456.
—. "Recent Developments with Respect to the Continental Shelf," 42 *American Journal of International Law* (1948) 849–857.
—. "Sedentary Fisheries and the Convention on the Continental Shelf," 55 *American Journal of International Law* (1961) 359–373.

(*c*) *The Shelf – descriptive and technical*

Bates, Charles C., and Glenn, Alfred H. "Oceanography in the Offshore Drilling Campaign," 127 (No. 13) *World Oil* (April 1948) 114–126.
Carsey, J. B., "Geology of Gulf Coastal Area and Continental Shelf," 34 *Bulletin of the American Association of Petroleum Geologists* (1950) 361–385.
Critz, James C., "Oil Possibilities on the Gulf Coast Continental Shelf," 124 (No. 6) *The Oil Weekly* (Jan. 6, 1947) 17–21.
Emery, K. O., "Continental Shelf – Southern California," 35 *Bulletin of the American Association of Petroleum Geologists* (Feb. 1951) 249–252.
Ewing, John I., Worzel, J. Lamar, and Ewing, Maurice. "Sediments and Oceanic Structural History of the Gulf of Mexico," 67 *Journal of Geophysical Research* (1962) 2509–2527.
Goedicke, T. R., "Areas of Interest in Marine Oil Prospecting," 143 (No. 6) *World Oil* (Nov. 1956) 116–127.
—. and E. R. Locke, "World's Offshore Oil Areas," 5 (No. 3) *Offshore* (Nov. 1956) 27–39, and 5 (No. 4) *Offshore* (Dec. 1956) 54–56.
Gray, Francis W., "Mining Coal under the Sea in Nova Scotia with Notes on Comparable Undersea Coal Mining Operations Elsewhere," in *Second Empire Mining and Metallurgical Congress* (Montreal, 1927), 2 *Proceedings* 1–191.
Latimer Jr., J. R., "The Search for Oil on the Continental Shelf," 129 (No. 9) *World Oil* (Dec. 1949) 50–58.
Mero, John L., "Minerals on the Ocean Floor," 203 (No. 6) *Scientific American* (Dec. 1960) 64–72.
Pratt, Wallace E., "Petroleum on Continental Shelves," 31 *Bulletin of the American Association of Petroleum Geologists* (1947) 657–672.
Umbgrove, J. H. F., "Origin of Continental Shelves," 30 *Bulletin of the American Association of Petroleum Geologists* (1946) 249–264.
Wiseman, John B. H., and Cameron D. Ovey, "Definitions of Features on the Deep-Sea Floor," 1 *Deep-Sea Research* (1953) 11–16.

DOCUMENTS

Food and Agriculture Organization. "Examination of Living Resources Associated with the Sea Bed of the Continental Shelf with Regard to the Nature and Degree of Their Physical and Biological Association with Such Sea Bed," in U.N. Conference on the Law of the Sea 1958, 1 *Official Records*, 187–197 (Doc. A/CONF. 13/13 in Doc. A/CONF. 13/37).
—. "Technical Particulars Concerning the Methods of Fishing Conducted by Means of Equipment in the Floor of the Sea," in U.N. Conference on the Law of the Sea 1958, 1 *Official Records* 176–186 (Doc. A/CONF. 13/12 in Doc. A/CONF. 13/37).
Organization of American States, Inter-American Specialized Conference on "Conser-

vation of Natural Resources: The Continental Shelf and Marine Waters." Ciudad Trujillo, 3 March 1956, Doc. 2, SG-2.

Organization of American States. *Final Act of the Inter-American Specialized Conference on "Conservation of Natural Resources: The Continental Shelf and Marine Waters."* Washington, D.C.: Pan American Union, 1956.

Pan American Union, Department of International Law. *Background Material on the Activities in the Organization of American States Relating to the Law of the Sea.* Washington, D.C.: Pan American Union, 1957; mimeographed.

State of Louisiana, Department of Wildlife and Fisheries. "Report of the Chief Biologist," by J. N. Gowanloch, in *First Biennial Report 1944–1945*, pp. 142–148.

U.N. Conference on the Law of the Sea, 1958. *Official Records.* 7 vols. Doc. A/CONF. 13/37–43.

U.N.E.S.C.O. "Scientific Considerations Relating to the Continental Shelf," in U.N. Conference on the Law of the Sea 1958, 1 *Official Records* 39–46 (Doc. A/CONF. 13/2 in Doc. A/CONF. 13/37).

U.N. International Law Commission. "Article 24 of the Statute of the International Law Commission," Working Paper by Manley O. Hudson, Special Rapporteur. *I.L.C. Yearbook 1950*, II, 24–35.

U.N. International Law Commission. "Comments by Governments on the Provisional Articles Concerning the Regime of the High Seas and the Draft Articles on the Regime of the Territorial Sea Adopted by the International Law Commission at Its Seventh Session in 1955," *I.L.C. Yearbook 1956*, II, 37–101.

–. "Comments by Governments on the Draft Articles Concerning the Law of the Sea Adopted by the International Law Commission at its Eighth Session in 1956," in U.N. Conference on the Law of the Sea 1958, 1 *Official Records* 75–113 (Doc. A CONF. 13/5 in Doc. A/CONF. 13/37.

U.N. International Law Commission. "Regime of the High Seas," by J. P. A. François, Special Rapporteur. *I.L.C. Yearbook 1950*, II, 36–52.

–. "Regime of the High Seas," by J. P. A. François, Special Rapporteur. *I.L.C. Yearbook 1951*, II, 75–103.

–. "Regime of the High Seas," by J. P. A. François, Special Rapporteur. *I.L.C. Yearbook 1953*, II, 1–51.

–. "Regime of the High Seas and Regime of the Territorial Sea," by J. P. A. François, Special Rapporteur. *I.L.C. Yearbook 1956*, II, 1–12.

–. Report of the International Law Commission to the General Assembly ... Covering the Work of Its Fifth Session in 1953. Chapter III: Regime of the High Seas. *I.L.C. Yearbook 1953*, II, 212–220.

U.N. International Law Commission. Report of the International Law Commission to the General Assembly ... Covering the Work of Its Fifth Session in 1953. Annex II: Comments by Governments on the Draft Articles on the Continental Shelf and Related Subjects Prepared by the International Law Commission at its Third Session in 1951. *I.L.C. Yearbook 1953*, II 241–270.

–. Report of the International Law Commission to the General Assembly ... Covering the Work of Its Eighth Session in 1956. Chapter II: Law of the Sea. *I.L.C. Yearbook 1956*, II, 254–301.

U.N. Secretariat. "The Breadth of the Safety Zone for Installations Necessary for the Exploitation and Exploration of the Natural Resources of the Continental Shelf," by M. W. Mouton. U.N. Conference on the Law of the Sea 1958, Preparatory Doc. No. 21, Doc. A/CONF. 13/26, 6 Jan. 1958.

–. "Memorandum on the Regime of the High Seas," *I.L.C. Yearbook 1950*, II, 67–113.

–. "Recent Developments in the Technology of Exploiting the Mineral Resources of the Continental Shelf," by M. W. Mouton. U.N. Conference on the Law of the Sea, Preparatory Doc. No. 20, Doc. A/CONF. 13/25, 3 Jan. 1958.

–. U.N. Legislative Series. Vol. 1: *Laws and Regulations on the Regime of the High Seas.* 1951. Doc. ST/LEG/SER.B/1. – Vol. 6: *Laws and Regulations on the Regime of the Territorial Sea.* 1957. Doc. ST/LEG/SER.B/6. – Vol. 8: *Supplement to Laws and ....* 1959. Doc. ST/LEG/SER.B/8.

U.S. Department of the Interior, Office of the Solicitor. Memorandum of 5 May 1961 to the Director of the Bureau of Land Management. Mimeographed Doc. 94127–61. M-36615.

U.S. House of Representatives, Committee on Interior and Insular Affairs. *Investigation and Study of the Seaward Boundaries of the United States,* Rep. No. 2515, 82d Cong., 2d Sess.

U.S. Senate, Committee on Interior and Insular Affairs. *Submerged Lands. Hearings.* Oct. 1949, 81st Cong., 1st Sess.; *Hearings* Aug. 1950, 81st Cong., 2d Sess.; *Hearings* Feb.-March 1953, 83d Cong., 1st Sess.; *Hearings* May-June 1953, 83d Cong., 1st Sess.

–. *Submerged Lands Act.* S. Rep. 133, 83d Cong., 1st Sess.

INDEX